VICTORIAN WOMEN'S FICTION: MARRIAGE, FREEDOM
AND THE INDIVIDUAL

Victorian Women's Fiction:
Marriage, Freedom and the Individual

Shirley Foster

BARNES & NOBLE BOOKS
Totowa, New Jersey

© 1985 Shirley Forster
First published in the USA 1985 by
Barnes & Noble Books
81 Adams Drive
Totowa, New Jersey, 07512
Printed in Great Britain

Library of Congress Cataloging in Publication Data

Foster, Shirley.
    Victorian women's fiction.

    Bibliography: p.
    Includes index.
    1. English| fiction – 19th century – History and
criticism. 2. Women in literature. 3. English
fiction – Women authors – History and criticism.
4. Women in literature. 5. Marriage in literature.
I. Title.
PR878,W6F67   1985   823'.8'09352042   84-24367
ISBN 0-389-20551-6

CONTENTS

ACKNOWLEDGEMENTS

This book is the fruit of a long-standing interest in Victorian women's fiction. I have been helped and inspired by discussion with many people, too numerous to mention individually, but prominent among whom are the American scholars especially concerned with women's writing and feminist criticism whom I met while on exchange at the University of Southern California in 1979–81, including Nina Auerbach, Barbara Kanner, and Elaine Showalter. I have, too, received invaluable assistance from Barbara Dennis, of St David's University College, Lampeter, who has been a constant source of guidance and encouragement from the earliest days of the project.

I should like to acknowledge permission to consult and quote from manuscript material in the following libraries: Department of Special Collections, Research Library, University of California, Los Angeles; Morris L. Parrish Collection of Victorian Novelists, Princeton University Library; Huntington Library, San Marino, California. I am also grateful to the University of Sheffield for a Research Grant which enabled me to travel in the United States and use this material.

The peculiarity of modern literature is, that women are addressed more as independent, and less as relative beings, — the possibility that they may remain unmarried is assumed, and dealt with. This alone marks an advance in common sense . . .

Geraldine Jewsbury,
Athenaeum, November 1857

1 INTRODUCTORY: WOMEN AND MARRIAGE IN MID-NINETEENTH-CENTURY ENGLAND

One of the commonest assumptions about the novel has always been that love is its primary concern. Most Victorian criticism takes it for granted that romantic interest is 'the one topic which forms the staple of most novels, and [is] a main ingredient in all';[1] one commentator even claims that contemporary fiction is so exclusively dedicated to 'the passion of love' that the very name 'romance' has been engrossed by the term 'novel'.[2] Not all were entirely happy with this state of things; though the form had expanded to embrace 'low-life' fiction of the 1830s and 'social-purpose' novels of the 1840s and 1850s, for some mid-century observers the domination of love and marriage in the contemporary novel represented 'a serious contraction of its capabilities'.[3] But for the majority of Victorian critics and novelists alike, affairs of the heart were the basic stuff of fiction, however restricting this might seem in practice. Even a writer like Elizabeth Sewell, who saw that her talents as a story-teller lay in quite other directions, felt obliged to try her hand at a 'regular novel, or a story in which love is the essential interest';[4] such a work, like one of her later ones, is 'unquestionably a novel' because it centres on 'love affairs'.[5]

For women writers, the association of romance and fiction was of particular significance. Lady novelists, forming a creative line that includes the romances of Aphra Behn, the Gothic novels of Ann Radcliffe, the sharply-observed social tales of Fanny Burney, and the coolly witty comedies of Jane Austen, had always focused predominantly on love. With the proliferation of female fiction in the Victorian period, however, this characteristic became a matter of artistic principle, as critical opinion increasingly insisted on the distinctiveness of women's writing, in both style and subject. Women, it was argued, wrote best about what they knew best; since, as a recent critic has put it, the central, defining preoccupation of the novel is 'the elaboration of an intensely personal experience',[6] the most obvious female fictional material is the treatment of emotions,

1

within a domestic context. Throughout the period, commentators claimed that the special merit of women novelists lay in their capacity for portraying love. G.H. Lewes, welcoming the advent of a new kind of fiction written by women and offering 'woman's view of life, woman's experience',[7] claims: 'The domestic experience which form the bulk of woman's knowledge find an appropriate form in novels . . . Love is the staple of fiction, for it "forms the story of a woman's life".'[8] Later in the century, reviewing the achievements of her predecessors, Mrs Humphry Ward posits that the strength of women novelists is 'their peculiar vision' of 'the one subject which they have eternally at command, which is interesting to all the world, and whereof large tracts are naturally and wholly their own . . . the subject of love . . . love as the woman understands it'.[9] Some critics even took the extreme line that the success of female fiction depended not only on the portrayal of romance, but on the writer's direct personal involvement with it. J.M. Ludlow, for instance, argues that because women's novels should emanate from the fullness of 'wifely and motherly experience',[10] unmarried women should refrain from writing them since they have never felt these emotions.

Discussion of appropriate subject-matter for women writers was closely linked to the notion that there were certain innately feminine characteristics which found best expression in romantic and domestic fiction. R.H. Hutton propounds such a thesis: women respond from the heart, not the head; their perceptions are 'finer, subtler, quicker than men's', and they have 'delicacy and skill in delineation', but they find it hard to reason abstractly and 'what they lack is an eye for universality, a power of seeing the broad and representative element';[11] therefore their art cannot successfully penetrate areas of professional and intellectual life, but does best in the emotional arena. Hutton wanted to see a widening in women's creative writing, achieved through better education, but other critics were anxious to maintain this sexual distinctiveness. Miss Stodart, in her *Female Writers: Thoughts on their Proper Sphere and on their Powers* (1842), was one of the first to suggest that womanly qualities of delicacy, sensitivity, quick sympathy, and powers of observation commit women novelists to a particular literary mode — the depiction of home and family; and, following her lead, other critics insisted that women novelists' 'keen sympathies', 'glowing sentiment', and 'sensitive consciences'[12] especially equipped them to deal with the emotional side of life. The high-lighting of such qualities — which, as we shall see, are intrinsic elements in the age's 'angel' ideology — reflects, like strictures on the appropriate material of women's fiction, current insistence on the supremacy of wifely and motherly functions. Anne Mozley posits that the most admirable female writers are those who turn their gifts to social and domestic account, who refrain from making themselves 'exceptions from the ordinary domestic type of women', and who write 'on subjects especially open to feminine treatment' with their natural 'delicate fingering . . . soft touch, and quick perception'.[13] Even George Eliot, hardly representative of the more traditional aspects of womanhood, claims that the peculiar beauty of woman depends on 'a class of sensations and emotions — the maternal ones — which must remain unknown to man'[14] and which will be part of her specialness as an artist. Lewes's praise of the particular merits of female fiction rests on the notion of biological separateness:

> The grand function of woman . . . is, and ever must be *Maternity* . . . the prolific source, not only of the best affections and virtues of which our nature is capable, but also of the wise thought-fulness, and most useful habits of observation, by which that nature can be elevated and adorned.[15]
>
> Woman, by her greater affectionateness, her greater range and depth of emotional experience, is well-fitted to give expression to the emotional facts of life.[16]

Many women novelists themselves recognised that this apparent tribute to female literary skills was in reality a thinly-disguised weapon of limitation. It not only subjected them to the notorious double standard in reviewing, but made it extremely hard for them to contravene the generally-upheld criteria. One reason for the central idealising focus on love and marriage in so much Victorian female fiction is certainly pressure from publishers, prudently responding to the tastes (which they had in part created) of a reader-ship which consisted largely of young women, themselves preoccu-pied with affairs of the heart. Harriet Taylor sums up the situation with cynical neatness: 'it is the personal interest of these [literary] women to profess whatever opinions they expect will be agreeable to men . . . [because] they depend on men's opinion for their literary as well as for their feminine successes.'[17] Only the strongest female authors could resist the tyranny of romantic conventions. Charlotte Brontë's refusal to comply with the urgings of her father and of

George Smith, her publisher, to change the last part of *Villette* so that the novel would convey 'the spirit of romance . . . far more flowery and inviting'[18] is an indication of her determined literary integrity; other women novelists, as a recent critic has demonstrated, submerged any unease they may have felt, perhaps in propitiation of male values, and complied with the demands of their intended audiences — women and families — who accepted traditional female roles and expected novels to depict them.[19]

As several contemporary commentators suggested, Victorian women novelists may have focused on romance and marriage also as a kind of consolation for personal dissatisfaction. Trapped in their private domestic sphere, they imaginatively enacted in fiction their own soothing dreams of blessed fulfilment. A *Saturday Review* contributor lightly describes 'the young recluse author', thrown back on herself within a monotonous round of domestic duties, 'put[ting] on paper what she would herself like to be'.[20] More sombrely, Anna Jameson, foreshadowing Lewes's assumption that women turn to writing 'always to solace . . . the sorrow that in silence wastes their lives . . . [to] escape from the pressure of that burden',[21] sees literary activity as a compensation for 'the void of existence', especially for single women:

> only in utility . . . only in the assiduous employment of such faculties as we are permitted to exercise, can we find health and peace, and compensation for the wasted or repressed impulses and energies more proper to our sex — more natural.[22]

To argue that preoccupation with romantic themes in Victorian women's fiction is either wish-fulfilment or capitulation to publishing convention — or a mixture of both — is not, however, to give the whole picture. There are even more cogent reasons why women at this time were exploring questions of love, marriage, and female domesticity in their creative work. In treating these topics, their narratives accord with one of the most sacred of Victorian canons, the appeal to realism; however much they may seem to be escaping from actuality into the idealising world of the imagination, mid-Victorian women novelists are in fact responding to contemporary conditions and ideologies. Foreign observers noted this fact with a degree of ironic amusement. In 1849, Eugène Forçade, comparing French and English novels, saw how the latter mirrored the social phenomenon in England that a woman's age of romance concluded with marriage,[23] while Taine, writing about his visit to England in 1859, observed that there was almost as much reverence paid to women and the institution of matrimony in real life as in literature.[24]

The subject which formed the basis of nearly all Victorian female fiction was of especial significance for the writers at this time. Victorian women, in fact, faced what many saw as a crisis in the affairs of their sex, emanating from conflicting cultural and social conditions. As has already been indicated, one of the most pervasive ideologies of the age rested on the assumption that the ideal womanly virtues — sacrifice, self-effacement, moral purity, service — were best expressed in the vocations of wife and mother. To be truly feminine, a woman must fulfil the beneficent functions which nature has assigned to her. She thus becomes the angelic figure which finds its best-known definition in Patmore's paean to married bliss, *The Angel in the House* (1855, 1856):

> Her disposition is devout
> Her countenance angelical;
> The best things that the best believe
> Are in her face so kindly writ
> The faithless, seeing her, conceive
> Not only heaven, but hope of it.
>
> (Book I, Canto IV, Preludes I)

The wife, in Patmore's vision, offers a haven of domestic peace and security:

> On settled poles turn solid joys,
> And sunlike pleasures shine at home.
>
> (Book II, Canto VII, Preludes I)

These sentiments are echoed in another much-quoted text of the period — Ruskin's 'Of Queens' Gardens', in his *Sesame and Lilies* (1865) — which similarly stresses the sacredness of woman's 'true place and power' in the Home, itself 'a vestal temple, a temple of the hearth watched over by Household Gods';[25] it also attributes quasi-divine power to 'the tender and delicate woman . . . with the child at her breast'.[26] Patmore's and Ruskin's attitudes towards feminine roles have gained such notoriety that it is easy to overlook the fact that the ideology was current much earlier in the period, and has antecedents in the previous century.[27] It is also tempting to claim that the relegation of woman to what, though spiritually elevated, was in reality a narrowed and restricted function, had its source in a masculine self-preserving strategy disguised as a doctrine of adulation. We should note, however, that many women themselves not only apparently accepted this view of their own sex but actually sought to promulgate it. Even if their response was unconsciously conditioned by male pressure, many nineteenth-century female writers earnestly voiced their belief in an exclusively domestic and maternal standard of womanly excellence. Mrs Sandford, in her *Woman in her Social and Domestic Character* (1831) posits that 'domestic life is the chief sphere of her [woman's] influence';[28] in the appropriate arena of home, she must be 'the tender nurse, the patient instructress, the sympathising and forgiving counsellor, receiving back from her children the recompense of her own filial affection'.[29] In her *Woman's Mission* (1839), Sarah Lewis similarly claims that woman's influence is dependent on maternal feeling, the basis for all good action, and must be exercised primarily within the 'sacred precincts of home'.[30] The best-known spokesman for this conservative view of womanhood is Mrs Ellis, whose series of guides to female conduct take it as axiomatic that a woman's responsibility is to make a happy home and devote herself to the service of others from within it. Since women are incontrovertibly 'relative creatures',[31] their noblest occupations are in the household sphere, fulfilling 'the domestic duties which call forth the best energies of the female character'.[32] The inherent sacredness of the wifely role means also that it is a woman's duty to uphold the sublimity of the marriage state itself; if a union fails, says Ellis crisply, the blame must be laid on the wife who has misled her suitor during courtship and whose subsequent 'falling off' towards him 'seems to indicate that her mind has been low enough to be influenced by a desire of establishing herself in an eligible home'.[33]

This ideology had a considerable effect upon middle-class Victorian women, in both social and personal terms. Because so much importance was attached to the roles of wifehood and motherhood, marriage was deemed the apotheosis of womanly fulfilment, alternatives to which were regarded as pitiable or unnatural. Emotional and psychological pressures on women to marry were thus added to the social and economic ones of earlier periods, when it was understood that pragmatism would be a primary consideration of female matrimonial aspirations.[34] These pressures were made more acute by particular ironies of the contemporary situation. As demographic figures indicate, the proportion of unmarried women in the total population expanded dramatically during the Victorian period. The census of 1851 showed that there were 2,765,000 single women over the age of fifteen, and by 1871 this figure had increased to 3,228,700.[35] According to Harriet Martineau, writing in the *Edinburgh Review*, in 1851 a third of females over twenty were independently supporting themselves and their households.[36] This percentage increased during the century as the number of 'surplus' women grew. Despite the fact that these figures include widows as well as those who never married, and that some social historians would argue that recent studies have exaggerated the numerical significance of Victorian single women,[37] the overall implications cannot be disputed. Partly because of sexual imbalance (by mid-century there were half a million more women than men), partly because many men were marrying later or not at all, and partly because of the growing numbers of eligible bachelors who emigrated to the colonies (leading several male commentators to suggest that 'redundant' spinsters follow them out there[38]), it is clear that a considerable proportion of females could never expect to experience matrimony. This produced the paradoxical situation that, setting aside the question of individual choice in the matter, fulfilment by all its female members of one of society's most insistent ideals was literally impossible. Given this state of affairs, it is not surprising that the issue of marriage became a primary source of anxiety for Victorian women, trapped between pervasive ideology and countering fact. Taught that a husband was essential to their existence, and all their training directed to the art of catching one, they had the choice of being relegated to the ranks of abnormality if they did not marry, or being forced into what many regarded as degrading sexual competition, in which the losers faced economic hardship as well as social obliteration.

Such frustration was compounded by the recognition that, ironically enough, singleness was in many ways a more attractive proposition than the married state. The disabilities suffered by nineteenth-century wives were notorious.[39] They could not act independently in court proceedings; they were legally and economically subject to their husbands and could obtain divorce only with great difficulty and at great expense; if separated, they could gain custody of children under the age of seven, but had right of access to older children only at stated times. Things gradually improved, with the

Matrimonial Causes Act of 1857 making for easier divorces (though reforms in the areas of maintenance for the woman and wider grounds for separation did not occur until 1878 and after), and the Married Women's Property Act of 1870 (expanded and made more effective in 1882) enabling wives to keep their own property and earnings. But there were still large areas of injustice, and these, coupled with the very real possibility of a husband's brutality, made marriage often far from the picture of bliss imaged by many contemporary writers. In addition, the all-too-common hazards of frequent child-bearing and the high infant mortality rate probably also caused many women to view the prospect of matrimony with some trepidation, particularly since contraception was not widely practised before the mid-seventies. In contrast to all of this, spinsters could own and acquire possessions, be bound by contract, be responsible for their own finances, and run their own lives; no wonder that such independence, lacking though it might be in emotional enrichment, had its strong attractions.

Matrimonial ideologies did not exist unchallenged, and whether in sorrow or in anger, many women sought to resist the creed that in missing 'her dream of a heart that she might indeed call her own, of a home and a husband', the spinster has 'in some sort, missed her destiny'.[40] But, as we shall see, the most characteristic female response was dualistic. Mid-Victorian feminists (many of whom would not even have included themselves under that heading) were both cautious in challenging their society's ideologies and themselves ambivalent about female desires and goals. In terms of the 'the woman question', the early and middle years of the century were poised between the radicalism of Mary Wollstonecraft in the 1790s and that of J.S. Mill in the 1860s. It was not until the 1880s that any substantial body of radical opinion began to make its appearance, and even then it was regarded with suspicion. Mona Caird's idea of a new kind of 'free' marriage, for example, called forth widespread defence of the status quo,[41] while Mrs Lynn Linton, her conservatism fuelled by her reversion from her youthful radicalism, poured out her endless vituperative attacks on 'modern' sexual mores.[42] In the period with which we are concerned, only a few revolutionary expressions of discontent made themselves heard. In an article in the *Westminster Review* of 1841, for instance, Margaret Mylne challenges the 'better-educated women make better wives' justification for improving female intellectual opportunities; for her, as it is essential that matrimony should not be a woman's

sole means of social position, so the principle of female independence should be a fundamental element in her choice of lifestyle.[43] In
A Plea for Women (1843), Mrs Hugo Reid, too, points ironically to
the gap between ideology and actuality:

> If all woman's duties are to be considered as so strictly domestic,
> and if God and nature have really so circumscribed her sphere of
> action — what are we to think of the dreadful depravity of thou-
> sands upon thousands of unprotected females, who actually pre-
> fer leaving their only proper sphere, and working for their own
> subsistence — to starvation?[44]

Like the more radical feminists, Reid saw the doctrine of woman's
'separate sphere' as a coercive social construct which needed to be
entirely set aside. Even more indignantly, Harriet Taylor attacks
current impositions against women. Denying the right of any one
part of humanity to decide what is the 'proper sphere' for another,
she interprets women's subordination as a male strategy for the
achievement of pleasure and power; this, and not inherent female
qualities, has produced ideals of womanliness such as 'abnegation
of self, patience, resignation, and submission to power'.[45] She also
argues that wifehood and motherhood should not be seen as the only
natural female functions:

> It is neither necessary nor just to make imperative on women that
> they shall be either mothers or nothing . . . There is no inherent
> reason or necessity that all women should voluntarily choose to
> devote their lives to one animal function and its consequences.
> Numbers of women are wives and mothers only because there is
> no other career open to them.[46]

It is a nice irony that one of the mid-century's most radical female
protestors was sainted for her quasi-maternal service and self-
abnegation. Quite averse to such sentimental idealism, Florence
Nightingale questioned the fundamental organisation of family life
and mocked at the inflated virtues of wifehood and motherhood.[47]
Longing for active employment, she herself rejected the social
restrictiveness of marriage because it would hinder the achievement
of self-expression — 'I have a mind, an active nature which requires
satisfaction'.[48] She was curiously hostile to the struggles of her sex as
a whole and had little sympathy with the Women's Rights Movement,

but was passionately convinced that until women freed themselves, as she had done, from the crippling bondage of family and matrimonial ties, they could never be true individuals. As she says bitterly in *Cassandra*, the present idealisation of the 'sacred hearth' of domestic life has made marriage women's 'only chance of emancipation',[49] which of course proves no emancipation at all.

Few women were prepared to reject as wholeheartedly as these speakers the traditions in which they had been brought up. Far more commonly, throughout the female pronouncements of the period there is a note of ambivalence, a tension between a desire to challenge and change current attitudes and a reluctance to disturb the status quo. Many women realised the extent to which the elevation of womanhood in terms of 'feminine' and wifely virtues was part of a campaign of male gratification. Thus to Frances Cobbe, the greatest barrier to legislative amelioration of matrimonial inequities 'is the sentiment entertained by the majority of men on the subject; the ideal they have formed of wedlock, the poetical vision in their minds of a wife's true relation to her husband'.[50] Others such as Anna Jameson, who stoutly embraced independence after the break-up of an unsatisfactory marriage, were more openly critical of the discrepancy between sexual ideology and the actual conditions of female life:

> Surely it is dangerous, it is wicked in these days, to follow the old saw, to bring up women to be 'happy wives and mothers' . . . as if for women there existed only one destiny, one hope, one blessing, one object, one passion in existence; some people say it ought to be so, but we know that it is not so; we know that hundreds, that thousands of women are not happy wives and mothers — are never either wives or mothers at all.[51]

Josephine Butler, a firm supporter of widened opportunities for women, was particularly angry about the cruelty of continuing

> solemnly to inform the women who are striving for some work or calling which will save them from starvation, and who have no human being but themselves to depend on, that their proper sphere is *home*, — that their proper function is to be wives and mothers, and their happiness is to be dependent on men![52]

Indeed, most female writers who took up the 'woman question' recognised the gross injustice of theories which sought to confine their sex to a purely relative existence. They were, too, ready to admit that conventional images of the pitiful, broken-hearted spinster were not true to life. As Frances Cobbe briskly argues, the traditional old maid is on her way out, and in her place is a new being, 'an exceedingly cheery personage, running about untrammelled by husband and children; now visiting at her relatives' country houses, now off to a favourite *pension* on Lake Geneva, now scaling Vesuvius or the Pyramids'.[53]

Almost all these writers, however, maintained a basic conservatism alongside their dissent. Even the most thorough-going feminists felt that wifehood and motherhood were the most important aspects of female experience; what was wrong was the pretence that these roles were available to all. Anna Jameson is sure that the maternal instincts are the most natural ones in women, and Josephine Butler, while arguing that there should be a place in society for unmarried women, asserts the supremacy of home-based values. Both suggest that the state of singleness is for most women a second-best. The deep-seated ambivalence which lies behind the conjunction of conventionalism and protest in mid-Victorian feminism is particularly aptly illustrated in the writings of Frances Power Cobbe, one of the best-known early reformers. Cobbe was an unashamed individualist whose own energetic life and tireless work for the woman's cause (she supported women's suffrage and campaigned enthusiastically for the Matrimonial Causes Act of 1878) vindicates her conviction, already mentioned, that an unmarried woman can be just as fulfilled as a married one. She deprecates the 'disgraceful and abominable' habit of making matrimony 'the aim of a woman's life',[54] and argues powerfully that 'the *knowledge* of the risks of an unhappy marriage' and 'the demonstrated danger of being inexpressibly miserable'[55] should make women extremely cautious of embarking on wifehood. On the other hand, she is sure that 'for the mass of mankind, marriage is the right condition, the happiest, and the most conducive to virtue';[56] it is one of the 'laws of nature' that when 'the great and paramount duties of a mother and wife'[57] have been adopted, all other feelings become subordinate. The appeal to nature is a constant feature of her thesis: marriage is 'the condition which God has appointed as the natural one for human beings';[58] it is 'the most natural and blessed of human ties and duties'.[59] Like the other early feminists, too, she believes that the widening of women's minds will produce the multiple benefits of better and more worthily-motivated marriages, and happier single lives. The 'two leading ideas' in her 1862 essay on 'Old Maids' — to 'seek how the conditions of single women may be most effectively improved' and to show 'the promotion of marriage . . . to be the best end at which such improvement will tend'[60] — most clearly reveal her attempt to reconcile the dichotomies in her attitudes towards female roles. Cobbe's dualism — both prescribing female individuality and holding it to traditional functions — represents the widely-felt uncertainty of Victorian women.[61]

This uncertainty had its effect on the direction of feminist agitation. Wider educational and employment opportunities for women were demanded because the 'facts' of increasing spinsterhood demanded them; the kinds of female employment recommended were those such as nursing, teaching children, and helping the poor, all of which embodied quasi-maternal virtues of service and self-abnegation. The campaigns for reform concentrated largely on the plight of single women so that there would be no apparent threat to the sacred roles of wifehood and motherhood; even the attempt to ameliorate the situation of wives was an attack on the abuses, not on the institution itself. It also makes a powerful mark on the area with which we are most concerned in this study — female creative literature. Victorian women writers were especially prey to the sense of duality because their professional status created additional tensions in their experience. As we have seen, certain criteria were laid down for female novelists, neglect of which led to charges of unwomanliness; an acute conflict of roles was almost inevitable for the woman writer, who, by the very act of entering the male world of letters, was challenging the traditional female spheres of private endeavour and economic dependence. Many sought to justify society's — and their own — doubts about their activities by adopting the same arguments as the reformers, and insisting that their occupation was compatible with domestic duties and femininity. Charlotte Brontë's reluctant — but fortunately temporary — acceptance of Southey's pronouncement to her that 'Literature cannot be the business of a woman's life, and it ought not to be. The more she is engaged in her proper duties, the less leisure will she have for it, even as an accomplishment and a recreation'[62] is recalled in many of her letters in which she earnestly emphasises that her writing is never undertaken at the expense of household and family responsibilities.

Yet Brontë also expresses her frustration at being forced to consider the needs and conditions created by her external environment.

She wrote in puzzled protest to Mrs Gaskell in 1853:

> Do you, who have so many friends, — so large a circle of acquaintance, — find it easy, when you sit down to write, to isolate yourself from all those ties, and their sweet associations, so as to be your *own woman*, uninfluenced or swayed by the consciousness of how your work may affect other minds; what blame or what sympathy it may call forth?[63]

Gaskell herself in her letters frequently expresses her sense of conflict between her roles as wife/mother and novelist; and in her *Life of Charlotte Brontë* she acknowledges, somewhat ruefully, that 'a woman's principal work in life is hardly left to her own choice; nor can she drop the domestic charges devolving on her as an individual, for the exercise of the most splendid talents that were ever bestowed'.[64] Elizabeth Sewell's wry recall of her youthful definitive opinion 'that women had no business to write'[65] similarly indicates the female author's uncertainties about the career of letters for women, just as her later tireless drive to combine literary and domestic activity reveals the equally strong pull of each. Indeed, most mid-century women writers suffer from the anxiety 'that they may give no occasion for vulgar men to say . . . that learning makes women unfeminine, and that literary ladies are likely to be bad wives'.[66]

These questionings find their way into the fiction, which not only reveals the kinds of paradoxes experienced by the writers but also shows how the novelists sought creatively to come to terms with their ambivalence. Their own lives embody their conceptual dilemmas. Many of them never enacted the pattern of romantic fulfilment which they created for their heroines:[67] some never married at all; some did not marry until they had written a considerable body of their fiction; some were widows; a few were in an anomalous position, either separated from their husbands, or, like George Eliot, in a sexual relation which conferred the emotional security but not the social advantages of legal matrimony. Of those treated in this study, only Mrs Gaskell bore children. They were all 'workers' who exercised their energies beyond the merely domestic, not only as novelists but often in other areas: Dinah Mulock, like Geraldine Jewsbury and Eliza Lynn Linton, was involved in the literary world as critic and publisher's reader; Marian Evans, before her union with Lewes, enjoyed a position of considerable, if unseen, power as co-editor of

Chapman's *Westminster Review*; the three Brontë sisters had brief careers as governesses; Elizabeth Sewell established and taught in two successful schools in the Isle of Wight; Mrs Gaskell took a prominent part in public affairs in Manchester. Most of them relished the enlarged freedom and opportunity for travel and social intercourse which their work made available to them. Yet their novels suggest that they accepted the romantic orthodoxies; in apparent contravention of their own experience, they focus centrally on courtship and marriage in their books and portray little in the way of alternative female occupation.

Recent feminist criticism, building on the idea of opposition between artistic conformity and personal conviction, has interpreted the contradictions and ambiguities inherent in mid-Victorian women's fiction as deliberate strategies to provide an oblique means of communicating the writers' unease to other women. Elaine Showalter, for instance, argues that many Victorian female novelists, fully aware of the frustrating dualisms of their lives, implement what she calls the 'tactics of sentiment', novelistic devices such as covertly rebellious language and projection on to male figures, 'by which sentimental narratives articulated female conflict about achievement and affiliation'.[68] In an innovative study of the women writers of the period, Gilbert and Gubar claim that female images of escape, and oscillation between overtly 'angelic' dogma and covertly Satanic fury, are oblique indications of protest against patriarchal tyranny,[69] a line developed further in Nina Auerbach's recent work on Victorian images of women.[70] These approaches are richly suggestive, but because they argue from the premise of the writers' deviousness and their 'covert/overt' strategy, they tend to play down the fact that puzzlement, as much as anger and rebellion, constitutes the female literary response to contemporary ideologies. Although it is true that Victorian women novelists often had to resort to obliquity in order to voice their dissent, it is also the case that many of them quite consciously articulate in their novels their ambivalence about sexual roles. The dichotomies in their work can be seen as direct confrontation of the discordancies of their world, an exploration of the dualistic nature of female experience, both protest against and accession to convention. So, while implementing traditional patterns of marriage and motherhood, they uncover the miseries of matrimonial bondage; they set a woman's desire for autonomous self-fulfilment against her need for emotional enrichment; they vent their anger at male cruelty and exploitation alongside their comforting portrayals of harmonious sexual relationships. Their uncertainties are thus an intrinsic part of the fabric of their fiction.

Not only the major writers express their discontent in this way. As we shall see, even those novelists who have been relegated to the ranks of the minor for the very reason that they appear to lack the creative imagination which transcends artistic conventionality and offers new insights into human experience, incorporate dissent within the traditional formulations of their narratives. They give glimpses of alternatives, sometimes hesitatingly, rarely radically attacking accepted ideologies, but clearly demonstrating their recognition that in reality sexual relationships are never exactly as imaged by the idealisms of their age. Whether duality is a central theme in their work, or whether unease manifests itself merely as tensions or discrepancies, they are all involved in the current debate about sexual roles.

Victorian women novelists, then, writing in the context of growing protest about the position of their own sex, echo the anxieties, anger, and ambivalence which, as we have seen, constitute the voice of mid-century feminism. The protesters, Janus-fashion, looked both ways: most of them genuinely believed that wifehood and motherhood represented the apotheosis of womanly fulfilment, yet they also recognised that since it was impossible that all women should achieve this fulfilment, society should stop promoting delusive ideologies and instead equip women to deal with the changed circumstances; they acknowledged, too, that spinsterhood had its own rewards and that it was reprehensible to deny this. The novelists also looked both ways, reflecting the attitudes of their more overtly propagandist contemporaries. Their challenge is wide-ranging, from a tentative assertion of womanly independence to a celebration of the blessings of the single life, from muted dissent from the ideology of matrimonial bliss to an outright attack on masculine deficiencies and tyrannies, but underlying all of it is an awareness of the profound tensions between new visions of womanhood and the old traditions upon which their lives were founded and to which they still in part adhered.

The range of novelists for discussion here is considerable. The better-known ones inevitably offer themselves because their particularly individual approaches to sexual themes mark them off from their less innovative contemporaries. Among the less familiar ones the choice is wide. Those selected for detailed analysis in this study have been picked out because their work is representative of the variety of response in the female fiction of the period, and because they help to confirm that it is possible to talk of a 'sisterhood' of women writers, sharing similar preoccupations and techniques. Before examining the work of the selected individuals, however, it will be useful to glance briefly at a few of the novelists not accorded detailed treatment. In some ways, these represent more extreme positions than the other writers, whether as romantics, reactionaries, or overt iconoclasts. But all show how stereotypicality and unorthodoxy can co-exist within a single work of art, and how duality can fruitfully be accommodated within it.

Julia Kavanagh is an example of a minor Victorian woman novelist whose work embodies all the romantic orthodoxies: her heroines' lives centre on love and its turbulent emotional crises; heavily influenced by the courtship theme of *Jane Eyre*, her narratives, as Mrs Oliphant puts it, do 'little else than repeat the attractive story of this conflict and combat of love or war'.[71] In many ways, Kavanagh is a 'pattern' single woman of her period. Shy, physically weak and unprepossessing, she substituted for wifely devotion a life-long dedication to her mother, writing in order to support both of them after her father, an eccentric author and philologist, had cavalierly abandoned his wife and child. The obsessively romantic content of her novels can be seen as a combination of wish-fulfilment — the imaginative enactment of personal fantasies — and pragmatic response to commercial demands. Yet, as Charlotte Brontë rightly surmised even before actually meeting her in 1850, Kavanagh was of sterner stuff than her literary tendencies might suggest. Brontë saw her as of the class 'in which endurance combines with exertion . . . self-reliance [is] unalloyed by self-complacency', a character developed by toil and struggle against adversity.[72] At least on one notable occasion she had to break through her female self-protectiveness and speak publicly as a writer in order to refute the dishonesty of her father when he coolly tried to pass off his own feeble novel, *The Hobbies* (1857), as the work of his now well-known daughter.[73]

Kavanagh's comments about women's literature also suggest that she did not take a wholly one-sided view of female characteristics and abilities. On the one hand, recognising that women have something special to contribute to the novel, she praises what she sees as distinctive female artistic qualities — respectability and refinement, 'the feminine attributes of delicacy, tenderness, and purity'[74] — for their power of portraying 'the internal woman, that mystery which man has rarely fathomed';[75] she also claims that women write from an 'intuitive knowledge of human nature',[76] and know 'how to appeal to the heart'.[77] Kavanagh echoes current convention in positing that love, the source of woman's influence, and passion, treated with 'lofty purity',[78] are the most suitable subjects for female fiction. As a character in her *John Dorrien* (1875) says, if a story is not a love-story it is no story at all. She is also convinced that 'not unwise is the law of old romances that closes a love tale with marriage', though her appeal here is to life — that once the 'exquisite moment' is reached it cannot be prolonged[79] — rather than to literary convention.

On the other hand, Kavanagh is aware of the limitations of such assumptions. She criticises the idealisation, the false depictions, of 'a world too sweet, too fair, too good',[80] which over-refinement in women's writing can produce; and she does not approve of the artistic distortions created by 'the predominance given to love as the great problem of human life'.[81] She is also firmly opposed to the literary portrayal of women as mere sex-objects, 'not wise . . . not lofty or intellectual . . . [but] silly young creatures made to delight man, to amuse, tease, and obey him',[82] preferring Fanny Burney's stouter-minded kind of heroine, who takes an innovative part in romantic relationships instead of just standing about waiting 'to be wooed and won'.[83] Interestingly, one of Kavanagh's reviewers suggests that she was not whole-heartedly drawn to neatly romantic conclusions: 'She occasionally half laughingly complained that Mrs Kavanagh's inveterate objection to sad endings somewhat hampered her in the conception of . . . [her] plots; for, as she argued, to make everybody happy all round, is unfortunately not exactly true to life.'[84] Unlike Charlotte Brontë, however, Kavanagh was unable to resist family pressure in this respect.

Kavanagh's own novels, as has been implied, are 'romantic' in a very traditional sense. Many of her heroines, passionate, rebellious, and often frustrated by their narrow existences, are, after lengthy misunderstandings or obstructions, finally purged of their wilfulness when they become good wives, prepared to honour and obey their mentor-husbands. The eponymous heroine of *Beatrice* (1865), for example, having at last achieved the fulfilment she has yearned for, and been transformed into a submissive and supportive helpmeet (with, it may be added, enough toughness to go out as a governess when her husband loses his job), upholds her creator's

belief that 'the true happiness of life — of woman's life especially — [is] love, home, and its joys'.[85] At the same time,
Kavanagh's vision of spinsterhood as a state of mournful resignation reinforces her stereotypical view of female needs. In *Nathalie*
(1850), the heroine's sister, Rose, is an instance of the single,
unloved woman who, feeling that she has been 'excluded from
existence'[86] and denied 'woman's destiny' (III, 184), is enabled to
bear her 'lonely fate . . . a quiet, obscure, and apparently useless
life' (III, 185–6) only by turning to religion and its creed of self-
sacrifice. The same kind of angelic self-abnegation is seen in *Rachel
Gray* (1856), in which the plain, sickly heroine dedicates her own
loveless life to the service of others; it also appears in *Daisy Burns*
(1853), in which the hero's sister has given up her suitor in order
to devote herself to her brother. Life without emotional fulfilment,
Kavanagh seems to be saying, can at best be only calm stoical
endurance.

Nevertheless, within this framework of conventional formulations, there are hints of questioning or dissent. In *Nathalie*, there is
an undercurrent of restlesssness which breaks out into directly
authorial protest:

> Amongst the 'wrongs of women', few are really more heavy and
> insupportable than the forced inactivity to which they are con-
> demned in all the life, fire, and energy of youth . . . They are
> social prisoners . . . a few . . . break through their bonds, and
> throw themselves into the social strife; but for one who wins the
> shore, how many perish miserably! (II, 104–5)

Nathalie's own turbulent emotions are satisfied by her eventual
marriage to an older, calmer man, but the suggestion of the attractiveness of womanly freedom lurks below the surface of the story. It
is there more strongly in *Adèle* (1858), where Kavanagh takes a more
penetratingly critical look at sexual relationships. In this novel she
follows many Victorian women novelists, including Craik, Sewell,
and Anne Brontë, in showing how marriage, while at its best the
supreme source of female happiness, may easily prove a delusory
paradise. Forewarned by the unhappy matrimonial experiences of
her friend who has been forced to accept an older and unsympathetic husband and now passively endures her dreary lot, Adèle
rejects the idea of marriage as a mere contract. She tells her cousin,
'do not ask me to marry a man whom I do not like; it is against my

honour to sell myself'.[87] When she impulsively agrees to marry a man with whom she is not really in love, she finds his newly-awakened passionate tenderness cloying and almost threatening. She longs to regain her lost liberty and to escape the bonds which seem to encircle her: 'it makes me mad to be married. . . . I feel fettered like one that is bound hand and foot — stifled like one that has not air to breathe' (II, 107). Beneath this somewhat naive expression of self-assertion, there are hints of sexual fear, combined with the torment of knowing that the choice was freely made. The importance of female self-respect within matrimony, too, is stressed in Adèle's angry reaction on learning that her husband initially married her in reparation for a wrong done to her family by his half-brother; again, the authorial voice is compelling:

> there is one feeling born and bred beyond all other feelings in a woman's heart — the pride of her being, the sense of her worth as a woman . . . when that feeling has been outraged . . . the woman who does not keenly feel that she has been cruelly wronged has not the nature of her sex. (II, 251–2)

The notion of the wrongs done to women by men (touched on in *Nathalie*, in the depiction of the unpleasant youth who relentlessly tries to force his unwelcome attentions on the heroine) is taken up again in *Beatrice* in the figure of Beatrice's governess, Miss Jameson, who, deserted by her former lover and badly treated in her previous employment, has become servile and shy, with 'a heart which might never have been great, but would have been good, had it not been profaned for a man's pastime' (I, 180). Beatrice herself is rewarded with a good man, but we are reminded that some women are less fortunate by the sufferings of her sister-in-law, an ill-used wife who, crushed by her husband's oppression, finally lapses into alcoholism. None of these themes could be called radical protest, and the 'anti-romantic' elements of Kavanagh's novels are often clumsily and unconvincingly interpolated into the narrative. Her depiction of conflicting feelings in the heroines themselves, as well as her own tentative affirmation of the importance of female individuality, do however indicate her reluctance to accept unquestioningly the sexual ideologies of her age.

Charlotte Yonge could be considered an archetypal Victorian conservative: firmly established in the middle class and unswervingly committed to Oxford Movement Anglicanism, she held rigidly hierarchical views about social status and sexual roles. The essentially orthodox stance of her fiction seems a direct reflection of these views as well as of her literary aims and methods. She always regarded herself as 'a sort of instrument for popularizing Church views'[88] and this, taken in conjunction with her firm belief in the serious moral purpose of all literary endeavour, accounts for the careful 'respectability' of her novels. Her prime interest in family, rather than sexual, relationships — perhaps a result of the apparent lack of romantic experience in her own life — also suggests that she has little of relevance to say about issues of particular concern to women. This latter view is, however, misleading. Yonge took an interest in the 'Woman Question', especially in its educational developments. She knew Elizabeth Sewell and her experiments in girls' schooling; Anne Moberly, First Principal of St Hugh's, Oxford, was a family friend; and her friendship with Elizabeth Wordsworth, founder and Principal of Lady Margaret Hall, Oxford, whom she first met in 1870, probably made her better-disposed towards the idea of higher education for women, although she was never wholly enthusiastic about institutionalised female education. Much of this interest comes into her novels: in *Magnum Bonum* (1879), Janet Brownlow goes to Zurich to study medicine (though, regrettably, her faith becomes unsettled there); in *The Long Vacation* (1895), Dolores Mohun and Gillian Merrifield go to university, proving their creator's willingness to keep up with the times. In a more general sense, too, Yonge was concerned with the problems of young women; within the religious and domestic settings of her novels she portrays the developments of female selfhood in the context of conflicting loyalties and clashes between personal ambition and external conditions.

Certainly, we can expect no radical pronouncements from Yonge. A sentence in the second paragraph of her own 'feminist' apologia, *Womankind* (published in 1887; serialised in the *Monthly Packet* from 1874 to 1877), sums up the basic conviction on which rests all her subsequent opinions: 'I have no hesitation in declaring my full belief in the inferiority of woman, nor that she brought it upon herself.'[89] She accepts unequivocally the traditional womanly virtues; for her, gentleness, modesty, and 'all the graces of humility, meekness, and submission [are] the true strength and beauty of womanhood' (240). She expects women to rely on men's superior powers and scorns those 'strong-minded' females who make themselves and their sex absurd by trying to emulate masculine behaviour. Her conventional view of womanhood is incorporated in her attitude towards wives and matrimony. In images reminiscent of Patmore and Ruskin, she describes the wifely role:

> Efficiency, sympathy, cheerfulness, unselfishness, and sweet temper: these are chiefly what go to make the real helpmeet wife . . . the true lady — or loaf-giver — is sure to make homes that radiate light and warmth from their glowing central hearth. (188–9)

Later, she repeats that 'Home-making is perhaps the most essential of all the duties of womankind' (264).

Not surprisingly, Yonge's novels reflect this traditionalism. Her heroines take on roles such as teaching in village schools and helping the poor, but express no dissatisfaction with the basic state of society and have to accept that personal aspiration must be resigned when domestic duty calls. 'Angel' wives, such as Amy in *The Heir of Redclyffe* (1853) and Violet in *Heartsease* (1854), embody the true wifely virtues in their humble submissiveness, which, combined with strong moral natures, enables them to exert an influence for good upon their husbands. In *The Three Brides* (1876), during a discussion of Women's Rights in which, as might be expected, an American female supporter of Equality of the Sexes is exposed to considerable authorial mockery, the conventional image of femininity is prescribed — 'the true wife and mother' provides that 'sweetness and tender innocence and purity that make a man's home an ideal and a sanctuary — his best earthly influence'.[90] This novel argues, too, that wives must show a proper submission to their husband's authority. Others of Yonge's characters who do not take matrimonial commitment seriously are punished: in *The Daisy Chain* (1856) Flora May's unwomanliness, evidenced by her marriage to a worldly man and by her involvement in outside affairs, is chastised by the death of her baby; in *The Clever Woman of the Family* (1865), Bessie Keith dies in childbirth because she has deliberately married a man to whom she is indifferent.

Yonge's sexual conservatism is, however, tinged with elements of unorthodoxy. Her own life illustrates the paradoxes in the lives of so many Victorian women. She was always dependent on male guidance (her father and John Keble read all her early work, none of which was published without their approval); she was a consistently dutiful daughter, devoting herself to her widowed mother and taking her with her on many of her visits from home; and she made no attempt to penetrate the literary coterie of her day. Yet she was well-educated, competent in Latin, Greek, French, Italian, and mathematics; she ran her magazine for young women, the *Monthly Packet*, for over thirty years and dealt with all its business almost single-handed; and she was widely involved in Church affairs. There are glimpses of this more independent spirit in *Womankind*, in those sections where she challenges some of the more reactionary opinions about women. She is sharply critical of 'weak, narrow-minded' (82) women who add themselves 'to the already overtoppling mass of froth of female silliness' (242), and argues that they need to develop their intellectual capacities, if only to make them more intelligent and agreeable companions to their husbands. While recognising that a wife must dedicate herself primarily to her family, she points to the important truth that 'pleasing her husband and making him comfortable and attending to her children is only a part of her office . . . what she *is*, the opinions she utters, the influence she exerts, have a power for which she is accountable' (297–8).

Yonge is also sensitive to the needs of single women. They must not be considered failures because they have missed matrimony, and their place in society, conferred by God, must be acknowledged:

There . . . comes in the woman's question of the day — Is she meant to be nothing but the help-meet? If by this is meant the wife, or even the sister or daughter, attached to the aid of some particular man, I do not think she is. It is her most natural, most obvious, most easy destiny; but one of the greatest incidental benefits that Christianity brought the whole sex was that of rendering marriage no longer the only lot of all, and thus making both the wife and the maiden stand on higher ground. (4)

Yonge sees a specific role for single women in the newly-developing Anglican sisterhoods,[91] but she envisages, too, the contentment of the spinster, ready to offer her sympathy to others but 'never happier than when alone' (272). The 'stuffy spinster, the scandal-monger of the country town' (321) has been replaced by an admirable, self-reliant individual in Yonge's vision here.

In her fiction, Yonge shows a similar awareness, especially of the needs of more exceptional women. She does, even here, implement two main strategies of conventional resolution — marriage as a salutary return to normality, and singleness accepted as devoted service rather than seen as a 'career' in its own right. But many of her novels explore individual female selfhood, eventually coming to terms with imposed circumstances but at least finding a voice of its own. Theodora Martin in *Heartsease* is a blueprint for the later more extensive portrayal of 'strong-minded' womanhood in *The Clever Woman of the Family*. Yonge mocks her eccentricities and exaggerations — Theodora loftily scorns all 'girlish, caressing ways'[92] and takes herself off to lectures on chemistry and Mesmerism — and also shows that much of her rebelliousness arises from self-will and jealousy of her brother's childlike wife. But she is not wholly unsympathetic to her heroine's earnest attempts to break free from conventionality, seen in her rejection of socially speculative marriage or her willingness to support herself if necessary — 'Independence is trusting for maintenance to our own head and hands . . . I would gladly get my own bread.'[93] In this novel, Yonge is too firmly tied to the ideal image of womanhood (embodied in Violet, Theodora's angelic sister-in-law) to allow her sympathy to venture far. Theodora has to recognise both the importance of female emotions (awakened in her, significantly, by her unwilled fondness for her baby nephew) and that her correct place is at home, helping to ameliorate the domestic troubles of her feckless brother and his long-suffering wife. Finally, having been spiritually purged when she is burnt during a fire, she achieves salvation through marriage to a good man who will guide and protect her.

Despite this conventional romantic ending, Theodora's portrayal reveals Yonge's cautious awareness that if female individuality is too rigidly confined it will seek dangerous outlets of expression, a view which she explores more fully in *The Clever Woman of the Family*. This novel is usually taken to be Yonge's most virulent attack on feminism and her most conservative depiction of womanhood, but it is worth looking a little more closely at this judgement. Rachel Curtis, eccentric, arrogant, and vigorously opposed to all 'systems', is certainly treated to strong authorial irony. Yonge mockingly depicts Rachel's resistance to conventional womanly behaviour, symbolised in a first venture into creative writing, whose 'slender thread of story' is heavily weighted 'with disquisitions on economy and charity', and which plans to place the heroines in 'various industrial asylums where their lot should be far more beatific than marriage, which was reserved for the naughty one to live unhappy in ever after'.[94] As could be anticipated, Rachel is a 'naughty one'. Her presumptuous experiments in the unfeminine world of professional life come to grief when she is duped by a free-thinking charlatan into putting money into an industrial school, whose appalling conditions cause the death of several children. Despite her earlier view of marriage as suffering and 'bondage' (228), and her determination to reserve herself for better things, she is saved by the traditional method — the protective love of a sensible man, Alick Keith, who leads her back to faith and a recognition of her own inferiority. Her new humility, indeed, seems so self-deprecating that it is tempting to see hints of authorial ambivalence — a sense of compromise, or a wry acknowledgement of the demands of orthodoxy — towards Rachel's vision of herself as 'commonplace' (337), fit only to be 'an ordinary married woman, with an Alick to take care of me' (410).

Yonge, however, does not close her case quite as conclusively as this suggests. In the first place, she is not totally dismissive of her heroine's aspirations. Rachel, like Eliot's Dorothea Brooke, represents the plight of a young, intelligent woman who needs an outlet for her energies and longs to do good in the world, but is frustrated by social circumstances. Yonge allows a personal note to enter her description of Rachel's predicament:

> she felt the influence of an age eminently practical and sifting, but with small powers of acting. The quiet Lady Bountiful duties that had sufficed her mother and sister were too small and easy to satisfy a soul burning at the report of the great cry going up to heaven from a world of sin and woe. (7)

In the second place, Yonge offers an alternative image of womanhood to counterbalance the absurdity/conformity polarisation which Rachel's career represents. The other heroine — acknowledged at the end of the novel by Rachel herself to be the real Clever Woman — is a sofa-invalid, Ermine Williams, who, as one critic has put it, subtly beats the feminists at their own game, showing how women can exert influence from behind the scenes.[95] Ermine writes periodical articles (a rare instance of this particular reflection of 'life' in Victorian female fiction), but anonymously; she fills her time intelligently with intellectual pursuits, and is in touch with all the latest opinions of the day. Though conventionally feminine in her unobtrusiveness, she is a staunch proponent of female individuality. Significantly, she admires Rachel, finds her company stimulating, and defends her against the typically conservative male view of her as a 'detestable, pragmatical, domineering girl' (113), declaring stoutly that 'I feel for her longing to be up and doing, and her puzzled chafing against constraint and conventionality' (114). She herself eventually marries her long-lost lover, but though she keeps her simplicity and genuine humility, she does not give up her writing and retains her independence of mind. Ermine hardly represents a radical feminism, but in that she reaches beyond the female norm (the nature of her invalidism suggests that she will never have children) and is able to express her selfhood from within traditional confines she embodies Yonge's sense of intrinsic potential in women.

Yonge's depiction of the single woman who escapes the 'bondage' of matrimony also suggests an extension of traditional womanly roles. Apart from occasional caricature — the eccentric Miss Marstone in *Heartsease*, or the prim, middle-aged fussy governess, Miss Winter in *The Daisy Chain*, for instance — her treatment of spinsterhood is perceptive and sympathetic. Her most famous 'unattached' heroine is Ethel May, introduced in *The Daisy Chain* and subsequently appearing in *The Trial* (1864) and *The Pillars of the House* (1873). From the first, the awkward, intelligent, idealistic girl was so popular that a family friend, Dr Moberly, was probably speaking for many of her public when he made Yonge promise that she would never alter the original conception of her heroine by letting her marry or her father die.[96] Ethel, like Theodora and Rachel, is one of Yonge's articulate, non-conforming young women, rejecting stifling conventionality and striving for noble attainment. With her, however, womanly maturity is achieved not through marriage but through learning the duties of a single woman, carried out in a spirit of faith. Ethel has to accept that her classical studies, undertaken in emulation of her brother, are interfering with her 'being a useful, steady daughter and sister at home';[97] she is granted the fulfilment of her church-building scheme, but her prime law must be self-sacrifice to family needs. Yonge kept her promise, and Ethel remains a spinster, an old maid without the exaggerations usually attached to such a figure. She represents the possibility of womanly satisfaction without marriage: an early romance with a cousin is quickly suppressed by Ethel's sense of duty, and we are assured that 'she had never given away the depths of her heart, though the upper surface had been stirred' (637); in *The Trial* any potential romantic feeling for young Leonard Ward remains idle fancy due to her ten years' seniority. There is, though, a note of wistfulness in her awareness, at the end of *The Daisy Chain*, that 'the unmarried woman must not seek individual return of affection, and must not set her love, with exclusive eagerness, on aught below, but must be ready to cease in turn to be first with any' (667). Yonge also sets her championship of singleness in an ideologically traditional framework; committed to the service of others, Ethel remains a daughter, denied the full maturity of independent womanhood, perhaps reflecting Yonge's own desire to remain filially dependent:

> I think the bereavement of the last parent is the sorrow that an unmarried woman always feels most, it seems so entirely to end the sense of being a child at home to be thought for and cared for, and to leave one so desolate without shelter from the world.[98]

Hopes and Fears (1861) — significantly subtitled *Scenes from the Life of a Spinster* — contains Yonge's most extensive examination of female singleness; written between *The Daisy Chain* and *The Trial*, the novel perhaps represents its creator's most acutely personal sense of the crisis of lonely middle-age. Like Ethel, Honora Charlecote is denied romantic fulfilment: her adolescent hero-worship of the young missionary, Owen Sandbrook, is punctured when he marries someone else and becomes a worldly-minded clergyman, while her changed feelings towards her kind but unglamorous cousin Humfrey, who has twice proposed to her in vain, are rendered fruitless by his sudden death. Though youth and early affections are past, Honora takes on a new lease of life as surrogate parent to Owen's two children and manager of Humfrey's estate, which he has bequeathed to her, thus acting out the roles and duties of both her ex-lovers. Honora's portrayal is remarkably free from the kind of satirical treatment accorded Theodora's and Rachel's attempts to break away from conventional femininity. Here, the heroine finds suitable occupation, cheerfully discovering that life has far more to offer than she imagined. Her management of the children and of estate affairs is 'real government';[99] she is as capable of subduing the passionate Lucilla as of dealing with a stubborn employee; she enjoys the freedom of moral and financial independence.

The novel's maturity is evident not only in its more positive assertion of female individuality but also in Yonge's honest depiction of the strains as well as the joys of womanly self-reliance. Unlike Ethel, Honora has only herself to depend on and she bravely faces the implications of her deficiencies, in particular her inability to keep up with the tides of modernism, represented by the Sandbrook children. Honora's self-knowledge becomes part of a historical process in which the older generation must give way to the new, and acknowledge its own redundancy. As Lucilla bluntly expresses it: 'the last generation was that of medievalism, ecclesiology, chivalry, symbolism, whatever you may call it. Married women have worked out of it. It is the middle-aged maids that monopolize it. Ours is that of common sense' (541). When Honora's other 'child', Phoebe Fulmort (a local businessman's daughter befriended by her), marries Humfrey's Canadian cousin and the new heir takes over the estate, past and present are reconciled, and the romantic 'middle-aged maid' willingly surrenders her power, confident that the 'goodly heritage' (640) will be well tended. Honora also, like Sally Mortimer at the end of Sewell's *The Experience of Life*, finds peace and contentment after her earlier cares and mistakes:

> the human affection that once failed her is come back upon her in full measure. She is no longer forlorn; the children whom she bred up, and those whom she led by her influence, alike vie with one another in their love and gratitude. (643)

Yonge's picture of spinsterhood here is not without its conventional aspects — it still emphasises self-sacrifice and the consolations of the world beyond — but it challenges the notion of female singleness as suffering and waste, and makes an honest evaluation of womanly capabilities.

With both Kavanagh and Yonge we have seen how essentially conservative women novelists — the one embodying romantic ideology, the other Christian codes of self-renunciation and submission — can question their own conscious conventionalism from within the orthodox framework of their narratives. Geraldine Jewsbury is an example of a novelist who expresses her dissent more overtly. As a recent article has argued, Jewsbury's fiction reflects the contradictions she herself experienced: the conflict of roles which, as we have seen, troubled many Victorian women writers, is expressed in her work through 'split' characters who enact the contrary pulls of womanly 'normality' and professional or spiritual independence.[100]

As her letters indicate, Jewsbury dissented from traditional ideologies more vigorously than either Kavanagh or Yonge. She delighted in her own unorthodoxy; she smoked cigars, used slang, relished the fact that her first novel *Zoë* (1845), which treated sexual passion and religious apostasy, was widely regarded as 'outrageous', and upheld 'George Sandism' as her model of female authorship. She enjoyed informal friendships with the men encountered in her literary work — there is an easy familiarity of tone in her letters to William Hepworth Dixon of the *Athenaeum*, for instance[101] — perhaps vindicating her belief in future comradeship between men and women in which the women's feelings would not all run to love, and they would not be 'reduced by their position to see them [men] as lovers or husbands'.[102] She was particularly critical of romantic creeds which forced women into undesired roles. Her strong sympathy for wronged wives, including Jane Carlyle, whom she regarded as the victim of a selfish husband and whose 'patience and endurance' (76) had done nothing but perpetuate her wifely misery, is based on indignation at male attitudes towards women. She is highly scornful of the 'civility, or the sort of gallantry (God save the mark!) that adulterates all the little bit of straightforward dealing women meet with from men, and is the reason they do so little that is really worth anything!' (204). Like the early feminist theorists, she views idealising images of womanhood as the creation of male fantasy; at present, she argues scathingly, 'the tendency of all the training they [women] get is just adapted to the prevailing fancy of men — a strong taste of housewifery in one generation, a dash of delicate 'feminine' stupidity in another, a gentle flavour of religion' (341-2). One of her dearest hopes for the future is that women will be released from constricting ideologies:

> I believe we are touching on better days, when women will have a genuine, normal life of their own to lead. There, perhaps, will not be so many marriages, and women will be taught not to feel their destiny *manqué* if they remain single. (347)

She and Jane, Jewsbury claims, represent

> indications of a development of womanhood which as yet is not recognised. It has, so far, no ready-made channels to run in, but still we have looked, and tried, and found that the present rules for women will not hold us; that something better and stronger is needed. (348)

For herself, 'all the eccentricities and mistakes and miseries and absurdities I have made are only the consequences of an imperfect formation, an immature growth' (348).

Despite this vision of a new species of womanhood, Jewsbury retained many of the traditional assumptions about her sex. The editor of her letters, Mrs Alexander Ireland, claims that she had a divided personality — 'Intellectually she was a man, but the heart within her was as womanly as ever daughter of Eve could boast' (vii–viii) — and this 'womanliness' (described with such arch sentimentality here) reveals itself in several ways. Jewsbury sees that love will always be central in women's lives, and though she is wry about her own love affairs — 'I don't think I ever shall have luck with my lovers' (235) — she clearly lived on her emotions, and suffered considerable pain from her romantic involvements, including her stormily passionate friendship with Jane. She also acknowledges the importance of the mother/child relationship, and accepts that home duties, such as looking after a sick brother, must come before literary activities. Furthermore, though she laughingly tells Jane, uneasy about the 'decency' of *Zoë*, that since all her efforts to make the novel 'proper behaved' have failed she must conclude that she has 'no vocation for propriety' (145), certainly by the 1860s, as a recent critic has shown, she had developed more conservative attitudes towards the portrayal of sexual attraction in fiction and was especially offended by those women novelists who openly flouted standards of decency.[103] Like other Victorian women novelists, Jewsbury experienced the stressful dualities involved in being both woman and writer:

> it is a problem that bothers me — viz., that when women get to be energetic, strong characters, with literary reputations of their own, and live in the world, with business to attend to, they all do get in the habit of making use of people, and of taking care of themselves in a way that is startling! And yet how are they to help it? . . . In short, wherever a woman gets to be a personage in any shape it makes her hard and unwomanly in some point or other. (367–8)

We see the same public/private dichotomy in Jewsbury's attitude towards Women's Rights. Though she read Frances Cobbe's writings and signed the petition for the Married Women's Property Act in 1857, she breezily dissociates herself from radical movements:

As to the 'emancipation of women' I really don't understand the subject. I have always been quite *content* with getting my own way — and I do not suppose that any of the sex desires more than that and I assure you I never either *write* or talk on that subject — it is quite as much as I can do to take care of myself![104]

What a phrenologist observer of Jewsbury termed her 'inconsistencies' (325), but what may more accurately be called her ambivalence, plays a direct part in her novels. *Zoë* is a much more searching depiction of female endeavour to reach beyond traditional confines than we find in Kavanagh or Yonge. The eponymous heroine diverges from feminine normality: educated like a boy and rebelling against social values, she is determined 'to make for herself, in spite of all obstacles, a destiny equal to all her vague dreams',[105] but because she is a woman subject to parental and societal restraints she has no employment for her energies. Marrriage comes to seem her only possible release, the only way of finding the freedom of a 'rational being' (I, 188). Jewsbury's stance is, however, ambiguous. She shows how an aspiring woman is driven into the delusive bonds of matrimony because she can find nothing to satisfy her artistic or intellectual impulses, yet she also argues that female sublimity can be achieved only through romantic passion, which, as one character expresses it, 'in its highest manifestations, ceases to be a mere passion; it becomes a worship, a religion; it regenerates the whole soul' (II, 261). Zoë falls in love with an apostate Roman Catholic priest, Everhard, who also has unfulfilled aspirations but who as a man can implement his unorthodoxy in an active vocation (he helps in a Welsh community, then goes to continue his work in Germany). Everhard's male achievement is contrasted with Zoë's female helplessness, while his love becomes a redeeming force, softening and purifying her and teaching her real 'moral beauty' (II, 308). Yet because such passion tarnishes the traditional image of sinless womanhood, it cannot stand as the apotheosis of womanly fulfilment. Everhard has to be rejected; and when Zoë's second lover, the masterful Byronic Mirabeau, urges her to flee with him, she refuses on grounds of self-respect (like Jane Eyre, she is not prepared to accept the insecurity of an illegal liaison) and of maternal responsibility (she will not abandon her children). She is finally left a chastened and disappointed woman, embodying a stereotypical female resignation.

In *Zoë*, Jewsbury directly expresses the same ambivalence about female roles that we saw in her letters:

> [women] are by the very constitution of their being, passive, receptive; in proportion as a true feminine disposition is developed, the positive, the active, becomes uncongenial to their nature; and in exact proportion as woman becomes active, self-sufficing, subjective instead of objective, she is a grander character, of stronger and more heroic mould, but she approaches the nature of a man. (III, 43-4)

The dualities of the novel indicate her inability to resolve this paradox. She wants to assert the primacy of female individuality, but cannot envisage it divorced from emotional satisfaction; she recognises the inadequacies of conventional marriage, but cannot propose a more radical alternative of 'free' womanhood.

In *The Half Sisters* (1848), Jewsbury breaks away from the impasse of defining womanly fulfilment solely in terms of idealised sexual passion. The two heroines — the half-sisters of the title — represent contrasting ways of confronting the restrictiveness of conventional female existence. Both aspire beyond trivial domesticity and both reject standard ideologies about female roles. But whereas the one's rebelliousness is positive and energetic, the other's is aimless and self-destructive. Alice Helmsby's aspirations are 'vague, undefined, restless',[106] and she cannot free herself from the small-town attitudes which teach that wives should be quiet, efficient housekeepers and that spinsters are poor dreary creatures. She marries Bryant — a respectable, preoccupied businessman who does not understand her — and is stultified by matrimony; able to conceive of no higher goal than an exclusive, adoring love, she indulges in an undutiful passion for the fickle Percy Conrad, the strains of which finally kill her. The half-Italian orphan, Bianca, on the other hand, aims beyond merely emotional gratification by resolutely embarking on an acting career. Her high goal is art, the 'sacred necessity' (I, 205), and her professionalism confers on her a kind of supra-personal individuality. Consecrated by the nobility of her aim, she finds her own voice through creativity.

This sharpness of contrast is not maintained. Alice's dismal fate highlights the predicament of a woman who wants to achieve self-identity but is too feeble to escape from the interlocked alternatives of restrictive matrimony or unlicensed passion. Yet Bianca, apparently triumphing over this predicament, herself returns to female conventionality when she accepts a marriage proposal from her admirer, Lord Melton; she willingly accedes to his request that she leave the stage, now recognising her emotional needs and convinced that dedication to art is not woman's highest vocation. This apparent inconsistency in the novel is directly examined, and the duality it represents becomes a central theme. In a lengthy discussion, Melton and Conrad debate the issue of wifehood versus careers for women. Conrad's complacent male egotism is revealed in his uncompromising assertion that

> 'A woman who makes her mind public, or exhibits herself in any way, no matter how it may be dignified by the title of art, seems to me little better than a woman of a nameless class . . . The intrinsic value of a woman's work out of her own sphere is nothing.' (II 18–19, 23)

For him, the ideal wife must have 'rational, though inferior intelligence . . . a gentle, graceful timidity . . . a sense of propriety . . . purity and delicacy of mind . . . she is the softened reflex of her husband's opinions — she does nothing *too* well!' (II, 25). Melton's scornful refutal clearly represents Jewsbury's own rejection of such chauvinistic conservatism. In contrast to Conrad, Melton believes that women 'never were intended to lead a purely *relative* life . . . I believe in the possibility of finding women who pursue art, for the love of art, and not for the glorification of themselves' (II, 30–1). His arguments are expanded in a later chapter in which he, his sister (who sponsors model educational schemes for lower-middle-class girls), and Bianca discuss 'the condition of women'. As Bianca sees it, 'the true evil' is the purposelessness of unmarried women's lives; they need 'definite employment' such as she has had, which has given her 'a sense of freedom, of enjoyment of my existence, which has rendered all my vexations easy to be borne' (II, 73–4).

Though no credence is given to Conrad's views, it is significant that both Melton and Bianca temper their protest with more conservative opinion. Melton claims that all women need 'wise guidance and government' (II, 26) in order for their aspirations to succeed, and Bianca, arguing for purposefulness in women's lives, resorts to the standard justification of early feminists:

> 'if you could furnish women with a definite object, or address motives in them fit to animate rational beings, you would have a

race of wives and daughters far different from those which now flourish in your drawing-rooms . . . they would be able to aid men in any noble object by noble thoughts, by self-denial, by real sympathy and fellowship of heart.' (II, 74)

The second area of debate in the novel considers how far female artistic expression should be divorced from emotional feelings. Bianca believes that the 'unutterable mysteries' (I, 249) of the dramatic impulse are consecrated only by dedication to an object of love; though she momentarily accedes to the view of an old actor friend that art must be its own inspiration, she soon reasserts her conviction that to live 'a calm, self-sustained existence . . . like that of a priestess, cold, strong and pure . . . would not do, she needed some more human motive to sustain her' (II, 238). The danger of an outer-directed woman's becoming 'cold' and unfeminine, touched on in *Zoë*, is illustrated here in the actress La Fornisari, who is egotistical and manipulative, and whose corrupted womanhood is symbolised by her guilty secret of a lost child. Bianca is saved from this fate: she retains true femininity through marriage and service to men. As in *Zoë*, Jewsbury reveals, but does not resolve, the dichotomies. She challenges limiting ideologies, but ultimately resorts to traditional images of womanhood — at the end, Bianca is merely a more successful version of Alice. As a contemporary reviewer sardonically observes, 'while Miss Jewsbury aspires to do battle with "Conventionalism" as a Dagon which is to be pulled down by every strong man and earnest woman, she adorns her heroine with most of its graces'; Conrad's fallacies with regard to womanly genius may be punctured, but 'the consolation which she accords to the unkindly used Bianca is a tacit admission of the justice of many of his — comments'.[107]

Jewsbury's later novels rely even more heavily on the conventionalism which she is apparently trying to undermine. In *Marian Withers* (1851), for instance, she both directs a quizzical look at marriage, especially when it is viewed merely as an escape from dreariness or a means of social elevation, and takes up her previous complaint that womanly genius can find no outlet or stimulation in a life of wearisome ennui. Her heroine, Marian, feels 'buried alive'[108] as she struggles to realise her unfocused aspirations. But Jewsbury's solution is to provide Marian with a good husband, who gives her a purpose in life and a healthier moral outlook, which in this case means recognising that true womanly fulfilment is attained through duty and service. Female individuality here is asserted not through challenge to traditional roles (a professional career or ennobling passion) but through the orthodoxies of wifehood and Christian self-discipline.

One of her last novels, *Constance Herbert* (1855), which George Eliot rightly criticised for its 'copy-book morality' and its confused approach to the subject of 'woman's true position',[109] leaves its heroine unmarried at the end, but far from championing female singleness it aims to illustrate the familiar Victorian female ethic that obedience to duty is more blessed than personal emotional fulfilment. The novel's extraordinarily confused and unconvincing plot is built around the central issue of inherited insanity: Constance, her future determined by the unlikely coincidence of madness in both parents' families, nobly rejects an offer of marriage from the only man she could ever love, so as to save future generations from her doom; she is strengthened in her resolve by the comforting notion of moral rectitude as well as by the knowledge of her aunt's unhappy matrimonial experiences. Despite Jewsbury's assurance that for a woman it 'is no ignoble destiny to be allowed to sacrifice her hopes of a happy marriage, and of being the mother of children'[110] for such a good cause, and that her heroine 'had not made the sacrifice of her life needlessly',[111] Constance's final state is distinctly dreary. Having nursed her father through his last illness — predictably involving mental collapse — she is left to run her own estate alone, having sacrificed her ideas of being loved to an acknowledgement of higher obligations than personal happiness; her only comfort (the false morality objected to by Eliot) is the realisation that the man she gave up was worthless anyway. Spinsterhood here takes on the stereotypical formulations of spiritually ennobling deprivation. Jewsbury's apparent increasing reluctance to confront openly the dichotomies she observes in women's experience is probably the result of the growing conservatism of middle-age. Her ultimate conventionality may seem disappointing, but she is nevertheless to be admired for directly voicing her more radical attitudes in her fiction and for allowing her novels to accommodate, if not satisfactorily to resolve, her own dualities.

Each of these three novelists, then, expresses in her fiction her recognition of the gap between accepted views of womanly roles and her own apprehension of them. Kavanagh's vision is essentially romantic, but she conveys an awareness of tensions beneath the surface idealism; Yonge, despite her sexual and ethical conservatism, sees that there is a place for single women in her society; Jewsbury voices a more open ambivalence about female roles, her traditionalism directly qualified by her more energetic assertion of womanly individuality. When we turn to the writers chosen for more extensive treatment, we shall see how their work further illustrates the varieties of creative dissent. In their fiction, the dualities are more integrated into the whole and there is often less artistic awkwardness in their presentation. But all share the same unease, and manipulate the conventional patterns of fiction in order to formulate their personal sense of the complexities of being female.

Notes

1. W.R. Greg, 'False Morality of Lady Novelists', *National Review*, vol. VIII (January 1859), p. 148.
2. Walter Bagehot, 'The Waverly Novels' (1858), in R.H. Hutton (ed.), *Literary Studies* (4th edn, London, 1891), vol. II, p. 148.
3. David Masson, *British Novelists and Their Styles* (London, 1859), p. 294.
4. Eleanor L. Sewell (ed.), *The Autobiography of Elizabeth M. Sewell* (London, 1907), p. 145.
5. Ibid., p. 196.
6. Patricia Stubbs, *Women and Fiction: Feminism and the Novel 1880-1920* (Brighton and New York, 1979), p. xi.
7. G.H. Lewes, 'The Lady Novelists', *Westminster Review*, vol. LVIII (July 1852), p. 131.
8. Ibid., p. 133.
9. Mrs Humphry Ward, Introduction to *Villette* (Haworth edition, 1899), p. xxvi.
10. J.M. Ludlow, Review of *Ruth*, *North British Review*, vol. XIX (May 1853), p. 169.
11. R.H. Hutton, *The Relative Value of Studies and Accomplishments in the Education of Women* (London, 1862), p. 20.
12. See, for example: 'Our Lady Novelists', *Dublin Review*, vol. XXIII (September and December 1847), pp. 178-203; 'Religious Novels', *North British Review*, vol. XXVI (November 1857), pp. 209-27; 'Miss Sewell's Novels', *Christian Examiner*, vol. LVII (1854), pp. 185-208.
13. Anne Mozley, 'Clever Women', *Blackwood's Edinburgh Magazine*, vol. CIV (October 1868), p. 427.
14. George Eliot, 'Woman in France: Madame de Sablé', *Westminster Review*, vol. LXII (October 1854), p. 448.
15. G.H. Lewes, 'Currer Bell's "Shirley"', *Edinburgh Review*, vol. XCI (January 1850), p. 155.
16. 'The Lady Novelists', p. 132.
17. Harriet Taylor, 'The Enfranchisement of Women', *Westminster Review*, vol. LV (July 1851), p. 310.
18. Letter to George Smith, 6 December 1852, *The Brontës: Their Lives, Friendships and Correspondence* ed. T.J. Wise and J.A. Symington (reprint, Oxford, 1980), vol. IV, p. 22.
19. See Susan R. Gorsky, 'Old Maids and New Women', *Journal of Popular*

36 *Introductory*

Culture, vol. 7 (Summer 1973), pp. 68–85.

20. 'Women's Heroines', *Saturday Review*, vol. XXIII (2 March 1867), p. 260.
21. 'The Lady Novelists', p. 133.
22. Anna Jameson, *Winter Studies and Summer Rambles* (1838). Quoted in E.K. Helsinger, R.L. Sheets and W. Veeder, *The Woman Question: Society and Literature in Britain and America 1837–1883* (New York, 1983), vol. III, pp. 23–4.
23. Eugène Forçade, Review of *Shirley*, *Revue des deux mondes*, tome 4 (15 November 1849), pp. 714–35.
24. See Hippolyte Taine, *Notes sur l'Angleterre* (Paris, 1872), especially Chapter 3.
25. John Ruskin, *Sesame and Lilies* (London, 1906) Section 68, pp. 137–8.
26. Ibid., Section 92, p. 173.
27. Two important studies which discuss the nature and sources of Victorian angelology are Alexander Welsh, *The City of Dickens* (Oxford, 1971) and Nina Auerbach, *Woman and the Demon: the Life of a Victorian Myth* (Cambridge, Mass. 1982). Further valuable information about Victorian attitudes towards women is to be found in Walter E. Houghton, *The Victorian Frame of Mind* (New Haven and London, 1957).
28. Mrs John Sandford, *Woman in her Social and Domestic Character* (7th edn, London, 1842), p. 2.
29. Ibid., p. 73.
30. Sarah Lewis, *Woman's Mission* (1839). Quoted in Helsinger *et al.*, *The Woman Question*, vol. I, p. 9. Lewis's work was an adaptation of Louis Aimé Martin's *De l'education des mères de famille* (1834), and was admired by many of her contemporaries, including Charlotte Brontë and George Eliot.
31. Mrs Sarah Ellis, *The Women of England: their Social Duties, and Domestic Habits* (1839; 10th ed., London, n.d.), p. 155. Mrs Ellis also wrote *The Wives of England* (1843) and *The Daughters of England* (1845), in which she reiterates her belief in the subordination of woman and the primacy of her role as wife and mother.
32. *The Women of England*, p. 21.
33. Ibid., p. 267.
34. For information about changing patterns of matrimonial conditions see Laurence Stone, *The Family, Sex and Marriage in England, 1500–1800* (New York and London, 1977). Mid-Victorian attitudes towards marriage and the spiritual idealisation of women are also examined in Fraser Harrison, *The Dark Angel: Aspects of Victorian Sexuality* (London, 1977) and Eric Trudgill, *Madonnas and Magdalens: the Origin and Development of Victorian Sexual Attitudes* (London, 1976).
35. Figures from J. and O. Banks, *Feminism and Family Planning in Victorian England* (Liverpool, 1964).
36. Harriet Martineau, 'Female Industry', *Edinburgh Review*, vol. CIX (April 1859), p. 298.
37. See for example Patricia Branca, *Silent Sisterhood: Middle-Class Women in the Victorian Home* (London, 1975), Chapter 1.
38. One such suggestion came from W.R. Greg whose essay, 'Why Are Women Redundant?', first published in the *National Review*, vol. XIV (April 1862), and later reprinted in his *Literary and Social Judgments* (1868), aroused considerable comment, particularly among those women whose singleness laid them open to his charges of 'redundancy'.
39. For some useful discussions of the social and legal sufferings of Victorian wives see Françoise Basch, *Relative Creatures. Victorian Women in Society and the Novel*, trans. A. Rudolf (London and New York, 1974); Banks, *Feminism and Family Planning in Victorian England*; Lee Holcombe, 'Victorian Wives and Property' in Martha Vicinus (ed.), *A Widening Sphere: Changing Roles of Victorian Women* (Indiana, 1977), pp. 3–28.

40. Dora Greenwell, 'Our Single Women', *North British Review*, vol. XXXVI (February 1862), p. 64.

41. See Mona Caird, 'Marriage', *Westminster Review*, vol. CXXX (August 1888) pp. 186–201, and 'Ideal Marriage' (November 1888), pp. 617–36. The articles gave rise to extensive correspondence in the *Daily Telegraph*; Caird's position was also challenged by Elizabeth Chapman in her *Marriage Questions in Modern Fiction* (London and New York, 1897).

42. Linton's opinions were most strongly voiced in the series of articles she wrote for the *Saturday Review* between 1866 and 1868, reprinted as *The Girl of the Period and other Social Essays* (London, 1883).

43. Margaret Mylne, 'Woman and her Social Position', *Westminster Review*, vol. XXXV (January 1841), pp. 24–52.

44. Mrs Hugo Reid, *A Plea for Women* (1843). Quoted in Helsinger *et al.*, *The Woman Question*, vol. I, p. 17.

45. Taylor, 'The Enfranchisement of Women', p. 301.

46. Ibid., pp. 297–8. Taylor, the long-standing friend and later wife of J.S. Mill, was a considerable influence on him; her arguments in this article anticipate some of those in his *The Subjection of Women* (1869).

47. The nature of Nightingale's unorthodoxy is analysed in Ray Strachey, *The Cause* (1928, reprinted London, 1978) Chapter 1, in Auerbach, *Woman and the Demon*, Chapter 4, and in Elaine Showalter, 'Florence Nightingale's Feminist Complaint: Women, Religion, and *Suggestions for Thought*', *Signs: Journal of Women in Culture and Society*, vol. 6, no. 3 (1981), pp. 395–412.

48. Diary entry of 1846. Quoted in Strachey, *The Cause*, p. 22.

49. Florence Nightingale, *Cassandra*, reproduced in Strachey, *The Cause*, p. 415.

50. Frances Power Cobbe, 'Criminals, Idiots, Women, and Minors', *Fraser's Magazine*, vol. LXXVIII (December 1868), p. 787.

51. Anna Jameson, *Winter Studies and Summer Rambles in Canada*. Quoted in Mylne, 'Woman and her Social Position', p. 37. Jameson, a friend of Elizabeth Barrett, separated from her husband who had gone to live in Toronto, in 1838, and was a firm defender of Women's Rights, though not a rabid feminist. Her own experience of having to support herself and several members of her family had confirmed for her the absurdity of teaching girls that their place was in the home.

52. Josephine Butler (ed.), *Woman's Work and Woman's Culture* (London, 1869), Introduction, pp. xxviii–xxix. Butler's most well-known work as a feminist was her campaign for the repeal of the Contagious Diseases Act.

53. Frances Power Cobbe, 'Celibacy v. Marriage', *Fraser's Magazine*, vol. LXV (February 1862), p. 233.

54. Frances Power Cobbe, 'What Shall We Do With Our Old Maids?', *Fraser's Magazine*, vol. LXVI (November 1862), p. 597.

55. Cobbe, 'Celibacy v. Marriage', p. 234.

56. Cobbe, 'What Shall We Do With Our Old Maids?', p. 595.

57. Ibid., p. 597.

58. Cobbe, 'Celibacy v. Marriage', p. 230.

59. Frances Power Cobbe, *Essays on the Pursuits of Women* (London, 1863), pp. v–vi.

60. Cobbe, 'What Shall We Do With Our Old Maids?', p. 599.

61. The characteristically cautious nature of early-Victorian feminism is emphasised in Olive Banks, *Faces of Feminism* (Oxford, 1981), Part I, 'The Early Years, 1840–1870', pp. 11–59.

62. Letter to Charlotte Brontë, March 1837, Wise and Symington, *The Brontës*, vol. I, p. 155.

63. Letter to Mrs Gaskell, 9 July 1853. Wise and Symington, *The Brontës*, vol. IV, p. 76.

64. E.C. Gaskell, *The Life of Charlotte Brontë* (2nd edn, London, 1857), vol. II, p. 50.

65. Sewell, *Autobiography*, p. 54.

66. Taylor, 'The Enfranchisement of Women', p. 30.

67. As Elaine Showalter has pointed out, only about 50 per cent of women writers born in the nineteenth century married, as compared with about 85 per cent in the general population — Elaine Showalter, *A Literature of Their Own* (London, 1978), p. 65.

68. Elaine Showalter, 'Dinah Mulock Craik and the Tactics of Sentiment: A Case Study in Victorian Female Authorship', *Feminist Studies*, 2 (1975), p. 5.

69. Sandra M. Gilbert and Susan Gubar, *The Madwoman in the Attic: The Woman Writer and the Nineteenth-Century Literary Imagination* (New Haven and London, 1979).

70. Auerbach, *Woman and the Demon*.

71. Margaret Oliphant, 'Modern Novelists — Great and Small', *Blackwood's Edinburgh Magazine*, vol. LXXVII (May 1855), p. 559. For a discussion of the literary relationship between Brontë and Kavanagh see Robert A. Colby, *Fiction with a Purpose: Major and Minor Nineteenth-Century Novels* (Bloomington, 1967), Chapter 6, pp. 180, 196–7, 343, and Shirley Foster, '"A Suggestive Book": a source for *Villette*', *Études Anglaises*, tome XXXV, no. 2 (1982), pp. 177–84.

72. Letter to W.S. Williams, 22 January 1848, Wise and Symington, *The Brontës*, vol. II, p. 182.

73. See the exchange of correspondence between her and T.C. Newby, the publisher of *The Hobbies* (and of the Brontës' first work) in the *Athenaeum*, June-July 1857 (Nos. 1546–9).

74. Julia Kavanagh, *English Women of Letters: Biographical Sketches* (2 vols., London, 1862; Tauchnitz edn, Leipzig, 1862), p. 3.

75. Ibid., p. 98.

76. Ibid., p. 28.

77. Ibid., p. 289.

78. Julia Kavanagh, *French Women of Letters: Biographical Sketches* (2 vols., London, 1862), vol I, p. 77.

79. Kavanagh, *English Women of Letters*, p. 203.

80. Ibid., p. 3.

81. Ibid., p. 96.

82. Ibid., p. 96.

83. Ibid., p. 97.

84. Mrs C. Martin, 'The Late Julia Kavanagh', *Irish Monthly Magazine*, vol. VI (1878), p. 97.

85. Julia Kavanagh, *Beatrice* (3 vols., London, 1865), vol. III, p. 143. Subsequent page references are to this edition and will be included in the text.

86. Julia Kavanagh, *Nathalie* (3 vols., London, 1850), vol. III, p. 183. Subsequent page references are to this edition and will be included in the text.

87. Julia Kavanagh, *Adèle* (3 vols., London, 1858), vol. II, p. 8. Subsequent page references are to this edition and will be included in the text.

88. Quoted in Georgina Battiscombe, *Charlotte Mary Yonge: the Story of an Uneventful Life* (London, 1943), p. 14.

89. Charlotte Yonge, *Womankind* (new edn, 1889) p. 1. Subsequent page references are to this edition and will be included in the text.

90. Charlotte Yonge, *The Three Brides* (London, 1904), p. 161.

91. Yonge herself became an Exterior Sister at Wantage. In her novels, Constance Somerville, who first appears in *The Castle Builders* (1854), founds an Anglican Sisterhood, and Angela Underwood in *The Pillars of the House* (1873) becomes a sister in this order.

92. Charlotte Yonge, *Heartsease, or the Brother's Wife* (London, 1880), p. 67.

93. Ibid., p. 35.

94. Charlotte Yonge, *The Clever Woman of the Family* (London, 1884), p. 187.

Subsequent page references are to this edition and will be included in the text.

95. See Patricia Thomson, *The Victorian Heroine: a Changing Ideal* (London, 1956), Chapter 3, 'Woman at Work', Section 3, pp. 74–85.

96. See Naomi Lewis, *A Visit to Mrs Wilcox* (London, 1957), p. 194.

97. Charlotte Yonge, *The Daisy Chain, or Aspirations* (10th edn, London, 1870), p. 181. Subsequent page references are to this edition and will be included in the text.

98. Letter to Miss Dampier, 5 July (n.y.). In the Morris L. Parrish Collection of Victorian Novelists, Princeton University Library.

99. Charlotte Yonge, *Hopes and Fears, or Scenes from the Life of a Spinster* (London, 1879), p. 84. Subsequent page references are to this edition and will be included in the text.

100. See J.M. Hartley, 'Geraldine Jewsbury and the Problems of the Woman Novelist', *Women's Studies International Quarterly*, vol. 2, no. 2 (1979), pp. 137–53.

101. Their correspondence is now in the Special Collections of the library of the University of California at Los Angeles.

102. Mrs Alexander Ireland (ed.), *Selections from the Letters of Geraldine Endsor Jewsbury to Jane Welsh Carlyle* (London, 1892), p. 347. Subsequent citations from Jewsbury's letters are from this edition, with page references given in the text.

103. See Jeanne R. Fahnestock, 'Geraldine Jewsbury: the Power of the Publisher's Reader', *Nineteenth-Century Fiction*, vol. 28 (December 1973), pp. 253–72.

104. Letter to Mr Sydenham Nodes (?), 21 July 1851. In Special Collections, UCLA.

105. Geraldine Jewsbury, *Zoë: the History of Two Lives* (3 vols., London, 1845), vol. I, p. 148. Subsequent page references are to this edition and will be included in the text.

106. Geraldine Jewsbury, *The Half Sisters: A Tale* (2 vols., London, 1848), vol. I, p. 31. Subsequent page references are to this edition and will be included in the text.

107. Review of *The Half Sisters*, *Athenaeum*, no. 1064 (18 March 1848), pp. 288–9. The reviewer, H.C. Chorley, argues that nearly all the recent novels which deal with actresses reveal the same trend — 'when the Delight of "shining theatres" is handed over the threshold of domestic life by Love, the career of the Artist comes to its close' (p. 288). In this context, he also refers to George Sand's *Consuelo* and Mme de Stael's *Corinne*.

108. Geraldine Jewsbury, *Marian Withers* (3 vols., London, 1851), vol. III, p. 125.

109. George Eliot, '*Westward Ho!* and *Constance Herbert*', *Westminster Review*, vol. LXIV (July 1855), pp. 295, 6.

110. Geraldine Jewsbury, *Constance Herbert* (3 vols., London, 1855), vol. I, p. 112.

111. Ibid., vol. III, p. 299.

2 DINAH MULOCK CRAIK: AMBIVALENT ROMANTICISM

Dinah Mulock Craik is a good example of the many Victorian female novelists whose creative work gives little obvious clue to the varieties of their own experience. She is a particularly interesting figure not only because of the discrepancies between her individual womanhood and her fictional version, but also because, of all the writers examined in this study, her life most fully illustrates the dichotomies of Victorian female roles. Self-dependent from the age of nineteen, she flourished professionally in a man's world, defending her own interests with an 'unfeminine' businesslike energy, yet she also craved for emotional fulfilment, and clung to an idealistically romantic creed. Moreover, during her career as a novelist, she made the transition from singleness to marriage, thus qualifying herself to evaluate personally the relative conditions of each state. Her experience of both sides of female existence sharpened her sense of its dualities, and made her acutely aware of the dilemmas faced by all her sex.

The novel which secured Craik's popularity in her own time — and her best-known today — is *John Halifax, Gentleman* (1856), perhaps because of its combined emphasis on the rewards of hard work and initiative and the blessings of happy married life. But it was the latter element, Craik's adherence to the romantic orthodoxies, which most positively established her success among her contemporaries, many of whom considered her main artistic strength to be her depiction of love. Jane Carlyle, for example, relished Craik's first novel, *The Ogilvies* (1849), because it was full of 'the old highflown romantic circulating Library sort of love';[1] despite her mildly cynical astonishment that the author could be so unquestioningly idealistic, she found herself captivated by it: 'It quite reminds one of one's own love's young dream. I like it, and I like the poor girl who can still believe, or even "believe that she believes", *all that*.'[2] Other readers were impressed by 'the powerful delineations of passion one meets with in her books',[3] and a common critical opinion was that 'sentiment . . . remains her forte'.[4] Some were less enthusiastic about Craik's treatment of romance. Harriet Martineau, who anyway felt that there was too much love in current female fiction, inveighed against its excesses in *The Ogilvies*,[5] while Henry James argued that, fine though her work was, it was often marred by a 'rose-colored' curtain of sentimentality.[6] Even an otherwise fulsome admirer in the *Victoria Magazine* admitted cautiously that 'only occasionally does she near the boundary line which divides sentiment from sentimentality . . . but when she does [cross it] the result is not invigorating'.[7] The conventional romantic patterning of Craik's fiction probably also accounts for George Eliot's lofty dismissal of a comparison made between her and the younger novelist by the *Revue Brittanique* in 1860:

> the most ignorant journalist in England would hardly think of calling me a rival of Miss Mulock — a writer who is read only by novel readers, pure and simple, never by people of high culture. A very excellent woman she is, I believe, but we belong to an entirely different order of writers.[8]

The majority of Craik's readers (those who bought the 250,000 copies of *John Halifax*), however, took her to their hearts because she told the age-old tale that 'there's nothing half so sweet in life as love's young dream'.[9]

Such a view, without wholly misrepresenting Craik's work, ignores other, less cosily traditional, elements in her fiction. Though the overt divergence between her life and her art is one source of her interest as a writer, equally noteworthy is the way in which the two impinge on each other. The dichotomies of Craik's experience, colouring her imaginative vision, enter her work in a manner which refutes easy labelling of it as 'romantic'; she explores creatively, albeit often obliquely, some of the questions with which her own life presented her.

From childhood, Craik led a much more unconventional existence than many of her female contemporaries. She was born in Stoke-on-Trent in 1826, and spent most of her early years in Newcastle-under-Lyme in an unsettled and precarious family environment. Her father, Thomas Mulock (dubbed 'Muley' Mulock by Byron), a native of Dublin, first came to the Potteries as a Baptist preacher, having already tried his hand at the law, journalism, and public lecturing. Impecunious, eccentric, and quarrelsome (sooner or later he offended most of his acquaintances), he was hardly a source of domestic harmony. In May 1830, he was imprisoned briefly for libel; by 1832, he had become so intolerable that, according to his own outraged account, his wife (the daughter of a respectable Newcastle tanner), abetted by her sister, 'actually *turned me out of doors*'[10] and, when he tried to return home, had him committed to Stafford County Asylum as a pauper lunatic. He spent the next seven years here, during which time Mrs Mulock single-handedly shouldered the family burdens; sometime in the late 1830s she established a small school in Newcastle, assisted by Dinah, barely in her teens. In December 1839, Mulock was released from the asylum and was reconciled with his family, though not until his wife had wisely ensured that her property was legally made over to her and her children, and thus secure from his clutches. In 1840 he took them all to London, but the domestic entente soon foundered. Though there is no proof that he ill-treated his dependents — indeed at this time he boasts how well his children are responding to his tutorship in classics and modern languages — his presence was clearly as unacceptable as ever. By 1845, his wife and children were again living apart from him, 'concealed from me and my nearest friends',[11] as he put it, disclaiming all responsibility for the breakdown.

In October 1845 Mrs Mulock died, and Mulock finally abandoned all pretence of paternal concern, quite literally writing his offspring out of his life — he wrote to his sister, 'Thus all communication between me and my children terminates'[12] — and leaving Dinah to support herself and her two younger brothers. With only their mother's small legacy to rely on, their financial position was extremely shaky, but the hardship was to prove a launching ground for Craik's future career; spurred on by necessity she began the literary activity which continued uninterruptedly until her death forty-two years later. Mrs Oliphant's obituary article gives a patronisingly sentimental, though admiring, picture of this period:

> The young heroic creature writing her pretty juvenile nonsense of love and lovers, in swift, unformed style, as fast as the pen could fly, to get bread for the boys . . . what a tragic, tender picture . . .[13]

The reality was far more hum-drum, and those who, like Mrs Gaskell, wished that Craik 'had some other means of support besides writing; I think it bad in it's effect upon her writing, which must be pumped up instead of bubbling out; and very bad for her health, poor girl',[14] were right to point out the physical and artistic hazards of such economic motivation. Craik, none the less, was energised by the challenge, despite moments of weariness and depression. Helped by Robert Chambers, who published some of her essays and stories in his *Journal*, she gradually gained a footing in the London literary world, achieving a distinctive self-reliance through her roles of guardian and wage-earner. She established herself on her own, first in Camden Town, then in Kilburn, and finally in Hampstead, and clearly enjoyed her unusual degree of independence. Catherine Shaen, a friend of Gaskell's, describes Craik's domestic arrangements in early 1851:

> We had been hearing much of [Miss Mulock] just then from Mrs Gaskell, who had been meeting her and Miss Frances Martin in London, as two handsome young girls, living in lodgings by themselves, writing books, and going about in society in the most independent manner, with their latchkey. Such a phenomenon was rare, perhaps unexampled in those days.[15]

At this time, Craik herself writes merrily to Gaskell about her and Fanny Martin's self-supporting existence — 'She, 22 — I, 25 — Are we not a steady pair of elderly women?'.[16] She had her own coterie of female admirers, and moved in literary circles which if not of the highest at least introduced her to some of the notable figures of the day: she was friendly with the playwright Westland Marston, and godmother to his blind son, Philip, later a poet; she knew Sydney Dobell, Frank Smedley, Gaskell, and Anna Maria Hall, the wife of 'the unscrupulous editor' Samuel Carter Hall,[17] at whose soirées she met other writers; another acquaintance was Jane Carlyle, who admired her self-assurance.[18] As Oliphant puts it, Craik rapidly became 'a writer with a recognised position, and well able to maintain it'.[19]

Craik's circumstances were to change when she married in 1865, but up to then her experience was teaching her the advantages as well as the limitations of self-reliant singleness. She became adept at asserting herself in her business affairs, stoutly defending her own interests in the male-dominated publishing world and, more firmly than many of her female contemporaries, demanding fair treatment from her publishers. She always claimed good terms for herself; having 'settled' with Hurst and Blackett for *John Halifax* in August 1855,[20] for example, two years later she reports delightedly to her brother that altogether she has 'cleared' £415 for the book.[21] Her publishers confessed themselves fearful of her 'sturdy, businesslike stand for her money',[22] as she argued over copyrights, asked for higher payments, and protested at injustices. As she proudly told the American publisher, J.T. Fields, in 1869, 'I have long been a "business woman" '.[23]

Craik's experiences also taught her to look to herself for emotional support. The myth of masculine superiority had early been shattered for her, as it had been for Elizabeth Sewell, though since in her case she was not squashed by overbearing male arrogance she was encouraged to take a more scornful attitude towards the opposite sex. Her relationship with her father is characterised by ambivalence. Well aware of his unreliability and hypocrisy, from an early age she fought against her distrust, even hatred, of him. After her mother's death, she wrote to him:

> Our characters, views, and opinions are so totally opposite that I must say without meaning to give offence, that our wisest course will be to live apart as we now do. This Mamma well knew, and therefore just before her death she made me give a solemn promise that I would never live with you — and from that promise nothing shall induce me to swerve.[24]

Later, though she felt obliged to assist him financially (he was imprisoned for debt in Stafford at least twice between 1855 and 1860), she experienced 'quite a morbid horror of him',[25] as well as contempt for his 'downright bad mean faults . . . his intolerable egotism — his violent temper — and his time-serving Irish ways'.[26] As she confesses guiltily, 'I have to think 20 times a day "he is an old man" to prevent actually despising him'.[27] Her younger brother, Ben, did little to compensate for Mulock's paternal failings. Probably permanently scarred by the tragic death in a naval accident of his elder sibling, Tom, in 1847 (and perhaps also feeling threatened by his sister's successes), he drifted from career to career and continent to continent, as a railway engineer in the Crimea, a prospective settler in Australia, a photographer in Liverpool and London, and a builder in Bahia; between these periods of employment he lived an aimless existence, supported by his sister and complaining about his misfortunes. He was finally committed to an asylum, escaping from which he was killed in an accident in 1863. Craik was emotionally bound up with him — her letters frequently stress that he is her sole object of affection — but there was too much in him which reminded her of their father to enable her to respect him. Irritated as well as saddened by his self-pity and whining complaints, she was deeply disappointed by his occupational and emotional failures, which gave her no encouragement to rely on him.

When Craik eventually married, at the advanced age of thirty-nine, she committed herself to a relationship the unusual aspects of which seem particularly appropriate. In February 1861, George Lillie Craik, already known slightly to her as the son of old friends, was seriously injured in a railway accident in London. He was nursed at her house, remaining there for nearly ten months, during which friendship blossomed into romance; the couple were married in April 1865. For Craik, the step was, overtly at least, singularly unorthodox. George was eleven years her junior and permanently disabled, and in many ways the union seemed to represent a reversal of roles — she the independent, successful public figure, he just embarking on his career as a partner in Macmillan's. The accusations made by her understandably piqued parents-in-law, who charged her with double-dealing, and with conduct quite unsuitable for one whom they regarded as 'an attached but elderly friend, whose position ha[s] quietly settled down into that of a lady occupying the place of an aunt rather than . . . any other relationship',[28] highlight the kind of prejudice which Craik as a single woman had to face. Moreover, her mother-in-law's criticism that Craik lacked 'the tender reverential tone that a woman ought to feel to the man she marries'[29] points suggestively, if not wholly accurately, to the nature of the union. Marriage clearly provided Craik with the emotional fulfilment she desired, but she continued to run her life in the way she wanted. Significantly, she refused to accede to her husband's wish that she give up writing; she maintained her financial autonomy, and, like Gaskell and Sewell, bought a house with her literary earnings.

As with the other women novelists of the period, we gain more direct knowledge about Craik's attitudes towards womanhood from her letters and non-fiction than from her fiction. Her best-known commentary, *A Woman's Thoughts about Women* (1858),[30] is specifically directed towards single women, who, Craik argues, have every justification for claiming 'the right of having something to

do'.[31] The work is not revolutionary — Craik disclaims all attempts
'to force women . . . into the position and duties of men'[32] — but it
contains enough unorthodox opinion for its author to demand
anonymous publication.[33] Her main protest here, as in her later
writings, is against the current ideology which classifies unmarried
women as redundant. Women should be free to choose their own
course — 'Is this Society to draw up a code of regulations as to what
is proper for us to do, and what not?', Craik cries indignantly.[34]
Like the early feminists, she accepts that marriage and motherhood
are the apotheoses of womanly fulfilment; spinsterhood is an
'unnatural condition of being'[35] and inevitably means some loneliness and disappointment. She however unhesitatingly condemns
stereotyped images of women as feeble creatures whose only duty is
to marry. Taking up the pragmatic arguments of the feminists, she
argues briskly that since half the present female population are
'obliged to look solely to themselves for maintenance, position,
amusement, reputation, life',[36] society 'must educate our maidens
into what is far better than any blind clamour for ill-defined
"rights" . . . the duty of self-dependence'.[37] Reiterating the point in
her later series of essays, *Plain Speaking* (1882), she insists that girls
must be made to recognise 'the right of independence; that every
unmarried woman who does not inherit an income ought to owe it to
neither father, brother, nor any other male relation, but to earn it'.[38]
Craik suggests positive means of achieving this: better female
education, and more professional opportunities for women as
clerks, book-keepers, poor-law guardians, and so on, one valuable
effect of which will be to prove that 'we can do [our work] as well as
most men'.[39] Throughout her writings on womanhood, she also
insists that female independence must include personal financial
responsibility; only thus can a woman avoid male exploitation and
enjoy the freedom which using her own money 'as she chooses . . .
without asking anybody's leave, and being accountable for it to no
one'[40] confers. As a self-reliant, free agent herself, she knows that
only challenging work, properly rewarded, will turn a discontented,
self-pitying spinster into a contented, fulfilled woman.

Craik's brisk unorthodoxy strongly colours her views on matrimony. In *A Woman's Thoughts*, she fulminates against false myths
of marital bliss:

> Every girl ought to be taught that a hasty, loveless union, stamps
> upon her as foul dishonour as one of those connexions which

omit the ceremony altogether; and that, however pale, dreary, and toilsome a single life may be, unhappy married life must be tenfold worse.[41]

In preaching the advantages of singleness, Craik is honest enough to admit the attraction of romantic fulfilment. She recognises that it may take much courage for a woman to replace the 'safe negativeness' of private life with the 'substantive position' of a profession:

But having chosen, let her fulfil her lot. Let there be no hesitations, no compromises — they are at once cowardly and vain. She may have missed or foregone much; — I repeat, our natural and happiest life is when we lose ourselves in the exquisite absorption of home, the delicious retirement of dependent love; but what she has, she has, and nothing can ever take it from her.[42]

Her language here reveals her ambivalence, as the crispness of conviction gives way to sentimentality, but the final statement re-asserts her pride in womanly individuality. Even after her marriage, Craik continues to stress the value of self-reliant womanhood. In her *Sermons out of Church* (1875), for example, she criticises exaggerated notions of female self-sacrifice, and reiterates her belief that 'anything less than a thoroughly happy marriage is to women much worse than celibacy';[43] few marriages are, she claims, entirely happy — 'as few, perhaps, as those single lives which are proverbially supposed to be so miserable',[44] she adds slyly. In *About Money and Other Things* (1886), she continues to urge that the 'ideal of a happy, single life'[45] be held up to all girls. And in her last, posthumously published work, *Concerning Men and Other Papers* (1888), she once more trims her romanticism with sturdy pragmatism: old-fashioned enough to believe that 'wifehood and motherhood [are] the highest and happiest destiny to which any woman can attain',[46] she is in no doubt that when marriage has become a source of suffering for a woman, 'noble endurance, falsely so called, is mere cowardice',[47] and separation should take place.

From her letters, we learn more about Craik's personal feelings and the stressful dualities of her own womanhood. Most notably, we gain glimpses of her more emotional nature. Though at eighteen she describes herself as 'a girl . . . who never was in love in her life, but . . . was always an odd, staid sort of personage',[48] she clearly had deep romantic needs. About this time, she fell heavily in love with a young Scottish painter, Joseph Noel Paton (later to become a famous artist and a Fellow of the Royal Scottish Academy), whom she met in London. The passion was not reciprocal and Paton, having returned to Scotland perhaps to flee from 'the too insistent pursuit of an admirer',[49] married in 1858 and had a large family. Craik remained friendly with him, and became godmother to his eldest daughter, but he always symbolised for her the ideal romance for which part of her yearned. Her letters to Ben reveal how she was torn between self-pity and tougher-minded self-respect:

> there's nothing for it but to put oneself in one's pocket for ever and ever Amen — and turn aunt and godmother to Joe's children. Perhaps life hasn't been such a very dreadful mistake after all — anyhow no one has been made unhappy except oneself: and one is not by any means unhappy now. Sometimes when I think of a few young people . . . it seems a bit hard that one never should have been *really happy* in all one's life — and one isn't quite a stone even at 34 — but I expect it's all right.[50]

The wistful tone here (expressed, interestingly, in the third person) recurs when Craik refers to her maternal longings. She frequently urges Ben to marry and have children so that she can enjoy vicarious motherhood; a visit to the large Macmillan family in Cambridge awakens a rare confession of real misery — 'many a time I had to run away to my bedroom to have a good cry — feeling so dreadfully desolate'.[51]

If such feelings are made light of because Craik sensed that Ben, bound up with his own problems, would have little sympathy with them, their deep reality is indicated by her expression of profound contentment in her own marriage, which even provided her with a fairy-tale child.[52] As she writes to her cousin in December 1865: 'Oh! Tom, people don't know what happiness is till they are happily married. After eight months, full of cares, difficulties, hard work and anxiety, I can truly say this!'[53] About the same time, she also writes to a friend, 'when people are happily married — they are so very happy!';[54] if in 1860, she could still feel that she loved Joe 'as I never loved anybody else and never shall',[55] five years later she can only rejoice that fortune has given her 'such an exceptional character as my husband'.[56]

Craik's acknowledgement of the blessings of 'normal' womanly fulfilment to some extent colours her views on more unorthodox female activity. Though she claims that 'the improvement of my sex has always been very near my heart',[57] like most of her fellow-novelists she has no desire for revolution. She adopts a tone of mockery towards the 'strong-minded' women she meets at a party in 1860, with their 'waistcoats, cravats, and short hair',[58] and she confesses that if a rumoured visit from Eliza Lynn Linton (in the 1850s still a radical of some notoriety) takes place, she will undoubtedly argue 'tooth and nail' with her.[59] Late in life she dissociates herself from the expanding women's movements:

> For myself, whatever influence I have is, I believe, because I have always kept aloof from any cliques. I care little for Female Suffrage, and have given the widest berth to that set of women who are called, not unfairly, the Shrieking Sisterhood.

At the same time, she shows a characteristic admiration for womanly individuality — 'I like women to be strong and brave — both for themselves, and as the helpers, not the slaves or foes, of men'.[60]

Despite this apparent cautiousness, many of Craik's letters place the same emphasis on female self-reliance which figures so prominently in her non-fiction. Her own existence as a single professional woman clearly affords her much pleasure. Rejoicing that she is 'in first-rate working trim',[61] she boasts of her intention 'to die with harness at my back'.[62] For her, one of the advantages of being single is the chance to explore her individual talents; another is the pleasure of being her own mistress. Like Virginia Woolf, she knows the value of a room of one's own: 'I have [not] the slightest wish of taking anybody to live with me — I like solitude much the best . . . [I] shall keep to the glorious independence of living alone',[63] she declares firmly. Even occasional loneliness does not mar her contentment: 'It is curious — but consolatory — that after all there is great peace in one's own company. I never come home from any household that I don't feel how very much happier Wildwood is than any of them.'[64]

The attractiveness of her lifestyle encourages Craik to welcome instances of energetic self-help in other women. She delights in the pioneering spirit of a young friend, Laura Herford, the first woman art student at the Royal Academy, and offers to assist another young girl who wants to become a concert singer. The tougher, less conventional side of Craik's nature also comes out when, setting aside her momentary depression, she takes a quizzical look at marriage. The numerous love affairs of her Scottish friends tickle her sense of humour: 'I do think all Scotland is gone daft about marrying',[65] she scoffs. While accepting that marriage based on real affection and respect is always worth while, she has no hesitation in condemning that motivated by social or economic considerations. She also has no time for women who sit helplessly waiting for circumstances to provide them with a husband. She is quite scornful about the case of a young friend, Minna Lovell, who at twenty-seven is still dependent upon her parents — 'I look upon hers as a completely lost life — with no usefulness in it and not a bit of happiness, either past, present or probable'.[66] She exhibits, too, a delightfully sly maliciousness towards 'typical' spinsters (among whom she clearly did not class herself). Tennyson's sister, she writes, having called on her, leaves the impression of being an ugly, sharp old maid, while Mary Craik, George's sister, is unfortunately 'growing rather old-maidish'.[67] Craik's own married happiness may have made her more sympathetic later towards the lonely single woman, but she never abandons her conviction of the positive value of female self-reliance. In the same letter in which she expresses her marital joys, she reminds her correspondent:

> I never alter my creed that a single woman may be perfectly happy in herself — if she chooses — and that a single life is far better than any but the very happiest married life.[68]

Conventional though she may now seem to her friends, she refuses to lie to them about the sense of dualities which her pre-marital experience has taught her.

*   *   *

As has already been suggested, Craik's fiction seems predominantly to voice her more conventional attitudes towards womanhood. The outspokenness of much of her non-fiction is curiously muted in her imaginative writing — a fact which implies that it is not only economic pressures (which affected all aspects of her work) which are responsible for the romantic patterning of her novels. Her narratives overtly enact the view that though 'there are other things in life besides love . . . everybody who has lived at all, knows that love is the very heart of life, the pivot upon which its whole machinery turns . . . A life without love in it must of necessity be an imperfect, an unnatural life'.[69] Romantic relationships form the core of nearly all her tales; most of her heroines accept the primacy of love, personally experiencing 'woman's highest, holiest destiny . . . that of a loving and devoted wife'.[70] Moreover, Craik appears to uphold the ideal of womanly submission in marriage, especially in her earlier novels. In *Agatha's Husband* (1853), for example, the advice given by an older woman to a young bride has authorial resonance: the husband is a tree upon which the wife can lean, but she must 'always remember that it is a noble forest-oak, and that you are only its dews or its sunshine, or its ivy garland. You never must attempt to come between it and the skies.'[71] This image, unlike the similar one at the end of *Jane Eyre*, gives little suggestion of mutual support.

Yet from within this framework of orthodoxy, Craik expresses dissent. If we dig more deeply into the texture of her novels, we find co-existing with the romantic idealism a tougher, more realistic appraisal of women's roles, a quite unromantic awareness of needs and conditions glossed over by her age's ideologies. Her own contemporaries were not blind to this aspect of her writing; an early reviewer of *A Life for a Life* (1859), for instance, recognises Craik as one of the 'sisterhood' of protesting women authors:

> She has the feeling that the woman's side of every question has yet to be asserted; that the time in the world's history has come for this new development . . . Her own sentiments . . . are evidently not founded on custom and received habits of thought; indeed . . . are more at variance with them than she likes openly to express.[72]

Modern critics have taken up the idea of covert rebellion in Craik's work. In an illuminating article, Elaine Showalter argues that like many Victorian women novelists frustrated by the dualisms of their lives, Craik, caught in the tensions of both wanting to be independent of society yet not willing wholly to reject its codes, uses her fiction to protest obliquely about contemporary attitudes towards women's roles.[73] Sally Mitchell includes Craik in her discussion of those Victorian women writers whose work challenges the double sexual standard.[74] Valuable as such criticism is, however, it fails to stress that Craik's unorthodoxy most prominently manifests itself as ambivalence, an awareness of dichotomies expressed through contrasts and juxtapositioning within her narratives. Like so many of her literary contemporaries, Craik enacts her response to female experience through questioning rather than outright rejection of current doctrines.

Craik's novels, oddly enough, contain relatively few spinsters. Despite her own experience of and statements about the blessings of singleness, she is reluctant to make female autonomy a central fictional theme. Furthermore, her portrayal of single women frequently depends on the very stereotypes which she herself, both personally and in print, refutes. Though she eschews the satirical portraiture of spinsterly eccentricity, brilliantly executed by Jane Austen with Miss Bates in *Emma* and widely echoed in the Victorian period (by Sewell and Gaskell among others), she seems drawn to the notion of the 'sad imperfectness'[75] and 'settled loneliness of heart'[76] of spinsterhood. For the critic R.H. Hutton, this was one of the chief defects of her otherwise excellent fiction. Objecting to the numbers of 'suffering and resigned angels' in her tales, he compares the sad-spirited Anne Valery in *Agatha's Husband* with 'Mrs Gaskell's wonderful sketch of "Miss Matty" in *Cranford*'; Miss Matty also has experienced romantic disappointment, but whereas she is 'bound to the present as well as to the past',

> Miss Muloch's [sic] suffering women live only 'for others'; the 'beautiful light' is always on their faces . . . they are never suffered to surmount their griefs quietly, and take living and characteristic interests in the living world.[77]

Hutton exaggerates somewhat, but Craik's old maids certainly survive through endurance rather than energy. Her view of spinsterhood as a poor alternative to a fuller emotional existence comes over most strongly in the fiction she wrote after her marriage. In *Hannah* (1872), for example, she paints a gloomy picture of the situation of those women who

> on the verge of middle age, find themselves without kith or kin, husband or child, and are forced continually to remember that the kindest of friends love them only with a tender benevolence, as adjuncts, but not essentials, of happiness. They are useful to many — necessary to none; and the sooner they recognise this, the better. (9)

In *The Woman's Kingdom* (1869), too, female self-dependence is seen as a grim recognition of necessity rather than a vitalising choice.

Craik's earlier fiction includes more cheerful versions of single-ness, but still depicts it as essentially a compromise. In *Olive* (1850), Miss Meliora Vanbrugh, a rather pathetic creature who has allowed her life to become dominated by her overbearing brother, is shel-tered from real misery only by her innocence: 'if her hopes never blossomed, she also never had the grief of watching them die'.[78] Others of Craik's single women are elevated to models of blessed resignation. In *The Head of the Family* (1852), the hero's maiden sister, Lindsay Graeme, lovingly self-sacrificial, owes her 'serene repose'[79] to her abandonment of the hopes, though not the memories, of a previous romance. In *Agatha's Husband*, Anne Valery, whom Hutton found so distressingly limp, is also effectively out of this world, racked by an organic disease and beatified by her disappointment. At thirty-nine, Anne considers that her life is over; it is hard to believe that her twenty-seven-year-old creator, though unable to foresee her own rebirth at the same age, really intended this as a sexual truism. Anne is a somewhat more outgoing character than Lindsay. She not only teaches Agatha to act decisively and win respect, but she also voices a doctrine of positive singleness:

'I have had a great deal to do always, and in all my labour was there profit . . . my life was not wholly thrown away, as many an unmarried woman's is, but as no one's ever need be . . . There are more things in life than mere marrying and being happy.' (346–7)

She hardly illustrates her own creed, however; after a brief recon-ciliation with her former lover, she dies, an image of incomplete female fulfilment. In *A Life for a Life*, too, Penelope Johnston, betrayed by her fiancé, becomes a faded, saint-like old maid, even though she at least lives on to be useful to others.

Such portraits, combined with the emphasis on matrimonial satis-faction in Craik's novels, would scarcely seem to suggest unorthodoxy, even ambivalence. But, as has been indicated, beneath her conventionality lies resistance to her own overt tradi-tionalism. She expresses this through particular artistic devices, the two most significant of which are common to many dissenting Vic-torian women novelists. The first, the portrayal of the strains and unhappiness of married life, highlights a contemporary reality pub-licly little commented on at the time; the second, the depiction of female energies operating both within and outside traditional roles, indicates an awareness of a more self-determining womanhood beginning to make its impact on orthodox values.

Craik's treatment of marriage is complex and bold; like Anne Brontë, Gaskell and Eliot, she shows that marital union, while it can be supremely satisfying, may prove a source of frustration and entrapment, crushing womanly individuality. Though none of her heroines is, like Brontë's Helen Huntingdon, subjected to a husband's drunken brutality, many of them are similarly lured into marriage by false idealism, and discover the penalties of what they have undertaken. *The Ogilvies* (1849), Craik's first novel, points out how easily a young woman's romantic notions may distort her personal judgment. Katherine Ogilvie is a victim of her innocence and lack of guidance; creating her ideal suitor out of her reading and 'her own fanciful dreams' (7), she thinks she has found him in the handsome and accomplished Paul Lynedon. When she finds that his advances to her have been mere self-amusement, in a spirit of vengeful disillusionment she marries her old admirer, her lumpish cousin Hugh, fully aware of the insincerity of her commitment. Craik does not entirely exonerate Katherine. But with chilling perceptiveness she describes the misery of a woman who has to suffer 'the daily burden of a loveless, unequal yoke — the petty jars — the continual dragging down of a strong mind to the weary level of an inferior one' (305), and who must, to the outside world, 'wear the mask of affection, or at least of duty; to display the mocking semblance of a happy home' (364). The ending of the novel contrasts markedly with its earlier insights, and demonstrates Craik's artistic immaturity as well as her uncertainty of stance towards sexual passion: Hugh dies and Katherine, reneging on her vow never to remarry, is re-united in matrimony with the now-repentant Paul, just before she dies of heart disease, thus providing a morally and emotionally respectable climax to the story. Yet firm hints of the more probing questioning of Craik's later work are unmistakable here, co-existing uneasily with the sentimentality.

In *Agatha's Husband* and *Christian's Mistake* (1865), Craik shows more forcefully how marriage can pervert or crush womanly individuality. The former explores the predicament of a young woman who, vulnerable to the temptations of security, thinks she can escape from her 'friendless desolation' within the 'contemptible, scheming, match-making' (36) society around her by marrying her guardian's brother, a man whom she hardly knows. As Craik wryly remarks:

To one whose heart is altogether free, the knowledge of being deeply loved, and by a man whose attachment would do honour to any woman, is a thought so soothing, so alluring, that from it springs half the marriages . . . which take place in the world (38)

Agatha is a victim of 'the terror that seizes a helpless young creature, who, all supports taken away, is at last set face to face with the cruel world' (49), and she accepts Nathanael Harper from ignorance rather than from wilfulness. Suffering follows almost immediately; her uneasy feelings of combined assurance and foreboding during the courtship are replaced after marriage by a strange 'mingling of attraction and repulsion' (228) towards her inscrutable husband. Images of repression and constriction describe Agatha's sense of restraint: early on, she feels 'the tightening pressure of that chain with which her life was now eternally bound' (121), and later the impenetrable barrier of Nathenael's reserve seems like 'a chain of iron wrapped round her' (216). Like a wild bird, vainly beating against a marble wall, she longs to break out from under the 'cloud' of his suffocating possessiveness into 'the sunshine of her careless, girlish life' (190) — a yearning for freedom which Kavanagh's Adèle also feels in a similarly restrictive marriage. Though hardly original, these images clearly express Craik's recognition of marriage as imprisonment. As with *The Ogilvies*, her idealism eventually triumphs; after an incredible series of misunderstandings, harmony is finally established between Agatha and Nathanael. But Craik here more openly explores the dualities of female needs. Agatha both wants to lean on her husband and resents his control over her; she also objects to being treated like a child and having 'secrets' kept from her. Their reconciliation may seem conventionally romantic, but Craik does not allow us to forget that there is a very thin line between mutual love and mutual irritation in sexual relationships.

Christian's Mistake appeared in the year of Craik's marriage and presumably represents her meditations on her own commitment to a more 'relative' position. Its examination of marital disharmony is psychologically more subtle than that of the earlier novel, with the focus primarily on the woman's emotions. Christian, a hard-worked governess, marries a middle-aged, respectable Cambridge don in an almost volitionless bid to escape the indignities of old-maidhood — 'the total desolation . . . [of being] exposed to every insult of the bitter world, or at least that bitter portion of it, which is always ready to trample down a woman if she is helpless, and to hunt her down if she is strong enough to help herself'.[80] Christian's ostensible 'mistake' is her failure to tell her husband of an earlier attachment about which she feels guilty since it aroused in her the passion which she cannot give him. The autobiographical links are obvious: Craik is here surely thinking of her own contrasting responses to George and Joe. But more boldly, the story also suggests that the marriage itself may have been a mistake. Even while the comforts of matrimony are still novelties for her, Christian regrets the loss of her 'fierce poverty-nurtured independence' (20), dramatically demonstrated by her symbolic attempts to pull off her wedding-ring and by her instinctive horror as she realises that she will never be alone again:

> The responsibility of being no longer her own, but another's, — bound fixedly and irrevocably, by the most solemn vow that can be given or taken, subject to no limitations, provisions, or exceptions, while life remained. Oh, it was awful — awful! (29)

As with Agatha, images of chains and captivity indicate Christian's new state: she is 'a free creature suddenly caught, tied, and bound' (27). The 'narrow gateway' and 'chilly cloisters' of her husband's college become metaphors for her imprisonment and exclusion from the 'existence of boundless enjoyment, freedom and beauty' (70) which she had envisaged for herself, as in *Middlemarch* Dorothea's traumatic disillusionment with her stifling marriage is imaged in terms of 'anterooms and winding passages which seemed to lead nowhither'.[81] The force of Craik's realistic insight is weakened by the conclusion, which shows Christian eventually finding happiness through her realisation that she loves her husband after all; the issue of the nature of marital affection also blocks more radical debate about matrimony as a social institution. But the novel unquestionably reflects Craik's unease about the loss of freedom and the restrictions on female individuality inherent in even the most apparently unexceptional unions.

The fiction which Craik wrote after her marriage on the whole offers a more rosy picture of wedded bliss. But one of her most interesting, if undisguisedly polemical, novels of this period vividly charts the breakdown of the union between a strongly individual woman and a weak, untrustworthy man. *A Brave Lady* (1870) was written in support of the Married Women's Property Act, finally passed in 1870, and of the ongoing debates about the reform of the Divorce Laws, and is impelled by considerable propagandist fervour. The brave lady, Josephine Scanlan (did Craik have her heroine's iconoclastic namesake, Miss Butler, in mind, one wonders), gradually recognises her husband's irredeemable failings and decides to fend for herself and her family. She earns money so that she need not depend on the vagaries of his labours, organises the household according to her requirements, and finally determines to flee from his corrupting influence. Her decision has full authorial approval: even at the cost of being 'forced into unnatural unwomanliness',[82] Craik argues, a wife is perfectly right to separate herself from a relationship which is spiritually destroying her and her children. As in her earlier work, Craik fails to maintain her subversion to the end. Josephine, learning that her husband has a terminal disease, remains with him after all, and after his death and those of all her six children lives out the rest of her life in sternly stoical widowhood. Once again, the challenge has been undercut by conventional values — here the ideal of martyrdom by which womanly self-sacrifice to duty is sanctified. None the less, Craik registers her protest: a life of marital wretchedness is not to be passively endured, and a wronged wife must initiate her own remedy.

In her questioning of prevalent matrimonial ideologies, Craik places particular emphasis on masculine deficiencies. Made wise by her own confrontations with male inadequacy, she imaginatively enacts a personal sense of outrage: 'having seen so much of the sufferings of my own sex from their own weakness and the wickedness of the other . . . I feel, like Jonah, "I do well to be angry".'[83] Like Gaskell and Sewell, she challenges blind faith in patriarchal superiority, aware that really good men are few and far between. So though admiring her 'heroes' such as John Halifax, or William Stedman in *The Woman's Kingdom*, she is uncompromisingly critical of the kind of male egotism which wreaks such havoc in *A Brave Lady*. Her shrill denunciation of Paul's cavalier treatment of Katherine in *The Ogilvies* is passionate, if stagey — 'You, O Man! who with your honey words and your tender looks steal away a young girl's heart for thoughtless or selfish vanity, do you know what it is you do?' (225). In her later works, her indignation is more controlled and her attack more effective. Figures such as the smooth, easy-going Ulverston in *The Head of the Family*, who runs off from the young woman he has persuaded to marry him, and the myopically self-centred Frederick Harper in *Agatha's Husband*, who ruins Anne Valery's life by coming between her and the man she loves, may seem somewhat pasteboard creations, but they function as telling indictments of masculine callousness. Craik is especially merciless towards the sort of moral deviousness which she saw in her father. The evasiveness of Josephine Scanlan's husband makes it impossible for her to deal with him head-on. In *A Life for a Life*, Dora Johnston's loyally patient sister, Penelope, is emotionally destroyed by the knowledge of her fiancé's mistress, a fact which he has carefully omitted to tell her; he himself is finally deemed worthless not so much because of his deception but because he is totally blind to Penelope's agonised feelings of betrayal:

> 'Her reason for refusing me is puerile — perfectly puerile. No woman of sense, who knows anything of the world, would urge it for a moment . . . I have done no worse than hundreds do in my position . . . and the world forgives them, and women too.'[84]

Craik's depiction of this aspect of male treachery reminds us of Gaskell's *Ruth*, but her unusually consistent tough-mindedness in this novel makes her less sentimental than her contemporary. Unlike Gaskell's Bellingham, Craik's faithless lover does not escape his responsibilities through death; he is humbled by the moral strength of the two women he has wronged, and is forced to undertake the duties which he had hoped to evade.

A total discountenancing of women as individuals, exampled in the artist, Michael Vanbrugh, in *Olive*, who tyrannises over his meekly submissive sister, appals Craik less than the patronising arrogance which disguises itself as adoring protectiveness. In several of her novels, sexual relationships are brought to the brink of disaster because of the man's refusal to confide in his partner. In *The Head of the Family*, Ninian Graeme's exaggerated sense of family duty, which prevents him from telling Hope Ansted that he loves her, and thus upsetting her, is, it is implied, partly responsible for her miserable union with a rascally bigamist. In *Agatha's Husband*, Agatha's happiness is wrecked by her husband's inability to express his passion for her, combined with his almost sinister iron will which refuses to bend to her pleadings for his confidence. Harmony eventually prevails in the romantic ethos of the novels, but not without a new respect for female feelings on the part of the erring male.

When tackling the question of womanly individuality more

directly, Craik reflects more of her personal unorthodoxy. To examine her treatment of a distinctive female selfhood, we can divide her heroines into three groups: the spinsters who defy the passively angelic stereotype; the wives who manage to exert power within the confines of marriage; and the women who, though eventually subsumed into sexual relativity, expand their own personalities before matrimony. Miss Flora Rothesay, Olive's aunt, is a welcome exception to Craik's limp-spirited single women. Like Sewell's Aunt Sarah in *The Experience of Life*, she is an energetic and resourceful spinster, who demonstrates that a woman's life 'never need be empty of love, even though, after seeing all near kindred drop away, one lingers to be an old maid of eighty years' (319). Though, like Anne Valery, she lives essentially in the past, having suffered the death of her lover many years before, she provides for Olive a model of self-reliant fortitude. Craik's most interesting portrayal of permanent spinsterhood occurs in a slight tale, *Bread Upon the Waters: a Governess's Life* (1852), which has several autobiographical features. The narrator/heroine takes herself and her two brothers away from an uncongenial home environment (her father has recently remarried); using her musical gifts and knowledge of classics and languages, she becomes a governess in order to provide for them. She finds the prospect of independent exertion invigorating: 'the very thought of toil gives me strength. It is like plunging into a cold bath, after being suffocated with foul vapory streams.'[85] Though some consider her behaviour 'strange' or 'improper', she has no regrets and works with cheerful energy. She too has lost a lover, but unlike most of Craik's other disappointed women, she puts her sorrow firmly away, and stoutly asserts the advantages of singleness:

> I go out into the world and see other homes full of selfishness, misery, and strife: — mine is all peace; there is never in it a shadow of disquiet or contention . . . I see around me restlessness, ennui, young lives wasted in doing nothing — until out of the dull void of an aimless existence gradually forms a chaos . . . Now, *my* life — steadily bringing its duties, and every night closing them in rest — would I change? No. (154)

There are clear echoes here of Craik's own declarations of independence. Regrettably, she once more fails to vindicate fully her lesson of womanly self-reliance, shying away from the implications of successful female autonomy. After all her confident self-motivation, the narrator suffers an accident which disfigures her for life, so that when her former lover returns and, out of pity, proposes to her, she can unhesitatingly refuse him.[86] Finally, she retreats to peaceful spinsterhood, existing vicariously through her brother's and her lover's children (a fate very similar to that of Susan Graham in Sewell's *Ivors*, who fades mournfully into the shadow of her rival's married happiness). Not only cautious about directly championing spinsterhood, Craik cannot abandon her conventional attitudes either; her self-abnegating heroine is left with neither husband nor independence, merely with the knowledge of lost possibilities.

Craik's depiction of female power within marriage challenges contemporary ideologies more subversively. Several of her heroines marry men who, while not actually evil, lack purpose or sensitivity; their wives, ostensibly fulfilling the traditional womanly roles of service and comfort, reveal more revolutionary qualities than the domestic angel is expected to possess, as they exert influence in a way which exploits without overtly rejecting their 'natural' sphere. So in *Christian's Mistake*, Christian, brought up by a father who if he neglected her 'had at any rate left her alone, to form her own mind and character, as best she could' (90), finds her true means of self-expression when called upon to act in a crisis. She comes into her own when one of her step-sons falls seriously ill; she handles the situation efficiently, and determinedly overrides opposition from interfering relatives. Undaunted by difficulties, she realises with pride that now 'she could rely only upon herself, and act for herself' (127), and her new role of authority gives her an energising 'consciousness of power' (239). Her growing self-confidence is fed by the knowledge that she is stronger than her husband — 'like many another good and brave man, he was in this matter quite paralysed . . . [she must] tell him what he was to do, and help him to do it, just like a child' (127–8). Craik suggests that one of the reasons for Christian's powerfulness is her youthful exclusion from the normal feminine world of 'small sillinesses, narrow formalities, and petty unkindnesses' (90), an exclusion which has saved her from 'women's smallnesses' (86). Craik, as always, is ambivalent about what constitutes true 'womanliness', and delegates Christian to the role of supportive helpmeet once the crisis is over. This, however, represents her heroine's own choice; her potential has been demonstrated and may be called out again at any time. In *A Brave Lady*, as we have seen, the exercise of female strength becomes a radical element in the wife's fight for survival. Even in the almost Edenic relationship between Edna and William in *The Woman's Kingdom*, Craik demonstrates her belief that 'it is women who are in reality the salvation or the destruction of a household' (169), arguing that the best wives must be able to rule as well as to obey. Edna is not William's slave — they are 'simply and equally friends' (182) — and, like Christian, she unhesitatingly copes with the family crises with which her husband proves incapable of dealing. Interestingly, all three of these novels are the fruits of Craik's early married life and may be fictional representations of her determination to resist wifely subordination — an instance of that unwomanliness which her parents-in-law found so alarming in her.

Craik's portrayal of women 'finding' themselves before becoming 'relative creatures' in marriage most vividly reveals her awareness of the conflicting impulses within her sex. *The Ogilvies*, crudely romantic though it is, shows how even in her literary novitiate Craik's unorthodoxy breaks into the conventional patterning of her story. The novel contrasts two instances of female assertiveness. Katherine's passionate wilfulness is injurious to herself and others, yet it leads her to self-knowledge; significantly, the chapter which describes her vengeful resolve to defy normal womanliness is headed by a quotation from Elizabeth Barrett Browning, voicing the spirit of rebellion:

> — Know you what it is when anguish with apocalyptic Never
> To a Pythian height dilates you and despair sublimes to power?
> (223)

In contrast, Katherine's angelic cousin, Eleanor, patiently waiting for the lover who she believes has rejected her, seems an archetype of female submissiveness and self-negation. Under her idealised self-lessness, however, she too possesses a distinctive individuality which demands expression. Eleanor shows unexpected determination in refusing to give up her fiancé even when threatened by her aunt's stony opposition; with surprising stubbornness, she puts self-interest before sacrificial duty, thus defying conventional notions of appropriate female behaviour. Additional strength is conferred on her by an inherited legacy, a material emblem of her independent spirit. Her eventual marriage represents her success in getting what she wants.

One of Craik's most interesting studies of female potential occurs

in *Olive*, a novel which examines singleness from a professional and
an emotional angle. At first glance, the heroine seems a perfect
subject for Craik's most sentimental treatment. Olive is born with a
deformity of the spine, which initially renders her repugnant to her
parents and makes her feel doomed to be cut off from normal
womanly fulfilment. Certain that she will remain an old maid, she
prepares to take on a spinster's role, devoting herself to her widowed
mother and seeking a means of supporting the two of them. Even at
this stage, however, Olive displays qualities which belie her apparent
feebleness. Her early sufferings promote an inner strength which
expresses itself as control and influence. After her mother dies, she
becomes 'the ruler of the household' (134), embodying, as her father
recognises, androgynous powers — 'a spirit equal to, and not
unlike, his own — a nature calm, resolute, clear-sighted; the strong
will and decision of a man, united to the tenderness of a woman'
(67). Reversing natural roles, he begins to rely heavily on her, eventually entrusting her first with the secret then with the care of his
illegitimate daughter; his appeal to her to absolve his memory in this
way authorises her as confessor and moral arbiter.

Other aspects of Olive's experience belie their seeming orthodoxy.
If she is not after all a pathetic single woman, neither does she prove
a totally submissive bride, though at first this seems likely. Despite
her conviction that she will never marry, Olive holds to her view that
love is 'life's crowning sweetness' (207), as, without optimism, she
falls for the recently-widowed husband of her best friend. When,
her deformity having mysteriously disappeared, Harold Gwynne
finally recognises her attractions, Olive readily gives up her independence, glad to have 'no interest in the world save what was linked
with him' (292). The novel concludes with a purely stereotypical
image, Harold loudly proclaiming his future plans and Olive nestling close to him, 'with her clinging sweetness, her upward gaze . . .
a type of true woman' (430). Such female perfection clearly greatly
impressed the reviewer in *Chambers*, who describes the novel as 'the
story of a Model Woman, not owing her power to superficial or
sensuous attractions, but to the high, holy, and yet simple character
of her mind and affections'.[87] The relationship, however, hints at
less traditional sexual patternings than the ones this critic
applauded. Harold also uses Olive as his confessor (though his
guilty secret is, less glamorously, religious apostasy, not sexual mis-
demeanour), giving her a sense of ascendancy over him, 'a strange
sensation . . . [a feeling] that she alone held the key of his soul'

(282). The closing chapters (in yet another contemporary echo of *Jane Eyre*) develop the suggestion of female strength triumphing over male weakness. While Harold is rushing to rescue Olive from a fire at her house, he is injured, and, reduced to helplessness, depends on her to nurse him to recovery.[88] Having healed his body and his soul — she persuades him to overcome his religious doubts and return to the fold of true believers — Olive briskly resolves his indecision about going to America and sets him on the track of a new life. Even in her wifely submission, she does not totally relinquish her power: while sheltering under his protection, she skilfully, if lovingly, 'beguile[s]' (429) her husband into doing what she thinks best.

Olive also examines another aspect of female self-assertion — involvement in the professional world. Craik, like other Victorian women novelists, uses the image of the female artist — painter, singer, actress — as a paradigm for her sex's strivings towards self-expression; the dualities of the role, itself an alternative to the 'natural' creativity of motherhood, symbolise the dichotomies of womanly experience. Her discussion of Olive's career as a painter reflects the mixture of enthusiasm and cautiousness with which, as we have seen, she reacted to the friend who became the first woman student at the Royal Academy; it also reveals her ambivalence about her own employment in the world of letters. Olive is initially impelled by financial necessity, and at first she regards her chosen career as a consolation for her emotional deprivation. Soon, however, she begins to sense within herself the power of Genius, 'the spirit whose pulses she could not mistake' (178). Recognising her own talent, Olive rejoices in her success, not only because it provides a means of sustenance but also because it satisfies her strong urge to express her own individuality. As a recent critic has pointed out, several epigraphs from Romantic poetry in the novel suggest that Olive identifies with the rebel artist figure, even aligning herself with a revolutionary Promethean spirit.[89] Craik's awareness of the paradoxes inherent in Olive's position echoes clearly the unease of all those early-Victorian women who sought to reconcile traditional and more radical female behaviour. They see that aspiring women like Olive, who strive beyond stereotyped female roles, have to adopt qualities of strength, assertiveness, and self-reliance, usually associated with masculinity; they cannot conceive of an alternative womanly voice independent of sexually-biased definitions of achievement. Yet, as Craik argues at some length in Chapter 21, the

'unfemininity' which artistic commitment involves actually releases
new energies in women: 'sometimes chance or circumstances or
wrong, sealing up her woman's nature, converts her into a self-
dependent human soul. Instead of life's sweetnesses, she has before
her life's greatnesses' (164). Being exempt (as she thinks) from 'a
woman's natural destiny' (165) enables Olive to live according to the
dictates of her individual talent and to find 'greatness and happiness' (166) beyond the conventional blessings of beauty and love.
Craik is still ambivalent, as her language here indicates: separation
from normal female experience represents loss, while it is also creatively enriching; womanly individuality may be possible only at the
cost of denying sexual impulses, but 'greatness' is offered as
compensation.

Craik investigates the relationship between professional commitment and female 'abnormality' in other of her works. In *The Head
of the Family*, Rachel Armstrong, an abandoned wife, has been
released by circumstances from her accepted role, and can thus give
full rein to her acting talent. Her chosen career, the embodiment of
her defiantly imaginative spirit, poses a far more serious threat to
her womanliness than Olive's does, and Craik, exhibiting a characteristically Victorian suspicion of actresses, solves the problem by
finally removing her heroine to a lunatic asylum, after a mental
breakdown. Rachel is nevertheless 'sublime' (336) in her acting, as
even the prim Ninian Graeme acknowledges; and Craik admires
(even if she also fears) her passionate individuality which is so much
more striking than the angelic meekness of Ninian's future wife,
Hope. The contrast between the two women, as well as the unease
about such female powers, recalls Jewsbury's treatment of the same
theme in *The Half Sisters*, which too, as we have seen, ultimately
reasserts the romantic orthodoxies. Others of Craik's heroines gain
'unwomanly' satisfaction from their artistic endeavours — the
unmarried singing teacher in 'Lord Erlistoun' (1857), for example,
or the plain old-maidish narrator of *The Little Lychetts* (1855) who
finds fulfilment in studying art, and is relieved from her feelings of
difference from other women by her creative absorption. Even
Christian, finding some joy as a wife and stepmother, experiences
through her newly rediscovered talent for singing 'that pure enjoyment which all true artists — be they singers, painters, poets —
understand, and they only — the delight in mere creation' (138); in
her depression and sense of uselessness, her artistic nature, the
expression of her true self, springs up in her 'like a living fountain'

(172). Women must be allowed to speak for themselves, Craik
argues; obedience to the creative impulse, despite its penalties, is
imperative.

Craik's most perceptive discussion of women's attitudes towards
love and marriage is found in *A Life for a Life*, a novel of which,
as her letters indicate, she was particularly proud. The work is tech-
nically and thematically innovative. It has a double narration in
the form of two parallel diary entries, one from an army doctor,
Max Urquhart, and one from a young woman, Theodora (Dora)
Johnston, whose life gradually becomes involved with his. The
device, as Craik explains in the Preface to the New Edition,
'appeared to me the best mode of evolving the two characters in
whose inward development and outward history lay the principle of
my book'.[90] It is not, however, merely structural experimentation,
but also encapsulates the thematic concerns of the novel. As well as
effectively charting the progress of the relationship between the two
characters, the adjacent accounts highlight the male/female contrasts and express Craik's dualism with regard to sexual roles. The
two histories complement and illuminate each other. Max is tormented by a guilty secret. Many years before, in a drunken fit, he
killed a man, an act for which, though he was provoked into it, he
feels endless remorse; having decided to confess and accept legal
punishment, he has to re-establish his own self-respect, and realise
that being socially branded as a criminal does not debar him from
marrying Dora, whose brother — in the one piece of incredible plot
machinery in the novel — turns out to be the very man he murdered.
Dora, plain, outspoken, and, at twenty-five, sceptical about marriage in general and about her own future prospects in particular,
defies social convention and parental opposition to unite with the
man she loves. Craik's radical attitude towards the legal and social
treatment of criminality is linked with her demand for a new view of
male/female relationships, as the *Christian Remembrancer* recognised: 'She has devoted unquestionable ability to no less an object
than changing the world's opinion on two important points. The
main and more prominent one — its conduct towards the criminal
. . . the other its views on . . . courtship.'[91] By juxtaposing the
narratives, both of which voice dissent from received assumptions,
Craik at one stroke boldly suggests that Max and Dora are equally
victims of oppressive social strictures, the one as a legally-defined
outcast, the other as an independent-minded woman.

Craik's challenge to sexual ideologies is most directly expressed through her heroine-narrator. Dora, bored with the trivialities of her everyday existence, yearns for occupation in the outside world:

> I longed for some change in my dull life; wished I were a boy, a man — anything so that I might be something, — do something. (70)
> To discover one's right work and to do it, must be the grand secret of life. (100)

Discouraged by her younger sister's frivolous attitude towards marriage, she looks instead for a means of usefulness and positive self-expression; like her creator speaking in *A Woman's Thoughts about Women*, she asks, 'What am I to do with [my life]?' (109). She is not granted the satisfaction of a career, but she is able to assert her individuality during her developing relationship with Max, taking his masculine exertions as a model, and refusing to be restricted by conventional notions of womanliness; undeterred by raised eyebrows, she works to re-integrate Lydia, the 'fallen' girl made pregnant by her elder sister's fiancé, into society by finding her employment. Dora flaunts her independence in defying her father and insisting on marrying Max; it is her suggestion, too, that they go to Canada, where they will both be free of prejudiced and petty creeds. The *Christian Remembrancer* was in no doubt that Craik was arguing for a radical rethinking about matrimonial union:

> What she evidently aims at is the greater equality of woman with man in the marriage relation . . . To this writer the idea of being sought, persuaded, wooed, is not congenial, — is almost repugnant. Mind should rather meet with mind on equal terms.[92]

As the reviewer recognises, the relationship between Max and Dora depends on the harmonising of personality and on mutual respect; the wife here will play an active, decision-making part, as a companion, not a subordinate.

The dualistic form of the novel also enacts the ambiguities which Craik sees underlying gender-oriented concepts of behaviour. Both narrators are curiously androgynous figures. Max represents the energetic purposefulness which Craik so much admired; as Dora realises, his active involvement in the outer world affords him some relief from the power of circumstances — an escape not possible for her. On the other hand, though he admires Dora for her unconventionality, he remains partially tainted by silly male sentimentality towards women; he envisages her as 'an angel, sliding down on a sunshiny cloud to a man asleep' (107), and at first refuses to believe that she can participate in a more flesh-and-blood way in his 'male' work. While Max's portrayal demonstrates the dichotomies of maleness, Dora's highlights those of femaleness. She desires both independence and the comforts of emotional support; she regards marriage as ultimate fulfilment, yet will not compromise her high evaluation of its conditions — 'I can understand women's renouncing love, or dying of it, or learning to live without it: but marrying without it, either for "spite", or for money, necessity, pity, or persuasion, is to me utterly incomprehensible' (205), she declares stoutly. Finally, it is the less conventional aspects of her womanhood which are vindicated in the novel. The more traditionally feminine qualities appear, oddly enough, in Max, in his self-obsession, his romantic visions of domestic bliss, and his elevation of pointless self-sacrifice into a moral law. These do not represent the positive side of femininity; Max needs Dora's tough-mindedness to lead him to a clearer understanding of himself and his role. Unorthodox femaleness triumphs, too, through Penelope, who resolutely rejects marriage when she discovers that her fiancé has betrayed her; her defiance of his strategies of deceit and his implementation of the double standard glorifies female integrity in the face of masculine faithlessness. In this work, Craik most directly and assuredly incorporates her unorthodoxies into her artistic vision.

Craik's novels are essentially explorations, not statements. They cling too closely to the romantic conventions to be considered revolutionary, and their undeniably sentimental elements indicate her creative, as well as personal, cautiousness. But, as *A Life for a Life* makes plain, their questioning of traditional sexual roles and their depiction of women attempting to 'find' themselves remind us that in her art, as in her life, she resists narrowly definitive views of womanhood. She will not completely overthrow the assumptions upon which her society is based, but she does ask that a fresh look be taken at them.

Notes

1. Letter to Helen Walsh, Sunday [November? 1849]. Quoted in *Jane Welsh*

Carlyle: Letters to her Family, 1839–1863, ed. Leonard Huxley (London, 1924), p. 335.

2. Letter to Forster, December 1849. Quoted in *Letters and Memorials of Jane Welsh Carlyle*, ed. James Anthony Froude (London, 1883), vol. II, p. 94.

3. Comment by Henry Sidgwick. Quoted in Amy Cruse, *The Victorians and Their Books* (London, 1935), p. 318.

4. G.H. Lewes, 'The Lady Novelists', *Westminster Review*, vol. LVIII (July 1852), p. 141.

5. Quoted in Cruse, *The Victorians and Their Books*, p. 317.

6. Henry James, '[Mrs Craik's] *A Noble Life*', *Nation*, vol. II (1 March 1866), p. 276.

7. 'Miss Muloch (Mrs Craik)', *Victoria Magazine*, vol. XXVIII (April 1877), p. 483. Ironically, in her own *Plain Speaking* (1882), Craik attacks sentimentality in fiction for its false view of life and hence potential immorality.

8. Letter to François D'Albert-Durade, 7 June 1860. In *The George Eliot Letters*, ed. G.S. Haight (New Haven and London, 1954–78), vol. III, p. 302.

9. 'Miss Muloch (Mrs Craik)', p. 479.

10. Letter to his parents, 9 July 1836. In Special Collections, Library of University of California at Los Angeles.

11. Letter to his sister, 5 November 1845. In Special Collections, UCLA.

12. Ibid.

13. Margaret Oliphant, 'Mrs Craik', *Macmillan's Magazine*, vol. LVII (December 1887), p. 82.

14. Letter to Maria James, 29 October [1851]. In *The Letters of Mrs Gaskell*, ed. J.A.V. Chapple and Arthur Pollard (Manchester, 1966), p. 167.

15. Letter to Emma Shaen, 15 January 1851. In *Memorials of Two Sisters: Susanna and Catherine Winkworth*, ed. Margaret J. Shaen (London, 1908), p. 64.

16. Letter to Mrs Gaskell, [19 April] 1851. In *Letters Addressed to Mrs Gaskell*, ed. Ross D. Waller (Manchester, 1935), p. 47.

17. W.J. Linton, *Memories* (1894; reprint, New York, 1970), p. 66. Linton, Eliza Lynn's husband, who met Craik at the Halls' and remembered her as 'an over-tall and in younger days somewhat spindly woman, not beautiful, but good' (p. 171), claims that Hall was the original for Dickens's Pecksniff. He had a somewhat poor opinion of the Halls' soirées, held at their house in Brompton, 'The Rosery' (nicknamed by the irreverent 'The Roguery'), at which 'we were entertained with small talk and smaller Marsala' (p. 74).

18. See letter to Helen Walsh, Thursday [July? 1852]. In *Jane Welsh Carlyle*, ed. Huxley, p. 363.

19. 'Mrs Craik', p. 82.

20. Letter to Ben Mulock, 22 August [1855]. In Special Collections, UCLA.

21. Letter to Ben Mulock, [20 April 1857]. In Special Collections, UCLA.

22. *The Autobiography and Letters of Mrs M.O.W. Oliphant*, ed. Mrs Harry T. Coghill (Edinburgh and London, 1899), p. 85.

23. Letter to J.T. Fields, 15 October [1869]. In Huntington Library, San Marino, California.

24. Quoted by Thomas Mulock in letter to his sister, 5 November 1845. In Special Collections, UCLA.

25. Letter to Ben Mulock, 3 January 1861. In Special Collections, UCLA.

26. Letter to Ben Mulock, 30 December 1861. In Special Collections, UCLA.

27. Letter to Ben Mulock, 4 November [1860]. In Special Collections, UCLA.

28. Letter from Thomas Craik to Dinah Mulock, 6 July 1864. In Special Collections, UCLA.

29. Letter from Mrs M. Craik to Dinah Mulock, 10 July 1864. In Special Collections, UCLA.

30. This was first published as a series of articles in *Chambers Journal* from May

to December 1857, appearing in book form in 1858.
   31. [Dinah Mulock Craik], *A Woman's Thoughts About Women* (London, 1859), p. 6.
   32. Ibid., p. 5.
   33. She herself said that she wished to remain anonymous 'for the sake of saying my say and [I] like to say it freely'. Letter to Ben Mulock, *c.* 1857. In Special Collections, UCLA.
   34. *A Woman's Thoughts*, p. 26.
   35. Ibid., p. 2.
   36. Ibid., p. 24.
   37. Ibid., p. 34.
   38. [Dinah Mulock Craik], *Plain Speaking* (London, 1882), p. 147.
   39. Ibid., p. 134.
   40. [Dinah Mulock Craik], *About Money and Other Things: a Gift Book* (London, 1886), p. 16.
   41. *A Woman's Thoughts*, pp. 344–5.
   42. Ibid., p. 63.
   43. [Dinah Mulock Craik], *Sermons Out of Church* (London, 1875), p. 124.
   44. Ibid., p. 239.
   45. *About Money and Other Things*, p. 156.
   46. [Dinah Mulock Craik], *Concerning Men and Other Papers* (London, 1888), p. 6.
   47. Ibid., p. 38.
   48. Letter to Rebecca Hallam, 1844. Quoted in Aleyn Lyell Reade, *The Mellards and Their Descendants* (London, 1915), p. 67. This work is the major source of biographical information about Craik.
   49. M.H. Noel-Paton, *Tales of a Grand-daughter* (Elgin, 1970), p. 16.
   50. Letter to Ben Mulock, 3 July [1860]. In Special Collections, UCLA.
   51. Letter to Ben Mulock, 18 November 1859. In Special Collections, UCLA.
   52. Craik achieved the fulfilment of her maternal desires in a most unusual way. In January 1859, an abandoned baby girl was found near the Craiks' house and was taken in by them for temporary protection. Craik decided to keep the child, who was formally adopted and christened Dorothy, the gift of God. She proved one of the greatest joys of Craik's life, after the novelist had managed to overcome George's initial doubts about taking such a step. Dorothy was a particular blessing because it seems that, perhaps due to his accident, the Craiks could expect to have no children of their own.
   53. Reade, *The Mellards*, pp. 90–1.
   54. Letter to Miss Ranken, *c.* 1865. In Morris L. Parrish Collection of Victorian Novelists, Princeton University Library.
   55. Letter to Ben Mulock, 14 July [1860]. In Special Collections, UCLA.
   56. Letter to Miss Ranken, *op. cit.*
   57. Letter to L.S. Metcalf, 14 November 1886. In Special Collections, UCLA.
   58. Letter to Ben Mulock, 15 January [1860]. In Special Collections, UCLA.
   59. Letter to Ben Mulock, 7 November [1854]. In Special Collections, UCLA.
   60. Letter to Mr Wilde, 17 July 1887. In Morris L. Parrish Collection, Princeton.
   61. Letter to Ben Mulock, 20 November [1855]. In Special Collections, UCLA.
   62. Letter to Ben Mulock, 7 November [1854]. In Special Collections, UCLA.
   63. Letter to Ben Mulock, 18 November 1859. In Special Collections, UCLA.
   64. Letter to Ben Mulock, 1 April [1860]. In Special Collections, UCLA.
   65. Letter to Ben Mulock, 14 July [1860]. In Special Collections, UCLA.
   66. Letter to Ben Mulock, 1 April [1860]. In Special Collections, UCLA.
   67. Letter to Ben Mulock, 6 June 1860. In Special Collections, UCLA.
   68. Letter to Miss Ranken, *op. cit.*
   69. [Dinah Mulock Craik], *The Woman's Kingdom* (London, 1870), p. 15.

70. [Dinah Mulock Craik], *The Ogilvies* (London, n.d.), p. 319. Subsequent page references are to this edition and will be included in the text.
71. [Dinah Mulock Craik], *Agatha's Husband* (London, n.d.), p. 328. Subsequent page references are to this edition and will be included in the text.
72. 'Our Female Novelists', *Christian Remembrancer*, vol. XXXVIII (October 1859), pp. 306–7.
73. Elaine Showalter, 'Dinah Mulock Craik and the Tactics of Sentiment: a Case Study in Victorian Female Authorship', *Feminist Studies*, 2 (1975), pp.5–23.
74. Sally Mitchell, *The Fallen Angel: Chastity, Class and Women's Reading, 1835–1880* (Bowling Green, Ohio, 1981), pp. 112–20.
75. *The Woman's Kingdom*, p. 12. Subsequent page references are to this edition and will be included in the text.
76. [Dinah Mulock Craik], *Hannah* (London, 1872), p. 19. Subsequent page references are to this edition and will be included in the text.
77. [R.H. Hutton] 'Novels by the Authoress of "John Halifax" ', *North British Review*, vol. XXIX (November 1858), p. 478.
78. [Dinah Mulock Craik], *Olive* (London, n.d.), p. 151. Subsequent page references are to this edition and will be included in the text.
79. [Dinah Mulock Craik], *The Head of the Family* (London and Newcastle, n.d.), p. 3. Subsequent page references are to this edition and will be included in the text.
80. Mrs Craik, *Christian's Mistake* (new edn, London, n.d.), p. 304. Subsequent page references are to this edition and will be included in the text.
81. George Eliot, *Middlemarch* (Penguin edn, Harmondsworth, 1981), p. 228.
82. [Dinah Mulock Craik], *A Brave Lady* (London, 1871), p. 111.
83. *Plain Speaking*, p. 137.
84. [Dinah Mulock Craik], *A Life for a Life* (new revised edn, London, [1860]), p. 313. Subsequent page references are to this edition and will be included in the text.
85. [Dinah Mulock Craik], *Bread Upon the Waters: a Governess's Life* (New York, 1887), p. 129. Subsequent page references are to this edition and will be included in the text.
86. Interestingly, several of Craik's male characters are cut off from romantic involvement by physical deformity, thus aligning themselves with the other-worldly single women. Most notable examples are the Earl in *A Noble Life* (1866) and Phineas Fletcher, the narrator of *John Halifax, Gentleman*; such men, as Hutton in his *North British Review* article suggests, are really women in disguise, reflecting their creator's ambivalence about sexual roles.
87. 'A Novel of the Season', *Chambers Edinburgh Journal*, n.s. vol. XV (January–June 1851), p. 7.
88. One wonders if, eleven years later, Craik was struck by the irony that she was now enacting her own art.
89. Showalter, 'Dinah Mulock Craik', p. 16.
90. *A Life for a Life*, p. iii. The Preface also explains how Craik had originally decided that Max should be guilty of intentional murder but that she changed this to manslaughter in the first edition in order to forestall disapproval; now, however, she realises that her first plan was the right one and appropriate for her argument that even the greatest crime can be redeemed by repentance. She was very enthusiastic about this novel: a letter to Ben of *c.* 1858, for instance, proclaims: 'My Max [her nickname for the book] is going on capital — two thirds of a novel already — and not yet at the climax. — I like it. I *feel* it's good — odd, very — and original.' (Special Collections, UCLA).
91. 'Our Female Novelists', pp. 306–7.
92. Ibid., p. 308.

3 CHARLOTTE BRONTË: A VISION OF DUALITY

As Charlotte Brontë's own contemporaries recognised, the striking originality of her novels lies not so much in the nature of her subject-matter as in her treatment of it.[1] Her work builds on the traditional staples of fiction — love and courtship, the progress of romantic involvement to its culmination in matrimony. Her heroines' deepest desire is for the satisfaction of sexual relationships; though they temporarily experience they do not whole-heartedly champion a single, self-contained existence. The power of Brontë's fiction, however, lies in its approach to the romantic orthodoxies, which at least one of her more hostile critics saw as socially subversive.[2] Brontë exploits these orthodoxies in order to express her reservations about her age's ideologies regarding women. More boldly than most of her fellow-novelists, she seeks to re-define feminine selfhood, freed from restricting images and assumptions. Her challenge is especially effective because she formulates it from within a conventional framework, arguing for new approaches to women's traditional needs. Inspired by her own awareness of the dichotomies of female experience, she is openly ambivalent about such needs, refusing either to deny their existence or to allow false idealism to suppress her sense of their problematic complexity. Her novels not only demand that sexual ideologies be re-examined, they themselves enact that re-examination, thematically and structurally.

Like so many mid-Victorian women, Brontë experienced the sense of a divided self. Described by the phrenologist who analysed her in 1851 as a mixture of self-doubt, intellectual strength, and poetical idealism,[3] she suffered in her own life the feeling of fragmentation or contradiction which her heroines encounter. Secluded in her dearly-loved yet imprisoning Haworth, she often longed for the freedom to range in the wider outside world, but was unremittingly obedient to the dictates of family and domestic responsibilities; instinctively pleasure-loving, she taught herself to endure the deprivation which she felt Providence had assigned her. She was

71

distressed, like many of her contemporaries, by the narrow scope for the employment of women's energies, yet she could not adopt the strident feminism of those such as her friend, Mary Taylor.[4] She saw the dangers of narrow preoccupation with marriage, but she herself, driven by her strong desire to be loved, could not abandon the belief that happy wifehood was the greatest fulfilment for most women. Mrs Gaskell considered that once Brontë began to publish she became two people — 'henceforward Charlotte Brontë's existence becomes divided into two parallel currents — her life as Currer Bell, the author; her life as Charlotte Brontë, the woman';[5] the dualities which this description so clearly illustrates are intrinsic to her art as well as to her life.

Brontë's correspondence indicates clearly the personal source of her artistic ambivalence. She hesitates to make definitive assertions about female roles and confesses herself unable to resolve her own dilemmas about the importance of romantic fulfilment. Her letters to her publisher, W.S. Williams, and to her former schoolteacher at Roe Head, Miss Wooler, contain her more general opinions on subjects such as careers for women and the relative advantages of singlehood and marriage; those to her long-standing friend, Ellen Nussey, express more private feelings and give us closer glimpses of the emotional strains of her personal life. On the whole, Brontë's letters, especially the earlier ones, reveal more scepticism than idealism about romance and marriage — perhaps a reflection of her morbid conviction of her own sexual unattractiveness. Her youthful scorn of what, in 1836, she dismisses as 'wretchedly insipid'[6] society grows into a more extensive condemnation of a social system which brings up girls to regard matrimony as their sole future. She has only pity for the position of young women such as the Robinson daughters, Anne's former pupils at Thorpe Green, each engaged but neither caring for her future husband, the one marrying out of self-interest, the other out of obedience to her mother's wish; both are victims of tyrannous social pressures.[7] Like the early feminists, and like her fellow-novelists Dinah Mulock Craik and Elizabeth Sewell, Brontë recognises the wide gap between the inculcated matrimonial ideal and the actual circumstances of most women. Writing to Ellen in 1843, with perhaps a touch of personal bitterness, she declares roundly:

Not that it is a crime to marry — or a crime to wish to be married — but it is an imbecility which I reject with contempt — for women who have neither fortune nor beauty — to make marriage the principal object of their wishes and hopes and the aim of all their actions — not to be able to convince themselves that they are unattractive — and that they had better be quiet and think of other things than wedlock.[8]

She also indignantly condemns (as well as chafes against) the almost universal assumption that in their social relationships with men women have but one intent. 'I know that if women wish to escape the stigma of husband-seeking they must act and look like marble or clay — cold — expressionless, bloodless — for every appearance of feeling of joy — sorrow — friendlessness, antipathy, admiration — disgust are alike construed by the world into an attempt to hook in a husband', she tells Ellen, coolly ironic about the male vanity of 'some pragmatical thing in breeches . . . [who] might take it into its pate to imagine that you designed to dedicate your precious life to its inanity'.[9] Women should raise themselves above such degradation by cultivating self-respect, she claims. Critical of the flirtatious habits of a family friend, Joseph Taylor, she would like to bolster up his victims to assert themselves against his manoeuvres and to develop 'the quiet strength of pride — of the supporting consciousness of superiority'.[10]

In attacking conventional attitudes towards female fulfilment, Brontë often expresses her scepticism about marriage itself, from the woman's point of view. With sober realism, she points to the glaring disparities between the ideal and the actual. Husbands may be cruel or selfish (and she knew several such cases), and wives may discover too late that they have trapped themselves in an intolerable situation, their dreams of love transformed into nightmares of bitterness and hatred. On several occasions, she speaks out against precipitate commitment: in March 1850 she tells Amelia Ringrose (later to marry the fickle Joe Taylor), 'I think it would be dreadful to take the most important — the most irrevocable step in life under the influence of illusive impressions — and when it was too late to retreat — to find all was a mistake';[11] and, voicing a common feminist sentiment of the period, she comments the following year, 'it is a terrible thing to be driven by a sort of despair from the evil of a solitary single life to the worse evil of an uncongenial married one'.[12] The cautionary note here must be placed in the context of Brontë's personal dilemma, since she was being courted by one of her publisher's partners, James Taylor, at this time, and is echoing here her own hesitancy about a particularly bothersome affair of the heart.

Frequent assertions of the blessings of independence complement her doubts about the value of matrimony. Writing to her ex-suitor, Henry Nussey (Ellen's brother), about his concern over his sister's marriage prospects, Brontë assures him that his anxiety is misplaced:

> We know many evils are escaped by eschewing matrimony and since so large a proportion of the young ladies of these days pursue that rainbow-shade with such unremitting eagerness, let us respect an exception who turns aside and pronounces it only a coloured vapour whose tints will fade on close approach.[13]

Less ironically, and with more heartfelt conviction, she expresses her admiration of Miss Wooler's contented retirement:

> it seems that even 'a lone woman' can be happy, as well as cherished wives and proud mothers — I am glad of that — I speculate much on the existence of unmarried and never-to-be married women nowadays, and I have already got to the point of considering that there is no more respectable character on earth than an unmarried woman who makes her own way through life quietly perseveringly — without support of husband or brother, and who, having attained the age of 45 or upwards — retains in her possession a well-regulated mind — a disposition to enjoy simple pleasures — fortitude to support inevitable pains, sympathy with the sufferings of others, and willingness to relieve want as far as her means extend.[14]

Though at this time she preferred to think of herself as one of 'those who have settled their bargain with celibacy',[15] eight years later and nearly four months after her own marriage, Brontë was still stoutly defending the unmarried state — 'When I go to Brookroyd [Ellen's home], if I hear Mr. Clapham or anybody else say anything to the disparagement of single women, I shall go off like a bomb shell.'[16]

Brontë reveals her concern with widening opportunities for single women in her letters to Williams of 1848 about whether or not one of his daughters should become a governess. Rather than attaining 'accomplishments', she argues, a girl should develop her particular talents, so that if she is 'fated to make her way in the crowd and to depend on herself' she may have the satisfaction of feeling that she is her 'own mistress'.[17] She is convinced that 'both sons and daughters should early be inured to habits of independence and industry', and approves of Williams's 'excellent sense when you say that girls without fortune should be brought up and accustomed to support themselves'.[18] In the same vein, she encourages Ellen in her desire to earn a little money for herself — 'even though you should not gain much — the effort is in the right direction — it will do you good — you will never regret it . . . it is so much gained in independence'.[19]

Despite her assertions that wholly domestic notions of womanhood must be replaced by a creed of female self-help, Brontë could not ignore the powerful counter-claims of emotional needs which a single life failed to meet. Another letter to Williams, written a year later when she was suffering the agonising sense of loss following the deaths of Branwell, Emily, and Anne, indicates her ambivalent outlook. Early in the letter, she declares that for unmarried women, 'an education secured is an advantage. Come what may it is a step towards independency — and one great curse of a female single life is its dependency', insisting that mental and moral health can be secured only by employment. A later paragraph, though, betrays that beneath her briskly-affirmed creed of self-reliance lurks the feeling that work is merely a diversion from the emptiness of singlehood:

> Lonely as I am, how should I be if Providence had never given me courage to adopt a career . . . something like a hope and motive sustains me still. I wish all your daughters — I wish every woman in England, had also a hope and a motive. Alas! there are many old maids who have neither.[20]

Such ambivalence characterises many of her statements about singlehood. Alongside her optimism about female self-dependence, her almost fearful reference to an unmarried teacher at the Pensionnat Heger who saw no future for herself except as a sister of charity,[21] her terror of becoming a stern and selfish spinster, and her sense of blankness 'because I am a *lonely* woman and likely to be *lonely*',[22] reveal her increasing unease about the viability of a fulfilling independent existence. Her inability to resolve the dilemma is due partly to her own deep need to love and be loved. Her passionate letters to M. Heger in Brussels, when she thought that he had forgotten her, show how much she depended on the reciprocation of affection; she longed for emotional fulfilment yet was gloomily convinced that her sorrow and dreariness would not be assuaged by the transcendent joy of loving companionship.

This dualistic attitude helps to account for Brontë's ambivalent response to her suitors. Despite her belief in her own unattractiveness, she had four offers of marriage between 1839 and 1852, and Arthur Nicholls, the man she eventually married, remained loyal to his pledge for over a year in the face of her apparent indifference and her father's bitter opposition. Yet her reservations about matrimony in general included her own case in particular. Of the initial two offers, she laughed off the second with mocking nonchalance ('I've heard of love at first sight but this beats all'[23]); and though she appears to have taken the first, from Henry Nussey, more seriously, her refusal on the grounds of conscience — it would be wrong to marry a man whom she could not make happy — is strengthened by her obvious disinclination to dispose of herself to such a solidly 'grave, quiet young man'.[24] As she grew older and more lonely, however, she became increasingly aware of the negative side of a non-matrimonial existence. Her earlier assurance, which briskly rejects both *grande passion* and calculated self-interest as motives for union, and which recommends sense over sentimentality in the choice of a marriage partner, becomes tinged with uncertainty. In September 1850 she writes to Ellen to refute rumours that she is about to be married: 'Whom am I to marry? . . . Doubtless there are men whom if I chose to encourage I might marry, but no matrimonial lot is even remotely offered me which seems to me truly desirable.'[25] Yet not long after, while fighting off the temptation of imagining union between herself and George Smith, she began to be besieged by the persistent attentions of James Taylor, towards whom she felt a mixture of 'apprehension and anger',[26] a fear of giving herself to him, and a prevision of the 'entire crumbling away of a seeming fountain of support and prospect of hope'[27] if she rejected him. Even after her definitive refusal ('I could not, *could not* look up to him. No — if Mr. Taylor be the only husband fate offers to me, single I must always remain'[28]), she continued to be racked by doubts, and her disappointment on hearing nothing from him in India (where the firm sent him perhaps at the instigation of the unsympathetic George Smith) was, in her own words, closely related to 'a state of absolute uncertainty about a somewhat momentous matter'.[29]

Most interesting of all are her reactions to Nicholls, whom she finally married in June 1854. At first dismissing him, together with her father's other curates, as one of the 'highly uninteresting, narrow and unattractive specimens of the coarser sex',[30] she was forced to reconsider her earlier judgement when he proposed to her. As her letters to Ellen indicate, she oscillated between the conviction that she could not love him and pity for his evident suffering. Struggling still with her doubts ('I may be losing the purest gem, and to me far the most precious life can give — genuine attachment — or I may be escaping the yoke of a morose temper'[31]), she decided to resign herself to the hands of providence — in her case, the vagaries of paternal reaction. When she at last decided to defy her father's opposition, and persuaded him to permit their engagement, her hopes of happiness were not unmixed with fears. Her letters announcing her engagement — to Ellen, Miss Wooler, Gaskell, and Smith — all contain repeated references to her 'doubts', her 'trust' that she will be able to love Nicholls, her 'battle . . . with myself', and her 'duty' of gratitude for his offer.[32] We have too little evidence from her married life to speculate what kind of long-term relationship theirs would have been. Certainly, though the note of uncertainty still sounds in her letters (she often mentions, somewhat wistfully, for example, that her time is no longer her own), she begins to stress Nicholls's real worth, and hints at the joys of 'true domestic happiness'.[33] Without falsely romanticising the actuality of what she had been debating theoretically for so long, she seems to have accepted a state which, on balance, she felt would give her more happiness than any available alternative. We cannot, nevertheless, assume that the ambivalence which permeates her letters and her fiction can have disappeared altogether; even a new kind of contentment cannot have obliterated her awareness that women's needs are not simply answered. The voice of protest, which first hit the outside world with *Jane Eyre*, would surely never have been entirely suppressed.

*   *   *

Ambivalence and ambiguity are the key-notes of Brontë's novels. In *The Professor* (1857), the oddly bi-sexual Crimsworth, who, unconvincing though he is as a character, illustrates two ways of responding to life, is partnered by Frances Henri, at once a self-contained, outward-looking 'career woman' and a willingly subservient dependent, pleased to rely on male support. The heroine of *Jane Eyre* (1847) rebels vigorously against orthodox definitions of femininity, and through her the author voices her well-known protest against women's enforced inactivity:

> Women are supposed to be very calm generally: but women feel
> just as men feel; they need exercise for their faculties, and a field
> for their efforts as much as their brothers do; they suffer from
> too rigid a restraint, too absolute a stagnation, precisely as men
> would suffer.[34]

Yet this passionate demand contents itself with a romantic sexual
relationship which, though not wholly conventional, vindicates the
private nature of female fulfilment. Similarly, in *Shirley* (1849),
Caroline Helstone and Shirley Keeldar look critically at their
society's ideologies about marriage, and challenge the notion that
singlehood inevitably means a wasted life for a woman. Shirley, in
particular, glorying in the pseudo-masculine freedom of her position as heiress and landowner, boldly asserts the advantages of being
her own mistress: 'when I feel my company superfluous, I can com-
fortably fold my independence round me like a mantle, and drop my
pride like a veil, and withdraw to solitude. If married, that could
not be.'[35] Nevertheless, by the end of the novel both girls have
retreated to a state of female subservience, united to the men who
have 'mastered' them, Shirley 'conquered by love, and bound with
a vow . . . vanquished and restricted' (592), Caroline nestling dove-
like in the arms of the stubborn mill-owner who once so cavalierly
rejected her. Even *Villette* (1853), with its more probing analysis of
the myth of romantic love and its more direct treatment of female
independence, still examines women's roles largely in the context of
sexual relationships.

These paradoxes, which attracted critical attention from the first,
have proved especially fruitful material for more recent discussion
of Brontë's work. Feminist critics in particular have taken her as a
paradigm for the many Victorian women novelists who, they claim,
express their sense of dualities through 'devious' or 'covert'
strategies. These critics argue that because the writers were unable to
dramatise directly the inner female life or to spell out their anger and
unease, they were forced to find oblique methods of articulation; we
must therefore look below the overtly 'angelic' dogma and the
explicit commentary to discover the real implications of the narrative. Brontë, they suggest, provides an admirable instance of the
tactics of subversion, because the archetypal patterns and structural
dualities of her work formulate, while at the same time disguising,

her protest. There are thus two 'levels' in her fiction, the one conscious capitulation to convention, the other dissent concealed by overt orthodoxy.[36] This approach is innovative and illuminating, but because it stresses the unsaid in Brontë's fiction it marks the subterranean elements as the most significant. It may be more in keeping with Brontë's own intentions to regard her novels as conscious explorations of personally important issues with whose complexities she is seeking to come to terms. The contradictory elements in her work may then be seen as avowed declarations of her ambivalence, and the ambiguities as an acknowledgement of the insolubility of the problems she depicts. In this way, we can reconcile a 'straight' reading of the text with the notion of its dissenting voice.

As has already been indicated, Brontë implements romantic and sexual orthodoxies in order to challenge some aspects of contemporary ideology. Her heroines' involvement in traditional roles enables them to question those roles. One way in which they do this is by closely examining their own needs and desires; another is by measuring themselves against contrasting images of womanhood; yet another is by evaluating their own position in differing sexual relationships. Their rebelliousness lies in their attitudes towards such relationships. It is noticeable that they rarely regard romantic commitment in terms of motherhood or even of dedicated service; their prime emphasis is always on personal fulfilment. According to conventional values, they are social and moral revolutionaries, selfish egoists demanding self-satisfaction; in female-oriented terms, they are merely asserting their creator's insistence that the special requirements of womanly selfhood be recognised. As her fiction develops, Brontë communicates with increasing confidence her vision of possibilities. Gradually moving away from the definitiveness of a totally 'closed' ending, she implements explorative analysis and dramatic debate, allowing the dualities of her novels to speak for themselves.

The first novel that Brontë wrote, *The Professor*, was not destined for success; it was rejected by publishers nine times in less than five years, and though it finally appeared after Brontë's death, due to Gaskell's urgings, it has never been as enthusiastically received as her other works. It is, however, of considerable interest, partly as a blueprint for *Villette* in its creative re-enactment of Brontë's experience in Brussels, and partly because despite its tentativeness and technical awkwardness it represents her earliest attempt at examining sexual roles and relationships. The most significant aspect of the novel is its use of a male narrator, who, though he has little psychological credibility, functions as a device for expressing Brontë's sense of dualities. She was probably initially inspired to take a man as her central character, as in her choice of authorial pseudonym, by her wish to conceal her own gender, but the strategy also demonstrates clearly her desire to explore notions of maleness and femaleness from an apparently uncontentious standpoint. Disguised as Crimsworth, Brontë can take a quizzical look at — and obliquely criticise — male assumptions about women; conversely, she can evaluate womanhood by stepping outside her own sex and giving a non-partisan view; she can also protest against restrictive codes of femininity by voicing her 'unacceptable' impulses towards power and self-assertion through the 'acceptable' mouthpiece of a male figure.

Crimsworth himself introduces the idea of duality, both sexual and psychological. Like the curiously feminine-natured male narrators in several of Craik's works, he seems in some ways a representative of his creator's sex; as R.H. Hutton crisply remarks, 'It is quite obvious to any reader who attends to the sketch of the character of the Professor, that the Professor is a woman in disguise'.[37] He shares many of the qualities of Brontë's subsequent heroines. Like them, he has no means of support, having rejected his uncles' patronage, and has to beg employment from his cold-hearted brother who has no time for family loyalties. Oppressed by his brother's hostility and his own self-doubt, he is forced into a subordinate role, imaged interestingly in female terms — 'weary, solitary, [I was] kept down like some desolate tutor or governess'.[38] While in Brussels, he is prey to fits of hypochondria, and has to call upon reason and duty to overcome his emotional yearnings. He is self-effacing, often deliberately taking on the role of observer and keeping his real character carefully concealed from scrutiny. At the same time, he exhibits traditionally masculine characteristics (which, as we shall see, are also exhibited by the heroines, especially Jane Eyre and Lucy Snowe). He can be self-assured, is unshakably resolved on his own independence, and refuses to be locked into situations which threaten his individuality. As a teacher, he triumphs over his unruly pupils and delights in the power of his authority. He thus embodies a sexual ambiguity which enables Brontë to confront some of the dichotomies in her thinking about male and female behaviour; as an androgynous figure he can act out rebellious female energies which his overt maleness validates.

Crimsworth assumes an evaluative function in the novel by commenting on the contrasting models of womanhood which he encounters, and again he speaks both as a woman and as a man, articulating his creator's ideals and indirectly indicating her reservations about masculine attitudes towards her own sex. At the Pensionnat des Demoiselles, for instance, he certainly speaks for Brontë in his scorn of the calculating and flirtatious schoolgirls, whom he at first mistakenly takes to be 'a kind of half-angels' (72), but later recognises as 'arrant coquettes' (81) who have but one object — to win a husband with their artificial charms. He also eventually sees through to the falsity of his employer, Zoraide Reuter, who, for all her mixture of capability and winning ways, is dishonest; though we can hardly believe in his momentary passion for her, Crimsworth's shifting response highlights Brontë's ambivalent attitude towards a woman who, while admirably exercising her talents in a successful career, is disloyal to womanly instincts of integrity and self-respect. Crimsworth's desire for a wife who is neither conventionally beautiful nor empty-headed, but who is intelligent and companionable, suggests an ideal of womanhood which Brontë wishes to recommend in the face of more conventional images. His eventual choice of Frances Henri is a vindication of this 'alternative' female type.

On the other hand, Crimsworth is himself representative of aspects of masculinity which Brontë sees as inimical to women. As a prospective husband, his complacency and male arrogance are potentially stultifying. Though justified in his rejection of Zoraide on moral grounds, he still exhibits an almost malicious pleasure in tormenting her, leading her on, then mortifying her with his merciless sneers. Foreshadowing Jane's interpretation of Rochester's attempt to possess her, Crimsworth's egotistical desire for dominance is revealed in telling imagery:

> There was at once a sort of low gratification in receiving this luscious incense from an attractive and still young worshipper . . . When she stole about me with the soft step of a slave, I felt at once barbarous and sensual as a pasha. (162)

His delight in mastery also finds expression in his relationship with Frances Henri, despite his recognition that her superiority to all the other women he has encountered exempts her from the usual approaches to her sex. He is flattered by her docility under his instruction, and enjoys the prospect of union with a heart 'over whose expression I had such influence; where I could kindle bliss, infuse awe, stir deep delight' (166). Even in a marriage based on mutual respect he cannot totally free himself from patriarchal attitudes, looking for the 'ray of gentle homage' beaming from the 'submissive and supplicating little mortal woman' (224) which Frances represents in the domestic context. Brontë's presentation of Crimsworth is too uncertain for him to provide a wholly effective commentary on sexual ideologies. We are never quite sure whether his contrasting responses to women are the product of his genuine ambivalence or merely of his creator's indecision about his function in the novel. It is also not clear how much authorial irony is directed towards him, with the less admirable aspects of his self-revelation indicating unawareness of his own deficiencies or delusions. He is, nevertheless, an interesting forerunner of Brontë's later and more successful female narrators who voice their creator's questionings more succintly and directly.

Frances Henri's role in *The Professor* both complements and contrasts with Crimsworth's. In some respects, she effectively reinforces the notion of sexual duality which he introduces into the novel, in particular suggesting the falsity of one-sided views of femininity. In other respects, she seems a puzzlingly inconsistent figure, sometimes a model of conventionality, sometimes an intrinsically subversive force. Her main function is to convey Brontë's consciousness of the complexities of the female condition. Frances is clearly not an overt rebel. She does not challenge the ideal of matrimony; just as Crimsworth takes a conventional view of old maids ('Anatomists will tell you that there is a heart in the withered old maid's carcase — the same as in that of any cherished wife or proud mother in the land. Can this be so? I really don't know; but feel inclined to doubt it' (193), so she sees spinsterhood as a dismal fate:

> 'An old maid's life must doubtless be void and vapid — her heart strained and empty. Had I been an old maid I should have spent existence in efforts to fill the void and ease the aching. I should have probably failed, and died weary and disappointed, despised and of no account, like other single women.' (226)

In her relationship with Crimsworth, she reveals a willingness to adopt a subservient role. Looking up to him as her mentor and master, even after ten years of marriage she continues to call him 'Monsieur', as she did when she was his pupil. Yet she is far from feeble-spirited, and a tough determination to fulfil her own talents underlies her apparent submissiveness. She tells Crimsworth that she intends to rise in the world through the education she has financed by her lace-mending. Her acceptance of his marriage proposal is also conditional on her being able to go on working, and her resoluteness triumphs: as eventual director of her own school in Brussels, she displays energy, efficiency, and authority. It is interesting that this is the only one of Brontë's novels that gives any extended treatment of the characters' lives after marriage, and that Frances is the only example of a wife's choosing to continue the career she had while single. Though a loyal wife, too, she is quite adamant that were her husband to prove cruel or bestial, she would revolt against the 'slavery' (226) and, like Helen Huntingdon in *The Tenant of Wildfell Hall*, would have no hesitation in leaving him.

The dualities of the female personality which she represents — nervousness, shyness, and the need for support, set against a strong sense of self and a desire for independent action — is explored more perceptively in the heroines of the later novels, but she alone achieves a pragmatic harmonisation of this duality. Moreover, her conscious exploitation of her two roles as working woman and wife/ mother, with their accompanying behavioural changes from the energetic resourcefulness of 'Madame the directress' to the willing homage of Frances Henri, the little lace-mender and home-maker, gives hints of subtle diplomacy aimed at getting the best of both worlds. Frances knows that her husband does not wholly understand her, and, like Jane and Lucy, chooses to keep the opposite sex in partial ignorance of her real self and intentions. He recognises the two sides of her character, naturally co-existing, but does not appreciate the full significance of her dual personality:

So different was she under different circumstances, I seemed to possess two wives. The faculties of her nature, already disclosed when I married her, remained fresh and fair; but other faculties shot up strong, branched out broad, and quite altered the external character of the plant. (221)

In *The Professor*, Brontë is clearly exploring the tensions between women's urge for self-expression and their need for emotional support. But there are too many dichotomies in the novel for her presentation to be completely satisfactory. In Frances herself, the notion of female duality is expressed through a split rather than a harmonised personality; she has to be two people, who are separate rather than integrated. Crimsworth, as we have seen, embodies both male and female characteristics, but in this he falls between two functions: as Frances's suitor and husband he represents the masculine role in sexual relationships; as an androgynous figure he is used thematically to put forward Brontë's ambivalent feelings about womanhood. Ultimately, too, each character contains such diversity that their relationship suffers in terms of psychological credibility as well as sexual significance. In her later novels, especially in *Villette*, her expanded and refocused version of *The Professor*, Brontë presents a much more assured vision of the ambiguities of female experience; her first work, however, contains in embryo all that she wanted to say about women in her society.

As has already been noted, the extraordinary impact made by Brontë's fiction was due not only to its emotional vitality but also to its outspoken unconventionality. *Jane Eyre*, her first published novel, was regarded by some as particularly subversive, a 'protest against social conventionalisms and inequalities',[39] and a potential threat to social and political order. Today it hardly seems a startlingly revolutionary work, especially in terms of sexual ideologies. It makes no specific reference to the social or political disabilities suffered by Victorian women, and protests directly about restrictive female roles only fleetingly. Though it certainly challenges contemporary attitudes, its questionings occur in the context of two basic assumptions — a belief in the primacy of love, and a conviction that the institution of marriage, in its best form, provides the only means of true emotional fulfilment for women. In her retrospective assessment of Brontë's achievement, Margaret Oliphant (taking a rather different line from her earlier criticism of Brontë's unwomanly portrayals of love[40]) points this out; the heroines, she claims, like their creator, demand a share in 'the natural openings of life',[41] and want to have 'their hands on the reins of common life, to build up the world, and link the generations each to each. In her philosophy marriage was the only state which procured this.'[42] This view needs modification, especially, as we shall see, with reference to *Shirley* and *Villette*, but it remains basically valid for *Jane Eyre*, which argues unequivocally for loyalty to the demands of the heart, even if not quite so simplistically as Oliphant suggests. In the novel, Brontë translates into artistic terms her firm belief in female 'self-sacrificing love and disinterested devotion'.[43]

One of Jane's earliest and most deeply-felt needs is for reciprocated affection. At Lowood, she declares vehemently to Helen
Burns,

> 'if others don't love me, I would rather die than live . . . to gain
> some real affection from you, or Miss Temple, or any other
> whom I truly love, I would willingly submit to have the bone of
> my arm broken, or to let a bull toss at me, or to stand behind a
> kicking horse, and let it dash its hoof at my chest.' (70)

The extremity of this attitude has to be tempered as Jane learns, but
its ideological foundation is not challenged. Throughout, Jane
speaks for feeling over reason. She recognises the coldness of Eliza
Reed's denial of all sisterly bonds; she is distressed by the 'obvious
absence of passion in his [Rochester's] sentiments' (188) towards
Blanche Ingram, whom she believes he will marry; and she has no
hesitation in vigorously rejecting St John Rivers's proposal of an
emotionless contractual marriage, in which, he believes, 'undoubtedly enough of love would follow . . . to render the union right even
in your eyes' (413). 'I scorn your idea of love . . . I scorn the
counterfeit sentiment you offer: yes, St. John, and I scorn you when
you offer it' (413), she flashes at him, in language whose vigour
recalls her outburst to Helen. We should therefore not regard the
conclusion of the novel as mere capitulation to romantic convention — albeit offering significant variations on traditional patterns
of female subservience — nor as a strategy of deceptive orthodoxy.
If we are to accept the sincerity of Brontë's declarations that
'genuine attachment [is] far the most precious [gem] life can give',[44]
and that after a woman of some prominence marries 'if true
domestic happiness replace Fame — the exchange will be for the
better',[45] we must surely accept the genuine fruitfulness of the union
between Jane and Rochester.

The novel in fact calls little attention to the conditions of female
singleness. We feel hardly any unease about Jane's destiny as an
isolated, therefore vulnerable, single woman. Though she is physically threatened as a child (attacked by her cousin, locked up, and
separated from the other girls at school), once she reaches womanhood, her sexual powerlessness is not emphasised. When she decides
to leave Lowood, her advertisement immediately brings her a post
which, if it contains hidden perils, certainly does not involve the

kind of suffering which Brontë herself underwent as a governess and to which she refers in her letters to Williams. Even Jane's briefly agonising fight for survival after she flees Thornfield is soon followed by a new security when she discovers the Rivers's. Her subsequent unexpected inheritance enables her to enjoy the prospect of a comfortable future, safe from the spectres of poverty and exploitation, even if it will not give her the emotional fulfilment she would like.

It is important also that in many respects Jane's self-reliance is a response to conditions rather than a chosen creed. As she tells St John, 'I am not ambitious' (360). Her exertions on her own behalf are a defence against self-extinction or threatening circumstances. At Gateshead and Lowood, self-preservation motivates her challenges to authority; her decision to leave Lowood is caused as much by her feeling that 'the reason for tranquillity' has gone with Miss Temple's removal (who, significantly, has entered the arena of womanly 'normality' by marrying) as by a desire to move into 'the real world' with its 'varied field of hopes and fears, of sensations and excitements' (85). Moreover, although both at this point and later at Thornfield, Jane invokes the images of distant hills to express her sense of frustration, her longing 'for a power of vision which might overpass that limit; which might reach the busy world, towns, regions full of life I had heard of but never seen' (110) disappears when she meets Rochester, and she is content for her horizon to shrink back to the limits of Thornfield. Her stirrings of protest against the confinement of women's lives are merely temporary, and, as Virginia Woolf rightly points out, her sudden explosion of anger about the futility of 'making puddings and knitting stockings' (111) seems out of place in the context of the story, though it plainly voices authorial indignation.[46] The almost fairy-tale atmosphere in which Jane's life unfolds here, even if it includes the tyranny of a Bluebeard and the malice of a demonic woman, makes reference to more narrowly contemporary grievances seem inappropriate; and whatever restriction or exploitation Jane suffers, they are clearly not of a traditionally domestic kind.

Once she has left Thornfield, Jane does become involved in the outer professional world, but again this is due to circumstances rather than to personal choice. She takes up teaching at Morton because the need to survive makes it 'urgent that I should have a vocation of some kind' (357); the readiness with which she abandons it when she receives her legacy, plus its inability to distract her from her longing for Rochester, remind us of the early feminist view that employment for the single woman is largely a substitute for or alternative to romantic fulfilment. Jane's other possible career, becoming a missionary 'partner', is, too, suggested to her by events; the force of another's will, not her own, drives her to consider a way of life for which she has no vocation.

Though *Jane Eyre* eschews obvious feminist protest and accepts the traditional orthodoxies of love and matrimony, however, it would be quite misleading to imply that its author was perfectly at ease with conventional sexual and romantic attitudes. It challenges contemporary sexual ideologies, arguing for revised notions of womanhood and womanly individuality, rejecting assumptions about male dominance, and offering a new vision of mutuality between men and women. To do this, Brontë uses a technique of contrast and comparison. Throughout the novel, Jane confronts contrasting models of her sex, according to which she is enabled to evaluate differing images of femaleness. She achieves her own version of womanhood by measuring and defining herself against these models. Though her final choice may seem conventional in its assumption of sexual relativity, she demonstrates her radicalism in defying externally-imposed definitions and creating her own identity.

At Gateshead, Jane learns that there are two aspects of girlhood — acceptable and unacceptable. Because she is physically and socially inferior to her cousins, she is made to feel unnatural as well as wicked: the adults continually remind her that she is not like normal little girls such as the conventionally pretty Georgiana with 'her pink cheeks and golden curls' (15) — as Abbott callously remarks, 'one really cannot care for such a little toad as that . . . I doat on Miss Georgiana' (26). Jane, though, will not accept that her odious cousin John is her 'master', and her refusal to submit to his masculine brutality challenges the traditional view of female subordination; her definition of herself as a 'rebel slave' (12) will be echoed later in the novel when she fights off Rochester's attempts to enclose her in his deceptively seductive harem. Her experience in the Red Room, where she sees her 'other' and almost unrecognisable self in the mirror and where for the first time she formulates her sense of being at odds with her environment, strengthens her awareness of her personal individuality and enables her to defy Mrs Reed and Mr Brocklehurst, both of whom seek to impose false versions of the self upon her.

In the Lowood section of the novel, Brontë explores the implications of another contemporary image of her sex, and again Jane's questionings express her creator's unease. At school, Jane encounters the creed of angelic womanhood in both its positive and negative aspects. The school itself is described as like a convent or a church, and its regime is forbiddingly monastic. Mr Brocklehurst attempts to deny female 'nature' (both in encouraging unhealthful abstinence and cutting off unruly hair) by imposing a false — and hypocritical — spirituality upon the pupils: 'my mission is to mortify in these girls the lusts of the flesh; to teach them to clothe themselves with shamefacedness and sobriety; not with braided hair and costly apparel' (65). While Jane has no hesitation in mutely rejecting Brocklehurst's doctrines, her response to Helen Burns is more equivocal. Helen herself is not of this earth; she exhibits a true spirit of martyrdom, and her smile is 'like a reflection from the aspect of an angel' (68). Immune to worldly afflictions because she looks beyond them, she tells Jane: 'Why, then, should we ever sink overwhelmed with distress, when life is so soon over, and death is so certain an entrance to happiness: to glory?' (70). Helen's angelic creed is a positive one, demanding courage and struggle with rebellious feelings, not merely passive non-resistance. But it is nevertheless the obverse side of Brocklehurst's pseudo-spirituality (later to be recalled in St John's cold religiosity) and as such it cannot satisfy Jane's ardent sense of self. From Helen she learns the need for self-control and the importance of personal integrity, but her passionate commitment to fulfilment in this life makes her reject Helen's belief in the primacy of heavenly reward; as she later insists, she is no angel, but a flesh-and-blood creature.

Brontë examines more closely the roles of women in social and sexual contexts in the next section of the novel. As at Gateshead and Lowood, at Thornfield Jane is once more confronted by influential images of femininity. Rochester's bevy of fashionable lady guests illustrates the social importance attached to women's appearances; in particular, Blanche Ingram embodies her own avowed doctrine that loveliness is 'the special prerogative of woman — her legitimate appanage and heritage! . . . an ugly woman is a blot on the fair face of creation' (181). Though Jane is constantly aware of her deficiency in this respect — 'I sometimes regretted that I was not handsomer . . . I felt it a misfortune that I was so little, so pale, and had features so irregular and so marked' (49) — she quickly recognises the limitations of such a creed. She sees immediately that

Blanche has no real individuality:

> She was very showy, but she was not genuine: she had a fine person, many brilliant attainments; but her mind was poor, her heart barren by nature: nothing bloomed spontaneously on that soil; no unforced natural fruit delighted by its freshness. (187–8)

If Blanche represents the hollowness of calculated appearance, the adult Georgiana Reed represents the flabbiness of superficial charms. On renewing her acquaintance with her after their long separation, Jane is struck by her cousin's silly and self-centred romanticism: her conversation runs solely on the London season and her many admirers there, and even in the most sombre of family circumstances, 'her mind seemed wholly taken up with reminiscences of past gaiety, and aspirations after dissipations to come' (236). Like Blanche and even the beautiful Rosamund Oliver (whom Jane finds 'charming . . . but not profoundly interesting or thoroughly impressive' — 373), Georgiaha is not a model for emulation.

Through her heroine, Brontë also challenges traditional notions of womanly behaviour within sexual relationships. Though emotionally bound up with Rochester, Jane will not allow custom to regulate their intimacy. She rejects the artificialities of formal courtship, and argues that his masculine claim to superiority is not inherent but 'depends on the use you have made of your time and experience' (135); for her, their union must be founded on mutual respect instead of on the 'bathos of sentiment' and 'turtle-dove sensibility' (276). Jane's outspokenness and bold unconventionality (as Rochester points out, she is actually the one who proposes marriage) are not just rebellion against empty form, however. Her assertion of her right to leave Rochester, both when she thinks he is about to marry Blanche and when she discovers the existence of Bertha, is based on a self-respect which denies the orthodoxy of female subservience to the male will. As she tells him on the first occasion,

> 'Do you think, because I am poor, obscure, plain, and little, I am soulless and heartless? You think wrong — I have as much soul as you, — and full as much heart!' (255)

and as she inwardly declares on the second,

'I care for myself. The more solitary, the more friendless, the more unsustained I am, the more I will respect myself'. (321)

Jane's point is that she deserves consideration as an individual and not merely as a representative of her sex.

Rochester is attracted to Jane because of her difference from other women, but he persistently views her in conventional images. Against his repeated identification of her as a fairy, an elf, a sprite, and an angel, Jane is driven to assert her own definition of herself developed from observation and experience; as she rejected a Christian female spirituality at Lowood, so now she rejects its secular version:

> 'I am not an angel . . . and I will not be one till I die; I will be myself. Mr. Rochester, you must neither expect nor exact anything celestial of me . . . I had rather be a *thing* than an angel.' (262–4)

More importantly, Rochester's transforming fantasies take on sinister overtones after their engagement. Jane rightly distrusts his offerings of jewels and clothes, not only because she feels they are inappropriate for her but also because the chains, bracelets, and rings with which he wants to adorn her are symbols of servitude; she compares his smile of triumph as he buys extravagant things for her to that which 'a sultan might, in a blissful and fond moment, bestow on a slave his gold and gems had enriched' (271), and, quite serious beneath her mocking tone, refuses to be included among the inmates of his harem. It is this prospect of enslavement, along with the cavalier attitude towards women which it implies, which in large part impels Jane's refusal to live, imprisoned, with Rochester in his white-walled Mediterranean villa.

The Thornfield section also reveals the ambivalence towards marriage, which, as we have seen, characterises Brontë's thinking. Her reservations about personal commitment are expressed through symbolism, a more covert means of protest than Jane's earlier declarations of independence. Jane's recurrent dream of a child who obscurely threatens her, suggests fear of child-birth consequent on matrimony. Similarly her shrinking from both her new name and her bride's clothes — that 'strange, wraith-like apparel' in the cupboard (278) — indicates her resistance to the violation of selfhood which sexual union increasingly seems to represent. It is important also that during her engagement, Jane writes to her uncle in Madeira about her 'independency'; the prospect of becoming a doll-like kept woman spurs her to seek means of reinforcing her self-reliant individuality. And since it is this letter which brings Briggs and Mason at the eleventh hour to stop the church ceremony, in one way at least Jane's self-protective instinct saves her from a socially and spiritually destructive union.

The figure of Bertha Mason offers perhaps the most revealing comment on matrimony at this point. Though, as is often suggested, she represents the bestiality of purely physical lust from which Jane needs to guard herself, she is also a wife and as such intervenes between Jane and marital fulfilment. It is never directly stated that Rochester has mistreated Bertha and thus exacerbated her insanity, but his extreme aversion to her, combined with his symbolic resemblance to Bluebeard, hint at the possibility that his conduct towards her may not have been blameless — a possibility which is realised in Jean Rhys's *Wide Sargasso Sea* (1966).[47] In these terms, the wronged wife steps in to rescue Jane from the suffering she herself has experienced at the hands of an unregenerate husband.

Jane's stay at Morton is a period of consolidation rather than fresh self-awareness, because by now she knows what she wants and sees any alternatives as compromise. Ironically, here for the first time she meets examples of womanhood whom she finds almost wholly acceptable: Mary and Diana Rivers are resolute, courageous, and warm; they are learned, which, in Hannah's words, makes them not 'like other folk' (347), but they also take pleasure in domestic pursuits. Even before discovering that they are her cousins, Jane feels that they are kindred spirits — 'Thought fitted thought; opinion met opinion; we coincided, in short, perfectly' (355) — and as with Miss Temple, the one other woman in the novel whom they resemble, she respects their authority. But her pleasure in their company cannot obliterate her constant yearning for Rochester. For the same reason, she cannot accept the alternative lifestyle of service and 'vocational' marriage which St John offers her. Not only, as we have seen, does she reject his idea of matrimony as a mere formal and passionless union (in which she would literally be a bodiless angel-wife), but she recognises that St John, as much as Rochester before him, is trying to force a false identity upon her. He wants her to 'disown half my nature' (403); for him, the individual is insignificant, and though he accurately perceives her courage and strong will, he regards her only as 'a useful tool' (421). He is a further instance of male dominance, this time in a spiritualised form (he is in part kin to Brocklehurst, as well as to Rochester), and Jane's escape, though artistically contrived, is psychologically necessary.

Appropriately enough, considering its mode of structural and thematic contrasts, the ending of *Jane Eyre* can be read in two different ways. On the one hand, it can be viewed as a final capitulation to romantic orthodoxy, either in conscious response to artistic convention or inspired by a genuine conviction that marriage constitutes the highest womanly fulfilment. On the other hand, it is tempting to see Jane's eventual reunion with the maimed Rochester, whom she has to sustain and over whom she enjoys a feeling of positive power, as Brontë's final vindication of female assertiveness; Jane, now truly her own mistress, can control not only her future but also her position in the relationship. Brontë's ambivalence about male and female roles thus seems to have resolved itself into the conviction that only with the man's emasculation can a woman achieve full self-expression. But as was suggested earlier, the most apt interpretation may lie somewhere in the middle. Neither wholly conventional nor militantly feminist, Brontë rewards her heroine with a union in which she finds emotional satisfaction but does not lose her identity. The images of balance and mutuality with which the novel concludes — the blasted tree needing the green plants to 'cover its decay with freshness', and they in their turn 'lean[ing] towards you, and wind[ing] round you, because your strength offers them so safe a prop' (449–50) — suggest a voluntary and mutual servitude; if we find the declaration of 'perfect concord' (456) by which Jane characterises their marriage a little too facile, this does not necessarily imply hypocrisy on the part of the heroine or her creator. The important point about this union is that Jane's final state reflects her own desires, not obedience to external pressures. In this novel Brontë has chosen to resolve her doubts in a vision of romantic harmony whose ideality depends on an untraditional view of marital relations.

Brontë's second published novel, *Shirley* (1849), is much more overtly propagandist than *Jane Eyre*. As has frequently been pointed out, a general concern with forms of powerlessness links the various narrative themes;[48] the exploitation of women in a male-dominated society, for example, is paralleled by the plight of workers in conflict with industrial changes and tyrannous employers. Most relevant to this study is the book's extensive exploration of singleness and matrimony; far more directly than *Jane Eyre*, it treats these topics from many angles, and seriously challenges the assumption that marriage provides a woman's highest fulfilment.

The novel contains much direct and closely-focused discussion about the contrasting states of female relativity and autonomy. Early on, Caroline Helstone, having concluded that she is not likely to marry, ponders the question 'which most old maids are puzzled to solve' (190) — that is, the purpose of existence without husband or children — and seeks to answer it by visiting the two spinsters, Miss Mann and Miss Ainley, in order to find out how they contrive to make their lives meaningful. Later, she indulges in a long and bitter inward meditation on the plight of single women, whose matrimonial aspirations are rendered derisory by their circumstances:

> The great wish — the sole aim of every one of them is to be married, but the majority will never marry: they will die as they now live. They scheme, they plot, they dress to ensnare husbands. The gentlemen turn them into ridicule . . . the matrimonial market is overstocked. (377)

There are also extensive exchanges between characters on the same subject. Caroline and Shirley debate the question of whether it is better for a woman to be unhappily married or to enjoy the blessings of self-respect and independence; Caroline and her mother, Mrs Pryor, voice contrasting attitudes to romantic love and the reasons why women marry; the vicar, Cyril Hall, commends to Caroline the admirably active lives of Miss Ainley and of his own spinster sister, Margaret; and among the scenes with the Yorke family, one of the most memorable is the heated discussion between Mrs Yorke, her daughter Rose, and Caroline, about the extent to which women can fully implement their talents within the domestic sphere of matrimony. Other more incidental expressions of opinion, particularly from the male characters, contribute to the debate: misogynistic remarks about marriage and female roles from Mr Helstone and Joe Scott, for instance, offer another interpretation of 'suitable' womanly activity, while conversations between Mr Yorke and Robert Moore treat the question of romantic love from a more sympathetic though still complacent masculine viewpoint. The nature of sexual relationships is indeed the most widely and thoroughly articulated theme in the novel, showing how the author's anguished loneliness at this time, when she was left the sole survivor of the Brontë children, was driving her to take stock of her own future.

The contrasts established by the various characters' opinions and circumstances express Brontë's ambivalence about issues of problematic significance to women. Whereas *Jane Eyre* hardly questions the supremacy of marital fulfilment, though it does distinguish between its differing patterns of relationships, *Shirley* examines and evaluates the dualities of both singleness and marriage. Its ambiguous approach to spinsterhood in particular highlights the inherent contraries which Brontë worries over in her letters. The lonely and dismally self-denying aspects of this state are emphasised in the lives of the two old maids, Miss Mann and Miss Ainley. Pondering on their existence, Caroline concludes, 'pure and active as it was, in her heart she deemed it deeply dreary because it was so loveless — to her ideas, so forlorn' (198) — a conclusion which the author seems basically to share. Even with these characters, Brontë reveals her ambivalence about the conditions of singleness. Her portrayal of the elderly ladies relies considerably on stereotype. Her initial description of Miss Mann comes close to the kind of caricature found in much early-nineteenth-century fiction:

> to avoid excitement was one of Miss Mann's aims in life: she had been composing herself ever since she came down in the morning, and had just attained a certain lethargic state of tranquillity when the visitor's knock at the door startled her, and undid her day's work. (193–4)

The portrayal of Miss Ainley, an almost saint-like figure who endures her deprivations in meek resignation, is stereotypical in another way, and reflects the sentimentality towards self-abnegating spinsterhood common among many women writers of the period. Yet Brontë is also anxious to point out that there is far more to these figures than their surface peculiarities would suggest. With Caroline, we learn that Miss Mann's harshness covers a brave and honest heart 'longing for appreciation and affection' (195), and that Miss Ainley's totally self-sacrificing spirit, which leads her to scenes of suffering where no one else will go, makes 'her life nearer the life of Christ, than that of any other human being . . . met with' (198). If, also like Caroline, we still find little to recommend in such an existence, it is because Brontë never allows a false glorification to distort the truthfulness of her picture.

In contrast to this somewhat sombre and negative vindication of spinsterhood, Brontë argues much more positively for the benefits of female autonomy through those women characters who defy matrimonial ideology. Shirley's bold assertion of her individuality, and Hortense Moore's eccentric but far from broken-spirited self-reliance give the lie to the view that single women are doomed to a life of hopeless endurance, while Rose Yorke's passionate outburst to her mother voices the belief that female energies must be given scope beyond the narrow confines of family domesticity:

'I am resolved that my life shall be a life . . . And if my Master has given me ten talents, my duty is to trade with them, and make them ten talents more. Not in the dust of household drawers shall the coin be interred . . . I will *not* commit it to your work-table to be smothered in piles of woollen hose. I will *not* prison it in the linen-press to find shrouds among the sheets . . . least of all will I hide it in a tureen of cold potatoes, to be ranged with bread, butter, pastry, and ham on the shelves of larder.' (384–5)

The sense of outrage in some of Brontë's correspondence is echoed in the novel when she attacks the assumption that marriage is her sex's only role. Caroline and Shirley energetically challenge the kind of scoffing dismissal of careers for women expressed by Helstone; and Caroline's passionate call to the 'Men of England!' to look to the condition of their daughters, pining away with nothing to do and forced by their 'narrow and fettered' minds either to become soured old maids or to employ despicable tactics to win the respect accorded matrimony but denied to celibacy (378–9), is one of the most personal and highly-charged passages in the novel. If *Shirley*'s attitude towards spinsterhood seems equivocal — should it evoke distaste, pity, fear, or angry protest? or all of these? — it is because Brontë herself recognises its irreconcilable paradoxes.

Brontë's approach to the issue of marriage is equally ambiguous. She has no hesitation in pointing out its snares and delusions. The conventional-minded Sympson and Nunnerly girls, for example, show the spiritual shrinkage caused by narrowly obsessive matrimonial expectations. Mrs Yorke, a woman soured by her marriage to a man who, having suffered romantic disappointment, is now largely indifferent to women's needs, illustrates the crushing effect on a strong female character when it wills its own resignation to the constraints of married life. Mrs Pryor embodies another kind of unhappy wifehood, more hopelessly resigned. With unaccustomed vigour she warns her daughter against the perilous creeds of romantic love; novelists' pictures are, she claims bitterly,

> 'not like reality: they show you only the green tempting surface of the marsh, and give not one faithful or truthful hint óf the slough underneath . . . [Marriage] is never wholly happy . . . it is as well not to run the risk: you may make fatal mistakes . . . let all the single be satisfied with their freedom.' (366)

Brontë presents a more strikingly antipathetic picture of marriage as female subjugation to male tyranny by articulating the cavalier attitudes towards women taken by misogynists like Helstone, or by pig-headed dogmatists like Joe Scott who has a wholly authoritarian view of marital relations — 'women is to take their husbands' opinion, both in politics and religion; it's wholesomest for them' (323). Even the Moore brothers' more liberal and discerning approach to women does not totally exclude certain limiting preconceptions which, as we shall see, insinuate themselves into their relationships with their future wives. Alongside this strong note of protest, however, Brontë continues to assert her belief in the blessings of true emotional fulfilment in matrimony. Always aware of the dangers of commitment, she has no wish to undermine wholly an ideal which held many attractions for her.

Brontë's discussion of singleness and marriage centres on her two heroines, Caroline Helstone and Shirley Keeldar. Whereas in *Jane Eyre* different images of womanhood were presented through the consciousness of the narrator/heroine as she progressed towards a self-defined individualism, here the alternatives are explored through a dualistic structural device. The juxtaposition of the two young women highlights their distinctive personalities as well as establishing a female bond between them; the dichotomies are thus integrated into the main narrative. Brontë's wish to maintain her sense of dualities as an intrinsic element of the plot perhaps accounts for certain unconvincing elements in the relationship between the two women. Why, for example, does Shirley not confess her love for Louis, or, more importantly, tell Caroline of her own lack of romantic interest in Robert, when she knows that the younger girl loves him? Why does she deliberately refrain from acknowledging her realisation that Mrs Pryor is Caroline's mother, again when she sees that such information would give her friend comfort and security? And why is Caroline not more jealous of Shirley, who, she is convinced, is about to marry Robert? The psychological awkwardness is however, counterbalanced by the thematic and structural effectiveness of the interaction between them.

Though the two women are not simple opposites, in many ways they act as foils to each other. Shirley — independent, courageous, and unconventional — represents a woman's right to free self-expression and her ability to manage her own affairs. Her assertiveness derives partly from her position as landowner and landlord, and partly from the fact that, as she explains, her parents, expecting a son, 'gave me a man's name; I hold a man's position: it is enough to inspire me with a touch of manhood' (213). It has been suggested that this masculine role-playing is in fact an expression of female powerlessness: unable to envisage a specifically feminine field of action, Shirley is driven to pretend that she is a man, thus acting out the values of her society and continuing the old pattern of sexual dominance.[49] We should note, though, that her assumption of masculinity is actually a positive challenge to claims of male superiority. Scornful of men's childish egoism, she knows how to deal with them to her best advantage; trading on her position as 'Captain Keeldar', she fires out against Yorke's taunts about her matrimonial plans, firmly dismisses the outrageous Donne, gets round Helstone better than any other woman, and defies her bullying uncle by asserting her right to choose her own husband. Confidently individualistic herself, she rejoices that women treasure an identity of which men have no conception:

'If men could see us as we really are, they would be a little amazed; but the cleverest, the acutest men are often under an illusion about women . . . their good woman is a queer thing, half doll, half angel; their bad woman almost always a fiend.' (343)

Shirley never betrays her own sex; she establishes a sisterhood with Caroline, and, like her creator, bitterly resents all charges of unwomanliness. At the same time she illustrates and enacts the positives of female self-reliance.

Caroline, in contrast, represents a much more conventional womanhood. Though she shares Shirley's belief in the need for expansion of female activity, and though she is able to defend herself against Mrs Yorke's vituperative attack on her sentimentality, she is essentially spiritless and lacks the native energy either to defy her circumstances or to carve out an alternative path for herself. Speaking movingly for the plight of single women, she herself is crushed by adversity and fades away in hopeless resignation. Ironically, she is literally brought back to life by being re-established in a parent/child relationship in which it becomes clear that her limp passivity is a maternal inheritance. Brontë's attitude towards Caroline seems equivocal. Caroline's unwavering belief in the supremacy of love reflects her creator's own idealism, but in her case it has near-fatal results. Obsessed with the desire for romantic fulfilment, she seeks work merely in order to obliterate the pangs of disappointed affection, and she is unable to contemplate future happiness in terms other than of marriage. We are surely intended to despise her ready capitulation to a vision of endless emptiness; Caroline's conviction, at eighteen, that life holds nothing more in store for her is coloured with the exaggerations of adolescent self-pity: 'an elegy over the past still rung constantly in her ear; a funeral inward cry haunted and harassed her: the heaviness of a broken spirit, and of pining and palsifying faculties, settled slow on her buoyant youth' (199). Her inability to rise above her admittedly depressing circumstances contrasts markedly not only with Shirley's triumph over emotional uncertainty (and she too lacks assurance that she is loved) but also with Brontë's own resilient spirit which, as we have seen, doggedly overcame despair and sought hope in fruitful occupation.

Brontë's ambivalence presents most difficulties for the reader at the end of the novel since here, unlike at the conclusion of *Jane Eyre*, there is a strong sense of unresolved tensions. Whereas Jane's union with Rochester represents a satisfactory harmonisation not only of male/female polarities but also of conflicting impulses within the heroine herself, the final position of the two heroines in *Shirley* seems artistically and thematically inappropriate. Both Caroline and Shirley are finally 'mastered' and tightly bound in matrimonial chains, a fate which strikes us as incommensurate with their earlier vigorously-voiced protest against restrictive sexual ideologies. Brontë's sharp perception of the dichotomy between the desire for emotional fulfilment and the urgings of individuality seems to have resolved itself into an unquestioning acceptance of romantic orthodoxies. One way of coming to terms with this anomaly is to regard the matrimonial unions as partial compromises, accepted as such by the characters and their creator, with the differences between the two marriages pointing to Brontë's recog-

nition of differing female needs. Thus in each case marriage represents both a response to certain aspects of individual personality and
an acknowledgement that the specific circumstances permit no other
equally desirable alternative.

With Caroline the problem is less acute because she is more traditionally 'feminine' in outlook than Shirley — indeed her moments
of rebelliousness seem oddly out of character — and her acceptance
of a subservient role in marriage is not so surprising. The relationship between her and Robert Moore does, it is true, express some of
Brontë's misgivings about the conditions of matrimony. Though
Robert, like Rochester, is regenerated through suffering, he retains
a totally conventional view of women. As his imagined portrait of
Mary Cave indicates, he sees them as angels, inspiring in men 'pure
affection, love of home, thirst for sweet discourse, unselfish longing
to protect and cherish, replac[ing] the sordid, cankering calculations
of . . . trade' (504) and he persists in defining Caroline as 'like the
loveliest of . . . pictures of the Virgin' (563). More insidiously, his
hope that 'the being I seek to entwine with my own will bring me
solace' (595) does not include equality of opinion; Caroline, unable
to change his intent of 'improving' the Hollow's Mill environment,
will have to remain content to adore and obey. Alongside this suggestion of female powerlessness, however, we are surely intended to
see that this is the only possibility for a character like Caroline who
essentially needs the support provided by matrimony. She is not
suited for a more aggressive role, and if her kind of marriage offers
no outlet for a more rebellious female spirit at least Brontë suggests
that she will be happier with Robert than left helplessly on her own
resources.

It is harder for the reader to come to terms with Shirley's apparent
surrender. The contradiction between her previous defiant self-
reliance and her final position of humility, kneeling at the feet of her
master, Louis Moore, certainly implies an uneasy capitulation to
romantic idealism, especially since it reflects a direct reversal of
roles; Shirley gives up her masculinity in order to enact a truly
feminine submission to male authority, while Louis converts a
somewhat womanish self-effacement into a strong assertiveness.
There is far more sense of authorial misgiving about this marriage.
Despite Shirley's seemingly willing acceptance of her future matrimonial role as pupil, having made her decision she shows a marked
reluctance to finalise their union; perhaps uneasy at Louis's refusal
to answer directly her question, 'Are we equal at last?' (578), she will

not let herself be easily 'tamed', and has no sentimental vision of a totally rosy future. Interestingly, Louis himself describes her as a wild animal still with 'dreams of her wild woods and pinings after virgin freedom' (584), and though we are told that her submission is part of a system to teach Louis to rule instead of her, the fact remains that the once free agent has become a captive.

The union is not, however, as thematically or psychologically inapt as this may suggest. Firstly, it is important to note that Shirley has never been totally unorthodox in her view of sexual relationships. In an early conversation with Caroline, she expresses her belief in noble manhood — 'I tell you when they *are* good, they are the lords of the creation, — they are the sons of God' (225–6) — and she confesses herself ready to look up to a truly superior man; as she tells her uncle, she will marry only one whom 'I shall feel it impossible not to love, and very possible to fear' (514). Secondly, she herself articulates Brontë's awareness of the conflicting needs and desires in women. As she herself both wants support and fiercely cherishes her independence, so the images by which she pictures womanhood illustrate its dualities. The pagan Eve she describes to Caroline combines the awesome power of a goddess, 'a woman-Titan', and the humility of the worshipper adoring her Maker 'with the softness of love and the lustre of prayer' (315–6). Similarly, her French essay on 'La Première Femme Savante' acknowledges a woman's need for a protecting presence as well as her longing to exercise the restless 'flame of her intelligence' and to express her feeling of her own 'God-given strength' (457–8). Shirley may not be able to harmonise fully the two sides of woman either in her imaginative portrayals or in her own life, but she openly admits their existence. When she eventually yields up her independence, it is to a man whose nature, despite his limitations, most closely complements hers. To some extent Louis sees Shirley in preconceived images; he too takes arrogant delight in achieving ascendancy over the female spirit. But, importantly, he shares with her a sense of the dichotomies of woman's nature. His awareness of her as both tyrannical and angelic, wild and submissive, shows that he has some understanding of the conflicting impulses of the female psyche. His dualistic images of womanhood are remarkably similar to Shirley's: his fiery Juno, enslaving then destroying her adorer, parallels Shirley's mermaid, coldly beautiful and luring men to a watery death. If both characters believe that women need men, so both at least acknowledge the potentials of female power. We may regret that ultimately this power cannot express itself autonomously, but our last glimpse of Mrs Louis Moore is not of a broken-spirited creature. As with Jane and Rochester, the notion of mutual help and respect underlies the union. Brontë may be enacting her own hesitations about matrimony through Shirley, but her ambivalence, while acknowledging the compromises inherent in her conclusion, is not despairing.

Villette, published early in 1853, is often considered Brontë's most accomplished novel and certainly offers her most interesting treatment of the single woman. It takes up many of the issues which she dealt with in *Shirley*, such as the nature of female independence, and the tension between the desire for self-expression and the need for emotional security, but this time the debate is more organically integrated into the narrative. By returning to the device of the narrator/heroine which she used in *Jane Eyre*, Brontë is able to explore the paradoxes of female experience through the varying attitudes and behaviour of one character, whose occasional 'unreliability' makes her more psychologically complex than her predecessor.

As before, Brontë expresses her ambivalence about women's roles partly by means of contrast and juxtaposition. Lucy Snowe confronts different examples of femaleness against which she measures herself. Her early experience with Miss Marchmont shows her one aspect of a single life — what it means to endure the loss of a lover, and live on in grim isolation. Miss Marchmont has an inner toughness which saves her from self-abandoning despair, and this lesson is to prove valuable for Lucy; but the negative side of her spinsterhood — her willed and other-worldly resignation — is no answer to Lucy's own suffering and disillusionment. In *Villette*, at the Pensionnat des Demoiselles, Lucy's employer, Madame Beck, presents an alternative image of womanly self-reliance. Madame Beck, a widow who has had to make her own way in the world, is in many respects an excellent example of female industry and determination; masculine in her energy and authority, she illustrates how a woman can build her own sphere and succeed in it.[50] Lucy admires and learns from her (she will become a new Madame Beck with her own school at the end of the novel), yet even before she comes up against the older woman's relentless jealousy which tries to separate her from M. Paul she is aware of the deficiencies of this kind of assertiveness: 'Power of a particular kind strongly limned itself in all her traits, and that power was not my kind of power: neither sympathy, nor congeniality, nor submission, were the emotions it awakened.'[51] Ultimately Madame Beck's cold ruthlessness, which divorces her from natural womanly instincts, disqualifies her as a model of female autonomy.

Miss Marchmont and Madame Beck represent womanhood which has either sublimated or denied the pull towards romantic involvement — Madame Beck's matrimonial hopes are certainly not based on notions of emotional commitment. Ginevra Fanshawe and Paulina (Polly) Bassompierre represent more normal patterns of romantic aspiration, though of very different kinds. Both girls assume that they will marry; the one openly angles for her goal, the other, with greater delicacy, waits quietly for it. By comparing herself with each of them, Lucy learns more about herself and about the complexities of female role-playing. Ginevra is pretty, selfish, empty-headed, and vain, a curious mixture of flirtatiousness and a quite unsentimental attitude towards men. With a typically naive yet cynical nonchalance, she explains why she is happy whereas Lucy is 'a poor creature':

> 'I am the daughter of a gentleman of family, and . . . I have
> expectations . . . I am just eighteen, the finest age possible. . . . I
> *am* pretty . . . I may have as many admirers as I choose . . . you
> are nobody's daughter . . . you have no relations; you can't call
> yourself young at twenty-three; you have no attractive accomp-
> lishments — no beauty. As to admirers, you hardly know what
> they are.' (215)

Not unmoved by the contrast, Lucy is nevertheless able to regard it quizzically, recognising, as her frequent sardonic comments to Ginevra indicate, that the younger woman is a totally different member of the species from herself. Yet the odd friendship between them teaches her the importance of self-protectiveness; Ginevra's callousness about breaking hearts is a betrayal of womanly integrity, but her determined self-consideration is a basic strategy of female survival. Paulina is a complete contrast to Ginevra: delicate, refined, gentle, and loving, she illustrates all the traditional virtues of womanhood. But she is no more a model for emulation than is Ginevra, even though to recognise this causes Lucy more anguish. Lucy's reaction to both young women is coloured by the knowledge of Graham's attraction to them, but whereas, like Jane with regard to Blanche Ingram, she can come to terms with his infatuation for Ginevra because she sees that there is no real love on either side, she finds it harder to accept his feelings for Polly. With the maturity born of suffering, however, she comes to realise that Polly, like Graham but unlike herself, is a child of fortune, destined for 'normal' emotional fulfilment, and that therefore their union is wholly appropriate:

> 'I think it is deemed good that you two should live in peace and be happy — not as angels, but as few are happy amongst mortals. Some lives *are* thus blessed: it is God's will.' (468)

Her refusal to take the post of companion to Polly or to act as her confidante on Graham's behalf is thus both a positive rejection of the disappointed spinster's self-abnegating role and an acknowledgement that enviable and fine as Polly is, their paths lie in different directions.

These alternative modes of female self-definition give Lucy the means of assessing and establishing her own selfhood; and it is in Brontë's presentation of her heroine's self-exploration that her sense of dichotomies is most vividly expressed. From the outset we are aware of contradictions in Lucy Snowe. On the one hand, she is passive, calm, and apparently resigned to a self-abnegating existence. Resentful when fate denies her the continuance of her narrow unchallenging servitude to Miss Marchmont, she persists in her belief that she is destined to a life in the shade; and she takes refuge from a painful sense of her own unattractiveness in a self-protective negativism — 'lover-less and inexpectant of love, I was . . . safe . . . in my heart-poverty' (186). On the other hand, she reveals an unquenchable resilience and capacity for self-reliance. She frequently surprises us by her ability to respond to new situations, and her moments of energetic assertiveness suggest not only unexpected reserves of strength but actual enjoyment of overcoming difficulties. Thrown on her own resources after Miss Marchmont's death, she knows that 'there remained no possibility of dependence on others; to myself alone could I look' (95), and she crushes her temporary sense of helplessness by resolving 'that it was better to go forward than backward, and that I *could* go forward' (107). With the recklessness of a gambler, she goes to a completely unknown town in a foreign country, wins herself a job through sheer bravado, and effectively crushes opposition from her rebellious pupils. Later, she overcomes her initial self-doubts about taking over at short notice a role in M. Paul's play, and startles herself and her audience by her dramatic talents. At the same time, she reveals depths of feeling which contrast sharply with her attempts to lead a passionless existence. Her highly-charged response to the loss of Dr John's letter, and her desolation when he ceases to write (recalling Brontë's own anguish at M. Heger's silence) show the extent to which she is the victim of her own emotional desires. She gradually arrives at a more objective assessment of these inner needs; ultimately, unlike Caroline Helstone, she will not allow her hopelessness to overwhelm her, and the will-power which enables her to bury Dr John's letters, and thus the illusory romance they symbolise, gives her a new determination to meet the future — 'I felt, not happy, far otherwise, but strong with reinforced strength' (381). The self-awareness which makes her recognise that Dr John could not bring her true contentment, enables her at the end of the novel to defy Madame Beck in order to claim M. Paul, knowing that this time the relationship is essentially right.

The dichotomies of female experience represented separately by the two heroines of *Shirley* are here internalised within one character, whose own knowledge of her divided personality enlarges the novel's vision of dualities. Early on, she describes herself as living 'two lives — the life of thought, and that of reality' (140); at this point, her sense of separation is essentially negative because it is unable to reconcile escapist imagination and a grimly stoical view of the external world. Later, her acknowledgement of the conflict within her between Feeling and Reason shows a more mature appreciation of the dichotomies of her selfhood because she sees that both have a part to play in her experience. Lucy displays awareness of her own complexity in other ways, too. She delights in playing a variety of roles. She refuses to answer Ginevra's persistent questioning as to who she is, and she inwardly revels in her ability to disguise herself in a multiplicity of outer images, none of which wholly accurately represents her:

Madame Beck esteemed me learned and blue; Miss Fanshawe, caustic, ironic, and cynical; Mr. Home, a model teacher, the essence of the sedate and discreet . . . the pink and pattern of governess-correctness; whilst another person, Professor Paul Emmanuel, to wit, never lost an opportunity of intimating his opinion that mine was rather a fiery and rash nature — adventurous, indocile, and audacious. I smiled at them all. (386)

This strategy, partly protective, partly self-bolstering (in that she derives strength from the knowledge that only she possesses the truth about herself) accounts for her deliberate concealment of certain facts from the reader — that she has recognised Dr John as Graham Bretton, and that the mysterious giver of the white violets to which she fleetingly refers was M. Paul. Her 'unreliability' in this respect, whose deep emotional source we recognise as a desire to co-exist as spectator of and participant in life, makes her evasiveness far more convincing than Shirley's unaccountable secrecies.

Lucy's awareness of the division between her inner and outer being is symbolised in the series of scenes involving mirrors, recalling a similar use of mirror imagery in *Jane Eyre*. On each occasion, Lucy sees her own reflection and perceives the discrepancy between the image and the reality. At Miss Marchmont's she sees herself 'in the glass, in my mourning-dress, a faded, hollow-eyed vision. Yet I thought little of the wan spectacle. The blight, I believed, was chiefly external: I still felt life at life's sources' (96). When she has been transformed by the coiffeur in honour of the school fête, she confesses that she 'could hardly believe what the glass said when I applied to it for information afterwards' (199), and likewise, unusually adorned for the concert to which she goes with the Brettons, she feels 'a jar of discord' when she realises that the 'person in a pink dress and black lace mantle' (286) in the mirror is herself. Her recognition of these disparities indicates her refusal to accept versions of femininity inappropriate to her, and her determination to cling to her complex and self-formulated identity. Her active exploitation of her own dualities is most strikingly revealed in the play scene. Asked by M. Paul to undertake a man's part, she accepts the male role while retaining her female identity by refusing to don masculine costume; her androgyny recalls that of Crimsworth, but whereas his suggests uncertainty of characterisation, Lucy's represents a deliberate strategy by which she can challenge conventional male attitudes towards women and implement her female power. By ousting the 'good' suitor and wooing Ginevra for herself, she not only symbolically triumphs over Dr John but also allows the new energy generated by her own love for him to promote imaginatively her own desires; temporarily liberated by her dramatic ascendancy, she both responds sexually as a woman and takes on a masculine strength.

The ending of *Villette* reinforces the ambivalence about female fulfilment which Brontë has expressed through her heroine's self-exploration. Lucy's need for emotional satisfaction is balanced by her appreciation of her separate personal identity, and therefore it is appropriate that she be left as both an affianced bride and a single woman. Neither Brontë nor her heroine totally rejects the notion of matrimonial contentment, but, unlike *Jane Eyre* and *Shirley*, the novel does not seek to harmonise its dichotomies with a definitive concluding vision. Furthermore, there is no sense of discrepancy between its statement of female self-reliance and its acceptance of emotional commitment. Lucy is both a normal woman and a free spirit who makes choices; she gains the prospect of happiness, but she is now far more realistic about the kinds of love available to her. Passing beyond her initial infatuation with Dr John, she detects his deficiencies, among them his myopia about women and his 'masculine self-love' (272). M. Paul, she sees, answers her needs far better; he understands her, recognising the spirit of rebellion beneath her orthodox exterior and seeing that she must have a sympathetic partisan who will activate her latent energies. Yet he, too, as she well knows, has his limitations: he is childishly vain and jealous, and his attitudes are often astonishingly conventional, such as his horror at Lucy's unabashed contemplation of the Cleopatra picture, and his half-serious alarm lest she should trespass 'the limits proper to my sex, and conceive a contraband appetite for unfeminine knowledge' (440). What Lucy respects in him — his complete sincerity, his intolerance of deceit, and his feeling for the female sex — leads her to open herself to him, but she realises that he must sometimes be resisted, that 'his absolution verged on tyranny' (438). Without radically asserting her rights, she will not rely wholly on the vagaries of romantic commitment but seeks to complement it with her own created destiny:

> 'With self-denial and economy now, and steady exertion by-and-by, an object in life need not fail you. Venture not to complain that such an object is too selfish, too limited, and lacks interest; be content to labour for independence until you have proved, by winning that prize, your right to look higher.' (450)

The fear of losing Paul for ever makes her reach desperately for the 'higher', and he becomes her king to whom 'to offer homage was both a joy and a duty' (587). Nevertheless, as has often been pointed out, Lucy's time as an independent schoolmistress, fully exercising her energies while waiting for M. Paul's return, 'were the three happiest years of my life' (593). Released from the constrictions of self-doubt and knowing that she now has real significance as an individual, she can relish the advantages of active self-expression, enjoying, like Frances Henri, the benefits of a 'career'.

The final statement of the novel is ambiguous, as Brontë intended. Her well-known refusal, recorded by Gaskell,[52] to make the ending more definitively conclusive, plus her failure to satisfy frequent enquiries as to M. Paul's ultimate fate, show her determination to leave us with her ambivalence. Barely two months before its publication Brontë was still uncertain about how to end the novel, and only knew that she did not mean to 'appoint her [Lucy's] lines in pleasant places'.[53] In the event, she chose to conclude with a final view of her heroine, which, while neither suggesting that matrimonial happiness is a total chimera nor proposing that a single woman can be completely fulfilled, is not depressing or despairing. Brontë's questionings remain, but the sense of possibilities inherent in Lucy's portrayal reveals the same honest confrontation of complexity as does her own self-scrutiny.

Notes

1. Brontë's earliest reviewers pointed out that the most notable aspect of her work was its powerful representation of love, striking in its freshness and originality. Some critics, however, found her unconventionality too much to swallow, accusing her of coarseness and unfeminine outspokenness. For a survey of contemporary opinion see Miriam Allott (ed.), *Charlotte Brontë: Jane Eyre and Villette* (London, 1973); Tom Winnifrith, *The Brontës and Their Background: Romance and Reality* (London, 1973); Miriam Allott (ed.), *The Brontës: The Critical Heritage* (London, 1974).
2. [Elizabeth Rigby], *'Vanity Fair and Jane Eyre'*, *Quarterly Review*, vol. LXXXIV (December 1848), pp. 153–85.
3. For an account of this visit, see T.J. Wise and J.A. Symington (eds.), *The Brontës: Their Lives, Friendships and Correspondence* (reprint, Oxford, 1980), vol. III, pp. 256–8. This work will subsequently be referred to as *The Brontës*.
4. Mary Taylor, the prototype of Rose Yorke in *Shirley*, emigrated to New Zealand in 1845 and set up a shop in Wellington. Always more revolutionary in her feminist attitudes than Brontë, she attacked her old friend for implying in *Shirley* that women may work only if they give up marriage and do not make themselves too disagreeable to men; Taylor felt that all women should work, and called Brontë 'a coward and a traitor' for suggesting otherwise (*The Brontës*, vol. III, pp. 104–5).
5. Elizabeth Gaskell, *The Life of Charlotte Brontë* (2nd edn, London, 1857), vol. II, p. 49.
6. Letter to Ellen Nussey, 10 May 1836. *The Brontës*, vol. I, p. 139.
7. Letter to Ellen Nussey, 28 July 1848. *The Brontës*, vol. II, pp. 239–40
8. Letter to Ellen Nussey, 1 April 1843. *The Brontës*, vol. I, p. 296.
9. Letter to Ellen Nussey, 2 April [1845]. *The Brontës*, vol. II, pp. 30–1.
10. Letter to Ellen Nussey, 26 August [1846]. *The Brontës*, vol. II, p. 108.

11. Letter to Amelia Ringrose, 16 March 1850. *The Brontës*, vol. III, p. 84.
12. Letter to Amelia Taylor, 11 June [1851]. *The Brontës*, vol. III, p. 245.
13. Letter to Henry Nussey, 11 January 1841. *The Brontës*, vol. I, p. 224.
14. Letter to Margaret Wooler, 30 January 1846. *The Brontës*, vol. II, p. 77.
15. Letter to Ellen Nussey, 25 April [1846]. *The Brontës*, vol. II, p. 90.
16. Letter to Ellen Nussey, [20 October 1854]. *The Brontës*, vol. IV, p. 155.
17. Letter to W.S. Williams, 12 May 1848. *The Brontës*, vol. II, p. 215.
18. Letter to W.S. Williams, 15 June 1848. *The Brontës*, vol. II, pp. 220-1.
19. Letter to Ellen Nussey, [22 April 1848]. *The Brontës*, vol. II, p. 205.
20. Letter to W.S. Williams, 3 July 1849. *The Brontës*, vol. III, pp. 5-6.
21. Brontë's comments were recorded by Mary Taylor in a letter to Mrs Gaskell.
See *The Brontës*, vol. II, p. 275.
22. Letter to Ellen Nussey, 25 August 1852. *The Brontës*, vol. IV, p. 6.
23. Letter to Ellen Nussey, 4 August 1839. *The Brontës*, vol. I, p. 184.
24. Letter to Ellen Nussey, 12 March 1839. *The Brontës*, vol. I, p. 175.
25. Letter to Ellen Nussey, 14 September 1850. *The Brontës*, vol. III, p. 157.
26. Letter to Ellen Nussey, 9 April 1851. *The Brontës*, vol. III, p. 222.
27. Letter to Ellen Nussey, 12 April 1851. *The Brontës*, vol. III, p. 223.
28. Letter to Ellen Nussey, 23 April 1851. *The Brontës*, vol. III, p. 229.
29. Letter to Ellen Nussey, 4 March 1852. *The Brontës*, vol. III, p. 319.
30. Letter to Ellen Nussey, 10 July 1846. *The Brontës*, vol. II, p. 101.
31. Letter to Ellen Nussey, 6 April 1853. *The Brontës*, vol. III, p. 57.
32. The letters containing these remarks were written between May 1853 and May
1854. Brontë married on 29 June 1854.
33. Letter to Margaret Wooler, 19 September 1854. *The Brontës*, vol. IV, p. 152.
34. Charlotte Brontë, *Jane Eyre* (Oxford, 1976), p. 110. Subsequent page references are to this edition and will be included in the text.
35. Charlotte Brontë, *Shirley* (Penguin English Library, Harmondsworth,
1979), pp. 223-4. Subsequent page references are to this edition and will be included
in the text.
36. Discussion of Brontë's work on these lines is to be found in Helene Moglen,
Charlotte Brontë: the Self Conceived (New York, 1976); Elaine Showalter, *A Literature of Their Own* (Princeton, 1977); Sandra M. Gilbert and Susan Gubar, *The
Madwoman in the Attic* (New Haven, 1979).
37. [R.H. Hutton], 'Novels by the Authoress of "John Halifax"', *North British
Review*, vol. XXIX (November 1858), p. 474. Hutton compares Crimsworth in this
respect with Craik's Phineas Fletcher, arguing that both characters demonstrate a
characteristic deficiency of women novelists, namely the inability to portray men as if
from a male viewpoint.
38. Charlotte Brontë, *The Professor* (Everyman's Library, Dent, London,
1983), p. 17. Subsequent page references are to this edition and will be included in the
text.
39. *Athenaeum*, no. 1149 (3 November 1849), p. 1107.
40. See her 'Modern Novelists — Great and Small', *Blackwood's Edinburgh
Magazine*, vol. LXXVII (May 1855), pp. 557-8.
41. M. Oliphant, 'The Sisters Brontë', *Women Novelists of Queen Victoria's
Reign: a Book of Appreciations* (London, 1897), p. 24.
42. Ibid., p. 47.
43. Letter to Mrs Gaskell, 20 September 1851. *The Brontës*, vol. III, p. 278.
44. Letter to Ellen Nussey, 6 April 1853. *The Brontës*, vol. III, p. 57.
45. Letter to Margaret Wooler, 19 September 1854. *The Brontës*, vol. IV, p. 152.
46. Virginia Woolf, *A Room of One's Own* (London, 1982), pp. 66-7, 70.
47. In this fascinating novel, Rhys depicts the events preceding those at
Thornfield, including the courtship and early married life of Bertha and Rochester in
the West Indies. Rochester, though not unsympathetically presented, is shown as a

moral coward who, when he learns of madness and miscegnation in his wife's background, totally rejects her.

48. See, for example, Helen Taylor, 'Class and Gender in Charlotte Brontë's *Shirley*', *Feminist Review*, 1 (1979), pp. 83–93.

49. See, for example, Moglen, *Charlotte Brontë*, Chapter 4.

50. Madam Beck is in many ways another Zoraide Reuter, though she lacks the latter's more obvious feminine wiles and is also more threateningly powerful.

51. Charlotte Brontë, *Villette* (Penguin English Library, Harmondsworth, 1983), p. 141. Subsequent page references are to this edition and will be included in the text.

52. Gaskell, *The Life of Charlotte Brontë*, vol. II, p. 266.

53. Letter to George Smith, 3 November 1852. *The Brontës*, vol. IV, p. 16.

4 ELIZABETH SEWELL: THE TRIUMPH OF SINGLENESS

At first glance, Elizabeth Sewell seems a paradigm of Victorian orthodoxy. Born in Newport, Isle of Wight, in 1815, the second girl in a solidly prosperous and middle-class household, she was a dutiful daughter and sister, who, since she never married, dedicated herself to easing domestic troubles, and always regarded family duties as paramount. Deeply devout, she built her life on Christian principles, and her moral and social attitudes derived essentially from her religious beliefs. As an educator of girls she was involved in a sphere of activity considered most suitable for her sex and position. As a writer, she produced a wide range of works, including thirteen novels and three volumes of short stories, religious and educational treatises, history and language textbooks, and travel books, most of which seem primarily inspired by a conventional didacticism. In general, the twentieth century has persisted in treating her mainly as a writer of juvenile and religious literature, focusing chiefly on her two early novels, *Amy Herbert* (1844) and *Laneton Parsonage* (1846), both of which concentrate on children's behaviour in relation to doctrinal issues.[1] It is however quite misleading to claim that Sewell had nothing to say to the adults of her generation or that she was totally unquestioning of her own society and its ideologies. As several recent critical studies have pointed out, much of her work is deeply concerned with problems crucial to her own sex, and establishes her within a sisterhood of Victorian women writers sharing similar preoccupations.[2] Her attitudes are often surprisingly unorthodox, and, without overt radicalism, she champions a far more challenging vision of independent womanhood than many of her contemporaries dared or wished to assert.

Sewell's background provided a network of traditional social and sexual assumptions which moulded her and from which she had to free herself before she could speak with her own voice. In childhood and adolescence, she experienced all the consequences of an ostensibly male-dominated family life. Her father, a prominent solicitor and land-agent in Newport, was a figure of some local importance, being twice mayor and at one time Deputy Governor of the Island. Her brothers, all older than she, were socially and professionally most successful: Richard Clarke was Fellow and Vice-President of Magdalen College, Oxford, and later accepted an invitation to become Reader in Law at Melbourne University; Robert carried on the family law firm in Ventnor; Henry held leading Government positions during the early settlement of New Zealand; William, a noted figure in the Oxford Movement, was Fellow of Exeter College, Oxford, and Professor of Moral Philosophy, as well as the founder of two public schools; James Edwardes was Fellow of New College, Oxford, and also Vice-Chancellor of the University for many years. In such a regime of male achievement, cultural and social family activities naturally centred on the men, whose wishes were deferred to and whose highly conservative opinions about women held sway.

The effect of this environment on the young Sewell, a sensitive and morbidly conscience-ridden girl, was to set up in her a life-long conflict between self-distrust and a desire for self-expression. In her *Autobiography*, a fascinating document of psychological as well as literary interest, she strikingly describes her relationship with the male members of her family. Chilled by her father's remoteness and vagaries of temper (significantly, she felt unable to tell him that she had published her first work of fiction, and like the autobiographical heroine of *The Experience of Life* [1853] probably recognised that 'in mental temperament we were far as the poles asunder'[3]), in her brothers she encountered the full force of masculine arrogance. Confident of their own superiority, the Sewell men had little time for women who were at all 'different'; they accused their sister of self-consciousness and affectation because she liked being by herself, forced her 'longings for something better, and vague dreams of distinction' to be 'kept under from the sense of being a girl',[4] and so much infused her with self-doubt that 'whenever I did compare myself with others it was to wonder at the extent of my own ignorance'.[5] Their tactic of disparagement extended well into Sewell's adulthood: when she was over twenty she was 'greatly humiliated' by William's crushing 'You can't understand that', when he saw her reading Butler's *Analogy*;[6] and, having attained considerable literary eminence, she was coolly dismissed by James as 'not remarkable in any way'.[7] She expands on the long-term results of such deflation of her ego in her semi-autobiographical

Letters on Daily Life (1885), where the narrator explains:

> My brothers were to me as so many fathers, I looked up to them
> and obeyed them; and it was not until I had long passed my girl-
> hood that I ventured to think that I could have a different opinion
> from theirs.[8]

Male dominance extended into her artistic activities as well: William
supervised and 'edited' her first five novels, and only in 1853 did she
first publish wholly independently of him. Her early doubts about
her creative abilities, remaining as a pervasive sense of 'literary
deficiencies'[9], must certainly have been exacerbated, if not actually
created, by such overwhelming pressures.

If Sewell's upbringing had been totally dominated by such traditional sexual patterning, she would probably never have made any
name for herself. In some respects, however, she was encouraged to
take a more challenging view of womanhood. Her mother, to whom
she was deeply devoted (twenty years after her death, Sewell still
records the anniversary in her *Journal*), was not only herself energetic and spirited, but also resolved that her daughters as well as her
sons should have a good education, 'because then they would be
prepared for any change of fortune which might meet them in life'.[10]
Thus at the age of four Sewell was sent to school and received formal
teaching for the next ten years, in Newport and in Bath, experience
which, despite its adverse effect on her moral sensitivity,[11] was to
prove invaluable for her own later teaching and self-education.
She was indeed always regretful that she had not had the chance of
a longer formal education, and continued to read widely, study
foreign languages, and attend University Extension lectures, until
well into old age.

Other aspects of Sewell's early experience provided a potential
source of unorthodoxy. Despite the outwardly conventional sex
roles in the Sewell household, in practice there was much to encourage disbelief in their sanctity. Mr Sewell's financial carelessness
landed the family with heavy debts after his death and it was many
years before they were cleared. Her brothers' similar airiness about
money matters prolonged the financial burdens, and for most of her
life Sewell was dogged by worry about how to make ends meet, as
the constant anxious references in her *Journal* indicate. The burden,
in fact, fell squarely on her and her sisters; until well on into her
literary career, all her earnings went to help prop up the failing

family business, and the small school she and Ellen, her elder sister, ran from their home in Bonchurch was begun in order to provide for family needs. As she observes somewhat bitterly, without her they would probably all have foundered.[12]

Her brothers' behaviour can hardly have endeared her to the notion of masculine superiority. William, whose apparent disregard of her idolising love for him precipitated an adolescent breakdown, caused her additional worries later by his mismanagement of affairs at Radley, the school he founded at Abingdon in 1847, which led the institution to the brink of closure; despite her loyal attempts in the *Autobiography* to whitewash his lack of business sense,[13] her sardonic comment in the *Journal* after yet another financial crisis that 'as usual [he] thought Bonchurch a kind of pit in which money was buried'[14] probably reflects more accurately her exasperation at his thoughtless ineptitude. She also felt the results of masculine irresponsibility when two other brothers, widowed early, left her and her sisters to bring up their children; in particular, Henry, who remarried quite soon after his wife's death and then refused to make a positive decision about his children's future home, caused Sewell considerable distress, between the pain of recognising their father's inadequacies, the burden of providing for them, and the hurtful accusation that by trying to sort out the difficulties she was being 'dictatorial'.[15]

Throughout her life, Sewell experienced the dualities of Victorian womanhood. On the one hand, she was committed to the traditionally female spheres of teaching and household management; her wry recall of her 'girlish declaration' that 'I would never be a useful aunt, for aunts, I felt, were put upon'[16] reminds us how inescapably circumstances had consigned her to a role of self-abnegating service. On the other hand, she exhibited a sturdy individuality which refused to capitulate to limiting ideals of femininity. Stimulated as well as fretted by the knowledge that 'I was to bear the burden for others as well as for myself',[17] she had no patience with 'too much womanish humility'[18] and was prepared to face the consequences of her self-reliance; 'I have gained for myself a character of independence, which will not be liked, but I cannot help it',[19] she says drily, convinced that because of the uncertainty of family affairs, 'I had better work for myself and trust to myself, humanly speaking'.[20] After her first 'perfectly independent step'[21] in 1852 (the decision to buy Ashcliff, the Bonchurch family house, by insuring her own life) she went on to demonstrate her administrative and intellectual abilities, not only running the small school at home but also founding a Church High School for girls in Ventnor in 1866 and supervising it efficiently for many years. When she was not involved in domestic and educational affairs, Sewell also indulged her passion for foreign travel which she regarded as a welcome escape from seemingly endless home cares. She first went to France in 1844, and from then until her mid-sixties she went abroad almost every year, delighting in the novelties of Continental life and amused rather than dismayed by the inevitable discomforts of journeying. Intrepidly she penetrated the less accessible areas of Spain, and in 1870, undeterred by the sudden outbreak of war between France and Germany which occurred during her visit, she marshalled herself and her three young protegées out of Germany to the safe conclusion of their tour. Like Frances Cobbe, she seized on the pleasures available to the adventurous single woman, relishing the chance of 'being so independent',[22] and could not help chafing at those family duties which curtailed opportunities for wider self-fulfilment.

Sewell's sense of the dichotomies of her own individuality (she comments in the *Journal*, 'I can quite recognise what I appear to others, but it only serves to bring out more strongly what I appear to myself'[23]) influences her attitudes towards womanhood in general. Her views about women occur throughout her non-fiction, especially in her educational treatise, *Principles of Education* (1865), and her *Notebook of an Elderly Lady* (1881). Like many other women writers of the period, she both recognises the importance of puncturing some of the current assumptions about female fulfilment and sees the need to uphold certain standards of womanly behaviour. Balancing her conviction that girls must be trained to develop self-sufficiency against her belief that 'women are not meant to stand alone, but are made dependent upon men',[24] she argues for a more positive approach towards female activity. There is no doubt in her mind that intellectually and physically women can never equal men and that therefore sexual rivalry is 'an absurd delusion';[25] as she briskly states,

> [A girl] is not meant to be a man, but a woman, with a woman's duties; and the best kind of education which can be given her, is that which will most obviously fit her for those duties.[26]

For Sewell, as for the early feminists, the sphere of womanly duty is naturally and primarily the home, and it is misguided to teach girls other than 'as women, to have women's minds, and do women's work'.[27] Typically, too, she did not actively support the more radical feminist demands. Airing, in her late seventies, her reservations about some of the most recent developments in female education, she adds cynically,

> It almost seems to me as I watch the spirit of the age, that the chief objects of some of its energetic women teachers, and workers, is to do their duty in that state of life to which God does *not* call them.[28]

At about the same time, in a letter discussing the Women's Movement with a young partisan, Sewell confesses her doubts about the usefulness of the protest, though she acknowledges how all those involved 'desire earnestly to do good'. With characteristic reasonableness, she recommends that the participants equip themselves properly for the task in hand:

> One thing I am sure of, that if the women who now come forward as leaders of the movement really desire to do permanent good they must devote themselves to a thorough study of the subjects about which they give their opinions.[29]

Tolerant but objective sympathy represents the limit of her involvement.

Alongside this conservatism there exists in Sewell a much more challenging attitude which rejects distorting images of womanhood. Scorning so-called 'finishing' education which leaves girls with a lot of useless accomplishments and superficial minds, she argues for far higher standards of female intellectual training — Latin as well as French, and wider curricula of literature, history, and science. She also urges greater female self-reliance to counteract 'that sense of helplessness and isolation which crushes a woman's spirit even before she begins to face the struggle of life'.[30] Sewell's dualism comes out most strongly in the *Notebook of an Elderly Lady*, a series of loosely-connected discussions between three women about female education and achievements. The conversations between the narrator, Mrs Blair (Sewell's persona) and the feminist Miss Brown (whose radicalism seems in part signalled by her single status) are the most interesting because they reveal Sewell's ambivalence. In the chapter on 'Higher Education', for example, while Miss Brown wants women to be educated exactly like men, Mrs Blair adopts a more conservative stance:

> As regards education and instruction . . . I should desire to give a girl all those attainments and accomplishments which would fit her as a woman — whether married or unmarried — to understand and sympathise with men's intellectual and political pursuits and interests, but not such as would be necessary if she had to undertake them herself.[31]

Similarly, whereas Miss Brown wholeheartedly supports the idea of women's colleges at Oxford and Cambridge, Mrs Blair would prefer girls to be away from direct competition with men, with their own institutions, and partaking of a less specialised university course. Again, in the chapter on 'Women's Rights', Mrs Blair, echoing the cautiousness of many women of her generation, cannot accept Miss Brown's radical demands for votes and public office for women, asserting instead that practical and purposeful action (she cites approvingly Florence Nightingale here) are the best means of promoting women's rightful claims.

On the subject of love and marriage Sewell is more coolly realistic than many of her female contemporaries. Unlike some of the other writers examined in this study, including Craik and Brontë, she seems to have escaped the emotionally harrowing conflict between romantic yearnings and the desire for independence. In her case the more intimate correspondence which might have provided evidence is lacking, and there is no reference to deeply personal concerns, except occasional religious ones, in either the *Journal* or the *Autobiography*. This perhaps substantiates her belief that there is much in an individual' life which 'ean never be told except to God'.[32] It does, however, seem that Sewell, whether from circumstances or inclination, was little romantically disposed. One of her friends suggests that she early learnt to suppress her emotions, turning instead to intellectual cultivation,[33] and despite the brief comment in the *Autobiography* about 'the life-long pain of disappointed affection'[34] suffered by one of her heroines, we have no reason to suspect a personal reference here. Her dry response to an acquaintance who presumed that she must have the typical single woman's eye to a matrimonial future ('I turned the conversation . . . leaving her in ignorance of my "ultimate views" which really are to help my family in the best way I can'[35]) indicates, overtly at least, that marriage was not part of her plans. As we have seen, her own experience had taught her only too well that men 'did not understand women in the least',[36] and she was doubtless wary of a state which required reliance upon such untrustworthy beings.

If inwardly Sewell did regret the lack of romantic fulfilment in her life, certainly she shows no outward hesitancy in condemning the false ideals inculcated by her own society. For her, marriage is an awesome and 'irrevocable' commitment,[37] but though she grants that 'as a general rule, men and women were intended to marry'[38] and that 'a happy marriage is the most happy of all events',[39] she also firmly believes that

> it is not the purpose and object of life, the final cause of woman's creation. It seems almost absurd to suggest the possibility of such an idea, and yet so-called rational human beings talk and act as if it was . . . Girls are so wrongly taught from childhood that they are led to stake their all upon this one cast.[40]

She is also well aware, like other thinking women of her time, that social circumstances make marriage an impossibility for many of her sex, and that elevating matrimony as the symbol of ultimate female achievement is both stupid and cruel. Moreover, like Cobbe, she vigorously refutes the notion that to be unmarried is to be 'condemned to a life of desolate repining';[41] on the contrary, she asserts cheerfully,

> An unmarried life, in truth, may be (if people choose to make it so) a life of great usefulness, great interest, bringing to the mind a pleasant sense of independence and freedom, blessed with much inward peace.[42]

Sewell's championship of singleness is reinforced, not undermined, by her strong religious convictions. Since everyone, married or unmarried, has an individual worth and function in God's hierarchy, a single woman, with her own particular set of duties, has as much personal significance as a wife, and should not regard herself as a useless parasite. Indeed, she argues, if life without the 'accident' of marriage is viewed as objectless, then it must be concluded that 'God has created a vast number of immortal beings without a purpose',[43] clearly a blasphemous notion. Since Sewell finds the commonplace image of spinsterhood as dreary martyrdom virtually irreligious, she is all the more eager to point out the positives of such a state. A single woman's happiness, she declares, lies largely in her own hands; there are more ways than one of achieving fulfilment.

*   *   *

Sewell's fiction, unlike that of many of the mid-century women novelists with whom we are concerned here, does not centre on the issues of courtship and marriage. Her novels concentrate mainly on domestic activities such as family duties and church and neighbourhood affairs, and her female characters are exercised more by the clash between personal aspirations and external circumstances than by the turmoils of sexual relationships. In this lies her artistic originality. Because she makes fewer assumptions than most of her contemporaries about the importance of marriage in women's lives, she is able to explore more fully the alternative ways in which individual female energies can express themselves; free from the kind of emotional traumas suffered by Charlotte Brontë's Lucy Snowe or Dinah Mulock's Katherine Ogilvie, her heroines function in the everyday world of duties and commitments familiar to their real-life counterparts.

Sewell's novels were, as she recognised, different from the conventional fiction of her day. At the opening of *The Experience of Life* (1853), the narrator indicates the nature of this difference:

> I am not going to write a tale, not at least what is usually so called. A tale is, for the most part, only a vignette, a portion of the great picture of life, having no definite limit, yet containing one prominent object, in which all the interest is concentrated. But this is not a real representation of human existence . . . (1)

Her reluctance to conform to prevailing literary trends is evident in her remarks on *Ivors* (1856):

> *Ivors* . . . was my first attempt at a regular novel, or a story in which love is the essential interest. Up to the time when I wrote it, I had always tried to show that life could be happy, and its events of importance apart from marriage . . . But love is, of course, a very prominent factor in human existence, and having fairly well established my reputation as a writer without it, I thought that I might venture to introduce it, endeavouring, if possible, to avoid

the usual ending — 'and so they were married, and lived happily ever after'.[44]

She herself clearly did not feel easy writing about romance, as another brief reference to *Ivors* in the *Journal* indicates: 'I am writing a love story, which I dislike extremely'.[45] Her rejection of the staple of 'regular' fiction may have been due to lack of personal knowledge, as has been suggested in the case of Charlotte Yonge, but it also clearly reflects her determination to be honest about female experience as she and many others knew it. Though constant financial anxiety made her only too aware of the need to please publishers and readers alike, she nevertheless strove for a faithful portrayal of her own vision.

Sewell's rejection of the centrality of love and marriage in her fiction leaves her more room to deal with the question of independent selfhood. Her depiction of female individuality outside total absorption in romantic relationships thus contrasts with the work of Brontë or Mulock who explore the complexities of womanhood from within an essentially romantic context. Sewell does not of course ignore marriage altogether; several of her heroines marry happily, and on many occasions she reminds us of the seriousness of matrimonial commitment. But without being radically unorthodox, she offers alternative images of female behaviour which often modify the traditional patterns more outspokenly than the work of her contemporaries.

Sewell approaches the subject of female independence both directly and obliquely. Her dissent from received ideas about appropriate sex roles comes out strongly in her sharply critical treatment of masculine deficiencies. Her novels contain numerous examples of feckless, selfish, or arrogant men who allow the havoc of their own misdemeanours to fall upon their women's shoulders. In *Gertrude* (1845), Gertrude Courtenay's weak-principled brother, Edward, becomes entangled in the financial and moral corruptions of a parliamentary career and is rescued only by his sister's sacrifice of her own small inheritance, intended for a long-cherished church-building scheme. In *Margaret Percival* (1847), the combined carelessness of a father who overspends and an elder brother who incurs gambling debts makes it necessary for Margaret to go out as a governess to keep her mother and younger siblings afloat. In *The Experience of Life* (1853), the heroine's older brothers complacently disregard their financial responsibilities, blithely oblivious to the sufferings of their mother and sisters. We do not have to look far for the source of this obsessive theme in Sewell's fiction.

In undermining ideologies of masculine authority, Sewell does not suggest that women should strike out totally on their own; she is as critical of women who seek to look or act like men (bossy or strident female personalities such as Miss Forester in *Gertrude* or Miss Manners in *Ivors* are depicted as absurd, even socially disruptive) as of men who abrogate their responsibilities. While apparently accepting, however, that women must be prepared for the burdens which a male-oriented society imposes on them, she implies that part of the female educative process is to learn to distrust or question male supremacy. A major theme of several of her novels is, significantly, a sister's gradual disillusionment with a much-admired elder brother. In *Gertrude*, both Edith and Gertrude come to see the falsity of their idolising image of Edward; in *Katherine Ashton* (1854), the heroine, a dutiful daughter and admiring sister, already discouraged by her father's narrow attitude towards female abilities (his crushing reply to her sensible views on local poverty — 'My dear Kitty . . . it's mere nonsense for a girl like you to give any opinion about such matters'[46] — reminds us of William's reaction to Sewell's reading of Butler), watches her brother John fall prey to the physical attractions of a vulgar, flighty woman, and follows his progressive failure as husband, farmer, and colonial pioneer. The most penetrating study of sibling disillusionment occurs in *Ursula* (1858), in which the orphaned heroine, brought up by her adored older brother, Roger, not only suffers his gradual withdrawal of affection, but is forced to acknowledge his deficiencies of judgment about women when he marries a pretty, childish girl whom he crushes by his lack of sympathetic understanding. Sewell is here clearly re-enacting her own painful re-assessment of William, but she moves beyond the merely personal to stress the potentially crippling effect of unquestioning female allegiance to notions of male infallibility.

Interestingly, Sewell sees that male thoughtlessness or deviousness, rather than actual treachery, is most damaging to women. Even the two-faced Mr Verney in *A Glimpse of the World* (1863), who leads on one woman while he is engaged to another, defaults through moral spinelessness, not cold-blooded villainy. As one of the female characters in the novel, speaking with authorial conviction, says indignantly, 'if there is one wrong greater than another of which men are guilty towards the women whom they profess to love — be they mothers, sisters, or wives, it is that of shrinking from inflicting necessary pain'.[47] Like Eliot and Gaskell, Sewell shows how slippery dishonesty, the result of a cowardly withdrawal from self-scrutiny, is not only the source of endless frustration but positively harmful; women, she argues, need to protect themselves from reliance on figures who, for all their apparent authority, can wreak emotional havoc.

Even Sewell's portraits of apparently worthy men contain subtle hints of protest at male authoritarianism. Saddled with inadequate fathers (who are often killed off during the course of the novel) and unreliable brothers, many of her heroines are guided by substitute mentor figures who teach their protegées to distrust or abandon individual desires. The saintly Mr Dacre tells Gertrude that she must dedicate her inheritance not to the building of a new church but to the assistance of the debt-ridden Edward; Mr Reeves, speaking with all the weight of clerical authority, reminds Katherine Ashton that family and parish duties must override personal inclinations. If on the face of it Sewell approves of such teaching, her insistent note of regret for the loss of 'the beautiful vision we so fondly cherished'[48] certainly suggests some ambivalence. She points most strongly to the crippling effects of male morality on female idealism in *Margaret Percival*, which penetratingly explores a woman's emotional fulfilment outside heterosexual relationships. Ostensibly written, at William's instigation, to warn of 'the danger of allowing our affections to be engrossed by persons who, however excellent in other respects, are likely to lead us into errors of faith',[49] the novel in fact derives its power from its moving portrayal of the passionate friendship between Margaret and the Roman Catholic Countess, Beatrice, and of the ensuing pain of separation, engineered by the triumphant hand of Margaret's staunchly High Church uncle. Though the overt 'message' is unequivocal (Margaret is saved from perversion to Roman Catholicism at the eleventh hour), Sewell's writing betrays her resistance to the authoritarian stifling of womanly emotion:

That peculiar feeling with which, from congeniality of taste, or even from accidental circumstances, we regard the individuals whom we love is theirs and theirs alone . . . there is for each a home in our hearts, which when vacant can never be filled again. We bear their images stamped upon our memories, to fade away indeed as the mists of time gather over the scenes of the past, but never to be effaced until we ourselves sink into the grave, covered with the scars of wounds which separation and death have caused. (510)

Sentimental though this seems today, the voice of feminine feeling asserts itself here against the coldness of male rationality.

Sewell's criticism of masculine supremacy is closely related to her discussion of the significance of matrimony for women. As we have seen, she wanted her fiction to depict 'reality', thus in *Ivors* she purposely rejects 'happily ever after' conclusiveness, because 'marriage is a beginning, not an end' and 'it is very misleading . . . to represent it in a different light';[50] in this novel, though one of the heroines eventually marries happily, the other, with whom Sewell avowedly had more sympathy, remains unattached in peaceful, if unexciting, spinsterhood. In her *Principles of Education*, Sewell spells out the difference between 'romance' and 'reality': 'Romance says, "And so they were married, and lived happily ever after". Reality says, "And so they were married, and entered upon new duties and new cares." '[51] The untold harm of novels lies in 'the untrue view which they afford of life, giving it but one object, one prize, and staking the whole of a woman's happiness upon this',[52] while offering an appallingly dismal image of spinsterhood: 'An unmarried life is, in fiction, a lot of sober sadness and regret, with no object and few duties, and which nothing but the spirit of resignation can make endurable.'[53] Sewell's own picture, she implies, will be far more bracingly cheerful.

Sewell conveys her scepticism about marital beatitudes by pointing unflinchingly to the causes and circumstances of unhappy marriage. Like Anne Brontë and Eliot, she grants that the woman may be partly responsible for the mutual suffering, but often in her novels the breakdown is attributable to the husband's domineering egocentricity. In *The Journal of a Home Life* (1867), the husband is even able to distress his wife from the grave, by exacting from her a quite unreasonable death-bed promise about the future of one of his children. *Margaret Percival* contains Sewell's most chilling portrayal of marital disharmony. Margaret's elder sister, Agatha, marries the crotchety Colonel Clive, thirty years her senior, deliberately blinding herself to his faults and lured on by the prospect of wealth and social standing. Her wilfully-crushed misgivings enact their revenge: the marriage proves disastrous, and, unable to bear her husband's obstinate ill-temper any longer, Agatha flees back to

her family after the death of her child, caused, she claims, by its
father's callous lack of concern. Sewell does not exonerate Agatha
altogether, and Margaret's urgings to her sister to return to her
wifely duties have authorial weight behind them. But she makes
clear how Agatha's upbringing has led her to her reckless choice.
Influenced by her mother's worldliness, Agatha makes the fatal
mistake of ignoring her 'dread of linking herself for life to a man
whom she could neither love nor respect' (96). Sewell shows a masterly grasp of psychological complexities — reminding us of Eliot's
brilliant treatment of Gwendolen's soul-destroying union with
Grandcourt in *Daniel Deronda* — in her depiction of the 'gnawing
regret and self-reproach' below Agatha's veneer of brittle gaiety,
whispering to her 'of those future years of married life . . . when the
delusions of the present hour would be passed away, and nothing
would remain to drive from her the conviction that she had sacrificed every better feeling of her heart upon the altar of Mammon'
(172). There is, moreover, a strong hint of sexual repugnance in
Agatha's hatred of her husband; her confession to Margaret of her
shuddering aversion to his blundering attempts at affection ('I could
have endured reproaches better . . . it is horrible' 602) touches on a
rarely-discussed aspect of Victorian married life.

Sewell depicts other instances of male selfishness or authoritarianism creating a near-fatal rift between husband and wife. The
theme is sketched in *Gertrude*, where Edward's refusal to confide in
his young wife prevents her from confessing her own financial difficulties. It is developed more fully in *Katherine Ashton*. Here, two
less-than-ideal marriages offer the heroine the chance to weigh
up the desirability of marital commitment. The union between
Katherine's brother and the pettish, spoilt Selina is fractured by
squabbles and domestic upheavals; as Katherine realises, much of
the discord could have been avoided had John had more strength of
mind. The union between Colonel Forbes (Sewell seems to have had
a weakness for the military, or else she felt that ex-soldiers made
particularly bad husbands) and Katherine's former schoolfellow,
Jane Sinclair, is more psychologically fraught due to the husband's
selfish refusal to compromise. Sewell etches his deficiencies with
cool incisiveness:

He loved her first because she pleased his taste, and approved
herself to his judgment of what the wife of a man in his position
ought to be . . . his constant thought for the future was not how

he could please her . . . but how she could please him . . . He did not really mean to be as unkind as he often was . . . but he was a cold man . . . cold because self was his centre, and the touch of self changes the rushing stream of love into an iceberg. (207–8)

Sewell's device for enabling Katherine to study this relationship at close hand — she becomes Jane's maid/companion — is somewhat awkward, but it serves its purpose. Katherine, whose energetic spirit finds Jane's total self-abnegation socially and morally distasteful, sees how a wife's constant deferral to her husband's whims actually reinforces his selfish dominance; as Sewell crisply remarks, 'had Katherine been in Jane's place, Colonel Forbes might never have become the tyrant which he was' (316). As in *The Tenant of Wildfell Hall*, in which Millicent Hattersley has to learn that complete submission to her husband only exacerbates his cruelty towards her, the narrative punctures the ideology of wholly compliant wifehood and argues for a more assertive expression of female individuality.

In *Ursula*, anti-matrimonial propaganda is more subtly integrated into the main plot. The marriage between Roger and Jessie Lee is closely linked to the book's overall theme of knowing oneself and others. In this respect, it is the most significant marriage in the novel, though the wretchedness of the long-suffering Mrs Weir, abandoned by her husband, and the discordant union between Ursula's other brother and his sharp-tongued wife serve to reinforce Sewell's by now familiar message. Roger — whose rigid uprightness and self-discipline, combined with a weakness for apparently helpless beauty, reminds us of the similarly fallible Adam Bede — fails to understand his pretty, empty-headed young wife, who in her turn is too much in awe of him to confess to her continuing entanglement in the complications of a former flirtation. When his false paradise is shattered, Roger will forget but not forgive; though Ursula manages to create an uneasy peace between them, complete harmony is impossible. As Ursula herself realises, incompatability of temperaments cannot be overcome by romantic idealism. The heroine's astute assessment of the situation, as her jealousy of her sister-in-law changes to a recognition of how Jessie too has been deluded, comes out of her growing self-knowledge and is thus an intrinsic element in the narrative. Ursula's critical perceptions are the author's, the more to be taken seriously because they are maturely considered.

Sewell's dissent from current romantic ideology is expressed more directly in her depiction of female activity outside marriage. Sewell's unmarried heroines are not of the 'shrieking sisterhood' and most of their energies are concentrated in the traditional womanly spheres of family and neighbourhood affairs, but they wield power and command respect within these spheres. As we might expect, Sewell rarely resorts to the conventional image of the 'old maid'; even the Misses Ronaldson, the fidgety 'do-gooders' in *Katherine Ashton*, and the nervous Miss Debrett in *Margaret Percival* are only lightly touched with satire, while Emily Morton, the long-suffering governess in *Amy Herbert* (1844), has just enough tough-mindedness to escape being the stereotyped pathetic spinster.

Most of Sewell's main heroines are independent-spirited young women who aspire beyond the restrictions of their environments. In many cases avowed authorial self-portraits, they yearn for self-expression and personal fulfilment. Margaret Percival, conscious of unsatisfied needs, her desire for a life of her own strengthened by the sight of her sister's wifely misery, longs for a wider field for her energies; her creator, abruptly abandoning her recommendation of traditional womanly roles, adds her voice to her heroine's rebellious cry of frustration, in a notable passage:

Exert herself for the Church [Margaret] did in her own limited sphere, by training the children, and whenever it was possible, suggesting right principles to the poor, and to the servants, or whoever might be placed within the range of her influence. But Margaret's mind could have taken a larger grasp. She had talents, and energies, and powers of self-devotion which burned within her, and would fain have found their exercise in some great scheme of usefulness. (347)

Margaret's sense of stultification is quite specifically linked to the disabilities of her sex. As she watches her brother and uncle cheerfully settle down to a morning's studying, conscious that she can read only in the intervals snatched from home duties, she protests wistfully against the common view of female intellectual shortcomings: 'Women are in general so shut out from doing good by their mental powers . . . and yet they possess them' (306). A lengthy and directly authorial passage fairly early in the novel suggests how much Sewell sympathised with her heroine's sense of outrage. Some unmarried women, she says, are content with their narrow lot, but

> there are others, the gifted, the enthusiastic, the poetical, con-
> scious of high intellectual powers, and believing themselves, per-
> haps justly, equal to men in all but physical strength, and sobriety
> of judgment, whose whole life is a struggle between the inferior-
> ity of their natural position and the cravings of an ardent, highly-
> cultivated mind . . . The wish, 'if I were but a man', passes the
> lips, and raises a smile, and is forgotten; but it is no transitory
> feeling which prompts it. (125)

Sally Mortimer, Katherine Ashton, and Ursula Grant, restlessly
fighting against the insignificance imposed on them as women, similarly embody their creator's protest.

Sewell's heroines, as has been indicated, never act directly in the
male world, but from their ostensibly subordinate positions they
frequently take on pseudo-masculine roles. Gertrude Courtenay,
for instance, despite having to sacrifice her inheritance, actually
thereby enjoys the power of preserving the family and saving her
brother from otherwise unavoidable disgrace. Likewise, Margaret
Percival's apparently traditionally feminine acts of intercession,
reconciliation, and self-sacrifice take on a more unorthodox significance; she becomes not only the active saviour but also a 'maker',
creating new lives for Agatha and for George, her younger brother,
who goes to college on the proceeds of her governessing.

In *Margaret Percival* and *Gertrude*, both written with a specific
didactic purpose (the one against 'perversion', the other against
neglect of home duties), the moral framework prevents full exploration of the heroines' urge for self-expression. In her later novels,
released from William's restrictive editorship, Sewell gives freer rein
to her personal convictions. Her three best works, *The Experience
of Life, Katherine Ashton*, and *Ursula*, proclaim the positives of
female self-dependence; the first treats the topic entirely outside the
marital sphere, the other two conclude with the heroine's marriages
but focus for the greater part on pre-matrimonial experience,
analysing the balance between a woman's emotional and mental
needs.

Though *Katherine Ashton* was inspired by discussions about
district-visiting,[54] its real interest lies in its treatment of the heroine's
struggle to find a purpose in life. The daughter of indulgent but
conventionally-minded parents, she aspires beyond her mother's

ideal of womanly excellence — 'keeping regular accounts, working quietly and neatly, and making good pies and puddings' (8) — feeling 'as if there was something in her kept down, imprisoned, as if there might be some object or aim in life which she ought to have, and had not' (17). Like Eliot's Maggie Tulliver and Dorothea Brooke, also trapped in a world of restrictions and local irritations, she longs for some definitive role. Sewell, herself ambivalent about the public exercise of female energies, cannot go so far as to propose a career for Katherine. But as with Margaret and Gertrude before her, she shows her heroine extending her range of action even within her limited environment. As we have seen, Katherine acts as peacemaker at home and in the Forbes household; after her father's death, she knows 'exactly what to do' (216), taking over her brother's position as family manager — 'she was the person to whom all looked for advice and support' (217). Moreover, at least to begin with, Katherine is healthily sceptical about marriage. Even before her vicarious experience of two unsatisfactory unions, she is coolly dismissive of a regime in which 'people fell in love, and after a good deal of fuss were married at last, of course, like everyone else; but afterwards they went on just as before' (17). Her scepticism is reinforced by her discovery of Jane's unhappiness:

> her own lot — its freedom and independence — stood out in brilliant light, compared with what she felt would be the irksomeness of such a perpetual restraint as that to which Jane submitted so willingly. . . . Katherine never felt more anti-matrimonially disposed in her life. (173)

Katherine's anti-matrimonial disposition is sometimes lightly touched with satire, recalling Charlotte Yonge's treatment of Theodora Martin and Rachel Curtis. Indeed, part of the plot's intrinsic irony consists of the undermining of Katherine's view that 'marriage was [not] in her way' (75). Even so, Sewell takes a very hard look at the realities of matrimonial commitment. If her introduction of romance into Katherine's life — her heroine is pursued by Charles Rolandson, an earnest young man who lurks unconvincingly on the fringes of the story — seems a capitulation to convention, it still contributes to the novel's overall questioning about female roles. Knowing that she does not love Charles, Katherine also knows that it would be self-destructive, as well as wrong, to accept his offer:

> For one instant she thought of herself as his wife, — home, friends, associations, all gone from her, — his wife! no one besides to look to, to lean upon, — and her heart sank. It was a sufficient answer to satisfy her conscience. (177)

For her, 'who had been free as air in thought and word, and almost in action', the idea of being continually with such an oppressive personality is 'unendurable' (184). Katherine's final acceptance of Charles, after he has demonstrated his worth by helping her out of her financial difficulties, seems something of a let-down, even though she continues to reveal her independent spirit by refusing to agree to a marriage date until she has fulfilled her prior commitment to Jane Forbes. Yet despite the limp conventionality of the book's last sentence —'The blessing of God was upon them, and for what further happiness need we seek?' (522) — Sewell does not let us forget her questioning of romantic ideologies. A few pages earlier, in a discussion with Charles about whether there can be 'anything better' than the prospect of marriage for a woman, Katherine's unhesitating response carries the weight of authorial conviction:

> 'Nothing better if it is a woman's voluntary choice, and she has plenty of time to think about it; and nothing worse, if she is forced into it, because it is all she has to look to. I do believe earnestly that one of the things most essential for a woman's goodness and happiness, is to be independent of marriage.' (514)

The novel itself does not entirely vindicate Katherine's conclusion, and as with much of Sewell's work the more unorthodox elements remain on the periphery of the narrative, as statement or interpolated argument. But it certainly qualifies unthinking idealism about matrimony, and at least suggests the possibility of alternative female self-definition.

Ursula is in some ways a rewriting of *Katherine Ashton*, its major themes including sisterly jealousy of a brother's wife and the clash between family and personal commitments. It is, however, better structured, and its characters, especially the main ones, are more convincing. Ursula herself is a particularly memorable heroine, partly autobiographical in her impatiently managerial spirit and her blunt honesty. The subtlety of her portrayal depends partly on her first-person narration, a technique which Sewell skilfully exploits to depict her developing knowledge of herself and others. Ursula's chief characteristics — vigour, intelligence and outspokenness — are directly linked to the central theme of female self-assertion. As a child she is, like Maggie Tulliver, a rebel, continually fighting against people's expectations of her. When Miss Millicent Weir tries to teach her how to darn a stocking, for instance, the young Ursula petulantly tears out all the stitches; later, on being told that she is to have a sister-in-law, she declares pettishly, 'I have done very well without one'.[55] Her sharp tongue and quick temper continue to get her into trouble in adulthood, especially in her prickly relationship with Leah, William's wife, though at the same time it is a mark of her increasing maturity that she can turn her own sense of the absurd against herself. Arguing with Leah about whether or not the chance of netting a husband can outweigh the dubious effects of 'fast' company, Ursula exposes herself with wry self-honesty:

> 'For twenty husbands,' I said, 'I would not go to Hove on a Saturday, to flaunt about the streets with Jane Shaw, and have all the idle folks in the country gossiping about me.'
> 'You are jealous, Ursie,' said Leah with some meaning. 'Jane Shaw is handsome enough and clever enough to have persons going after her who would never look at you.'
> 'Very likely,' I said, carelessly, not choosing to show that I was annoyed; though I must own that, as Leah spoke, I glanced at the old mirror over the fireplace to see if I was really so plain that no one would ever look at me. (75)

Ursula's irrepressibility, depicted here with such humorous and colloquial incisiveness, makes her seek for more positive freedom of action than that desired by either Sally Mortimer or Katherine Ashton. Motivated by the desire to 'provide for myself, and make my own way in the world' (187), she reaches a position of considerable power and independence as Roger's housekeeper and Mrs Weir's adviser. When she has to make her home with William and Leah after Roger has gone to Canada, the arrangement is on her own terms; she bluntly tells her sister-in-law, 'the long and the short of the matter . . . is, that it is my duty to do the best I can for myself' (127). Ursula has to learn the difference between a healthy assertion of individuality and wilful egoism. Miss Millicent Weir, with her strange, mannish appearance, her odd habits (which include wandering about the sea-shore collecting specimens), and her lack of consideration for others' feelings, serves as a warning against female 'strong-mindedness'. But Ursula's determination and sturdy efficiency, as capable of escorting a querulous elderly woman on the Continent as of dealing with troublesome relations, are a vindication of self-reliant womanhood.

Like Katherine Ashton, Ursula is finally united to a man she has known since childhood, but the conclusion strikes us as less conventional than that of the earlier novel. Ursula's changing attitude towards marriage, from scepticism to acceptance, is more carefully detailed; only after she has herself overthrown the 'idol' which her imagination has made of Roger can she recognise the worth of John Hervey's loyal and loving comradeship. Her relationship with him is based both on knowledge of her own emotional needs and on a realistic assessment of what marriage entails. Ursula, like her creator, is not blindly idealistic about romantic commitment, and her union will presumably be one of balance and mutual respect. Significantly enough, the most enduring image of the heroine in this novel is of a vigorously independent woman, not a sexually 'relative' creature.

The Experience of Life, written when Sewell was in her mid-thirties, self-proclaimed author and firmly established in the self-reliant role which was to be hers all her life, is her most positive statement about the single life. The plot is slight, consisting of the elderly narrator's recall of personal and family affairs, but, as she explains at the beginning, this is the normal reality for most people:

> For one person whose life has been marked by some very striking event, there are hundreds who pass to their graves with nothing to distinguish the different periods of their probation, but the changes which steal upon them so naturally as scarcely to occasion a momentary surprise. (1)

From this rather drab premise, the novel creates its own artistic originality. Its whole point is that the spinster will find fulfilment in the unexceptional sphere of ordinary circumstances, not in extraordinary activity. There is much autobiographical material here. Sally Mortimer, another first-person narrator, is an outsider in the family, her temperamental 'difference' accentuated by her physical weakness; but she too becomes a prime source of moral and practical support. She acts as an adviser to her elder siblings, and provides for her mother and the younger ones after their father's death by setting up a small school. She struggles to achieve an independent yet morally viable selfhood, a process which involves overcoming her tendency towards self-pity, displayed in her dispirited assumption of her Cinderella role:

> Sickly, plain and indifferently educated, what better could I expect than to live in shade, whilst others glittered in sunshine? To what duties could I look forward, except those which were scarcely deemed worthy of thanks? (30)

The answer is, of course, as she herself soon realises, that there is 'no "must" be miserable' (32); with determination, a woman can always make a life of her own.

This novel provides the heroine with an actual model for female self-reliance in the figure of Sally's much-revered Aunt Sarah, a lively and unregretful spinster. Aunt Sarah shows Sally that a single life is 'so much of a blessing' that a woman should never exert herself 'merely to escape from it' (147); she also teaches her the valuable lesson that self-denial must not be confused with self-annihilation. When Sally proposes to take the whole burden of the collapsing family finances on her own shoulders, Aunt Sarah briskly deflates such elevated idealism:

> 'Generosity is a valuable quality, but justice is so too . . . And if you ever wish to be generous, you must begin by being just, — just to yourself as well as to your neighbours.' (230–1)

Combining tough-mindedness with deep piety, the elderly spinster voices most directly Sewell's own rejection of stereotyped images of the single life.

The Experience of Life also contains Sewell's most extensive discussion of marriage, much of which, as in Jewsbury's *The Half-Sisters*, is conducted through meditation or debate. After a conversation in which Sally has stoutly refuted her sister's whining complaint that 'anything is better than being an old maid' (144), she ponders,

> in novels . . . there was nothing else worth a moment's thought. If women were not married, they were either soured by the disappointment, and lived to be the torment of their friends; or, after concentrating into a few years the sorrows of a long life, they invariably died of consumption.

And was this then the true statement of the case? If the opportunity of marrying from affection should be denied me, must my existence be indeed so lonely, so burdensome? And was there no mode of escape from such wretchedness but that of sacrificing taste and feeling by consenting to be the wife of the first man of ordinary respectability who would give me the honour of his name, and a share of his fortune? (162)

Again, of course, the answer is 'no'. Sally's single state offers her new horizons of attractively positive action:

There was, indeed, no one to depend upon but myself; and as the thought forced itself upon me, fully and plainly, my spirit rose, and the full energy of my mind seemed, for the first time, realized to myself. (170)

As Sally also recognises, freedom from matrimonial ties enables her to undertake her chosen role with greater efficiency. Coolly realistic about her situation — 'I had reached the age of eight-and-twenty, not only without having had the opportunity of marriage, but without having seen a single person who, I felt, could make me happy in such a life' (171) — she enjoys the satisfaction of seeing the fruits of her labours. And even when the marriage of her younger sister and a legacy from her aunt permit her to give up the school-teaching which is injuring her health, she continues to take on private pupils and to study, because she still needs the 'variety and occupation, and the sense of usefulness, without which, after the employment to which I had been accustomed, I could never have been happy' (341).

The prime message of *The Experience of Life*, then, is that 'a single life need not be solitary and unblest' (341). The novel offers a quiet statement of unorthodoxy rather than any striking challenge to current sexual ideologies. It is also more honest than Sewell's other works in that it does not attempt to deny that a spinster's existence can be lonely nor that marriage sometimes seems highly desirable. Only in one place in the novel does Sewell's awareness of the complexities of female experience remain as 'unconverted' ambivalence instead of direct expression. Quite unexpectedly, Sally tells us of an attractive offer of marriage which she turned down because of family commitments. As her wistfulness reveals, she is clearly conscious of the personal sacrifice this has entailed:

I will not pretend to say that the necessity of refusing did not give
me a great pang . . . There was a curious mixture of sadness and
relief in my mind when the affair was quite at an end . . . it was
very pleasant to think of resting upon another instead of depend-
ing upon one's self; and the idea of an affection exclusively one's
own was more tempting than words can tell. (259)

There is more to this than mere adherence to romantic convention
on Sewell's part, but the issue is developed no further. When, in
justifying her refusal, Sally declares that she has decided not to tell
Aunt Sarah because she wishes to spare her pain, we suspect ration-
alisation. As Sally must well know, might not the old woman have
told her niece not to be a goose (one of her favourite terms) and deny
herself happiness? Sally seems here guilty of the delusive self-
sacrifice she was encouraged to reject, yet the psychological implications are too vague to be effective.

Taken as a whole, though, the novel offers a more positive and
committed approach to singleness than almost any other woman's
novel of its time. A brief comparison with Brontë's *Villette* is
particularly illuminating in this respect. Both works explore the
theme of women on their own, developing the self-reliance which
comes from their anomalous position in the 'normal' social world,
but whereas in Brontë's novel the idea of female self-fulfilment,
independent of male support, is only cautiously and obliquely suggested, in Sewell's it is directly examined. We may believe that Lucy
Snowe will go forward without M. Paul, but Brontë cannot openly
propose a womanly existence devoid of romantic emotion. In contrast, at the end of *The Experience of Life*, Sally, an active and
contented spinster, demonstrates her creator's firm belief in the
rewards of a single life, despite its apparent compromises. Less
passionate and artistically imaginative than her fellow-novelist,
Sewell has perhaps more to say to the women of her generation.

Notes

1. For discussion of Sewell as a religious and children's writer see Gillian Avery,
Nineteenth Century Children (London, 1965); Amy Cruse, *The Victorians and Their
Books* (London, 1935); Andrew L. Drummond, *The Churches in English Fiction*
(Leicester, 1950); Margaret Maison, *Search Your Soul, Eustace* (London and New
York, 1961); Vineta Colby, *Yesterday's Woman: Domestic Realism in the English
Novel* (Princeton, 1974). Sewell herself disliked being regarded as merely a writer for
the young, and most of her fiction from the late 1840s onwards is essentially adult in

interest. The novels which have been selected for detailed examination here are chiefly those of her middle period (1847–58), which represent her greatest artistic achievement; her two final works, *The Journal of a Home Life* (1867) and *After Life* (1868), which recreate some of her European travel experiences as well as her duties as guardian of her many nephews and nieces, reveal a certain artistic fatigue and are also less relevant to the issue of marriage *vis-à-vis* singleness.

2. The best examples of this approach are in Elaine Showalter, *A Literature of Their Own* (Princeton, 1977) and Nina Auerbach, *Woman and the Demon: the Life of a Victorian Myth* (Cambridge, Mass., 1982).

3. Elizabeth M. Sewell, *The Experience of Life* (new edn, London, 1886), p. 4. Subsequent page references are to this edition and will be included in the text.

4. Eleanor L. Sewell (ed.), *The Autobiography of Elizabeth M. Sewell* (London, 1907), pp. 15–16.

5. Ibid., p. 55.

6. Ibid., p. 53.

7. Ibid., p. 96.

8. Elizabeth M. Sewell, *Letters on Daily Life* (London, 1885), p. 148.

9. Sewell, *Autobiography*, p. 95.

10. Ibid., p. 24.

11. The absolutely rigid insistence on truth-telling at her first school, kept by a dragon-like Miss Crooke, created in Sewell a life-long obsession with guilt and, she claims, 'laid the foundation of a sophistical habit of mind' (*Autobiography*, p. 27).

12. Her *Journal* contains frequent references to her role as saviour of the household; what she found particularly galling was the fact that despite her hard work to keep them all afloat William still controlled her business dealings with her publishers. As she confessed, 'What I earnestly longed for was to get my money into my own hands, and draw it when and how I liked' (Elizabeth M. Sewell, *Extracts from a Private Journal kept from 1846 to 1891* [Edinburgh, 1891], p. 75).

13. See Sewell, *Autobiography*. pp. 165, 204–5.

14. Sewell, *Journal*, p. 75.

15. Ibid., p. 59.

16. Sewell, *Autobiography*, p. 155.

17. Ibid., p. 69.

18. Ibid., p. 131.

19. Sewell, *Journal*, p. 33.

20. Ibid., p. 57.

21. Sewell, *Autobiography*, p. 140.

22. Sewell, *Journal*, p. 135.

23. Ibid., p. 150.

24. [Elizabeth M. Sewell], *Principles of Education* (London, 1865), vol. II, p. 221.

25. Ibid., vol. II, p. 22.

26. Ibid., vol. II, p. 287.

27. Elizabeth M. Sewell, *Notebook of an Elderly Lady* (London, 1881), p. 108.

28. Sewell, *Autobiography*, p. 203.

29. Letter to Margaret Chanler, 20 June 1894. In Radley College Archives.

30. Sewell, *Principles of Education*, vol. II, p. 231.

31. Sewell, *Notebook*, p. 110.

32. Sewell, *Autobiography*, p. 163.

33. Ibid., p. 236. The chapter in which this comment is made was written as a memorial to Sewell by one of her oldest friends, Mrs Reginald Clayton.

34. Ibid., p. 146.

35. Sewell, *Journal*, p. 15.

36. Ibid., p. 9.

37. Ibid., p. 97.

38. Sewell, *Principles of Education*, vol. II, p. 112.
39. Ibid., vol. II, p. 105.
40. Ibid., vol. II, p. 105.
41. Ibid., vol. II, p. 106.
42. Ibid., vol. II, p. 113.
43. Ibid., vol. II, p. 107.
44. Sewell, *Autobiography*, pp. 145–6.
45. Sewell, *Journal*, p. 90.
46. Elizabeth M. Sewell, *Katherine Ashton* (new edn, London, 1886), p. 35. Subsequent page references are to this edition and will be included in the text.
47. Elizabeth M. Sewell, *A Glimpse of the World* (new edn, London, 1886), p. 206.
48. Elizabeth M. Sewell, *Gertrude* (new edn, London, 1886), p. 249.
49. Elizabeth M. Sewell, *Margaret Percival* (new edn, London, 1886), p. 1. Subsequent page references are to this edition and will be included in the text. Interestingly, this is the only instance in Sewell's work of a close relationship between two women. Though she was very keen on the idea of sisterhoods (she wrote two articles about Protestant deaconesses for *Macmillan's*, January 1870 and September 1873), she never suggests that friendship between women is a substitute for marital union.
50. Sewell, *Autobiography*, pp. 145–6.
51. Sewell, *Principles of Education*, vol. II, p. 103.
52. Ibid., vol. II, p. 116.
53. Ibid., vol. II, p. 113.
54. See Preface to *Katherine Ashton* (written 1 June 1858), p. 1.
55. Elizabeth M. Sewell, *Ursula* (new edn, London, 1886), p. 51. Subsequent page references are to this edition and will be included in the text.

5 ELIZABETH GASKELL: THE WIFE'S VIEW

In May 1850, Elizabeth Gaskell wrote to Lady Kaye-Shuttleworth, 'I am always glad and thankful to Him that I am a wife and mother and that I am so happy in the performance of those clear and defined duties'.[1] This declaration takes us straight to the most obvious difference between Gaskell and the other women novelists examined in this study: she actually participated in the 'norm' of female experience about which they could write only at second-hand; her conviction that marriage and motherhood represent the apotheoses of womanly fulfilment thus carries the weight of personal validation. Gaskell seems largely to have escaped the emotional crises and role-questioning which affected many of her female contemporaries. Basically stable and optimistic by nature, she married early, and her union with William Gaskell, despite later laboured interpretations to prove the contrary,[2] was on the whole successful. If, as seems a reasonable assumption, Gaskell's fictional portrayals of unhappy marriages indicate her recognition that matrimony as an institution has its limitations, this is not to say that she was dissatisfied with her own state. Her rueful remarks about William's reserve and his unwillingness to be bothered with domestic tribulations or family arrangements — even her well-known account of how he 'composedly buttoned . . . up in his pocket the proceeds of *Lizzie Leigh*[3] — hardly negate the very powerful sense of contentment which emanates generally from her letters. Her warm concern for her children, also described so delightfully in her correspondence, reinforces this image of her and gives small grounds for theories of her unwilled or resented 'relativity'.

Gaskell's evident womanliness, described by Margaret Shaen as 'queenly' charm[4] and by Mrs Lynn Linton as 'graciousness and feminine dignity'[5] did not endear her to the more rebellious spirits of her generation; Jane Carlyle, for instance, felt that there was 'an atmosphere of moral dullness' about her,[6] and Geraldine Jewsbury could not get on with her.[7] It has also encouraged critics to regard her as a spokesman for traditional sexual values, whose work firmly supports the status quo and has little of interest to say about the more contentious or problematic aspects of female experience. Such a view, however, needs qualification. Without attempting to acclaim her as a sexual iconoclast, we must recognise that she too plays a part in the mid-Victorian female challenge to society's ideologies. Her treatment of the 'woman question' is not as straightforwardly conservative as may at first appear, and even while upholding intrinsically orthodox romantic attitudes she voices her own dissent from contemporary mores.

Gaskell's perceptions of the complexities underlying even the most apparently fulfilled womanhood were, ironically enough, strengthened by her own situation. As a working wife she was in theory subject to the law that she could not keep her own earnings, and she also faced possible husbandly disapproval of her literary activities. As it happens, neither restriction became a serious problem for her, but she was certainly not unaware of their potential threat. The conflict between the expression of individual talent and the pressures of domestic duty, which exercised so many Victorian writing women, was, too, particularly acute for her, as mother of four and wife of a busy Unitarian minister. Her more public or traditional responsibilities in addition probably made her especially sensitive to the criteria imposed upon the woman writer. She somewhat shamefacedly confesses to her own deceitful capitulation to literary demands, in contrast to Charlotte Brontë's honesty:

The difference between Miss Brontë and me is that she puts all her naughtiness into her books, and I put all my goodness . . . my books are so far better than I am that I often feel ashamed of having written them and as if I were a hypocrite.[8]

Recognising that speaking 'as the character in a story — or even as the author of a book'[9] is not the same as speaking as a private person, she growls comically to her old friend Eliza (Tottie) Fox that, contrary to her inclination, she is always 'obliged to write as if I loved [my species];[10] beneath the humorous tone lurks resentment at being unable to enjoy a 'free swing'[11] in her work.

As with so many of her female contemporaries, Gaskell's recognition of the dualities or tensions of her womanhood expresses itself as ambivalence, either directly or more obliquely. Her strong sense of the powerfulness of accepted sexual ideologies, wryly acknowledged in her admission of literary role-playing, is revealed succintly in her *Life of Charlotte Brontë* (1857). Full of admiration for the younger novelist and aware of her notably individual artistic voice, Gaskell was nevertheless clearly influenced by the nature of her task. Her biography, a commisioned and protective tribute to her friend, is more a depiction of the ideal figure she wanted the world to approve than of the artist/woman she knew. Thus she chooses to emphasise Brontë's feminine qualities — her womanly purity and self-sacrifice — rather than her creative originality or her professional-mindedness. She stresses Brontë's readiness to fulfil a 'woman's simple duty'[12] of practical household work and the 'sacred pious charge'[13] of looking after her father. She also underplays Brontë's determined self-reliance, assuring her readers that her subject was no wilful rebel by pointing to her 'womanly seeking after protection on every occasion, when there was no moral duty involved in asserting her independence'.[14] Her anxiety to establish Brontë's female normality also makes her give particular prominence to her emotional needs. Presenting her as the victim of loneliness and lack of support, she eagerly offers romantic fulfilment as the remedy. Her confident assertion that 'one of the deepest interests of her life centres naturally round her marriage . . . that short spell of exceeding happiness . . . that calm sunshine of domestic peace'[15] not only attaches exaggerated importance to the event in the novelist's career, but also ignores Brontë's own misgivings. Those of Brontë's letters to her at this time which Gaskell quotes express clear if guarded reservations:

> my time is not my own now; somebody else wants a good portion of it . . . it generally seems the right thing . . . My own life is more occupied than it used to be . . . I believe it is not bad for me that [my husband's] bent should be so wholly towards matters of life and active usefulness; so little inclined to the literary and contemplative.[16]

Yet, either deliberately disregarding or blind to their significance, Gaskell enthusiastically calls them 'the low murmurs of happiness'.[17] Unwilling to mar her portrait by suggesting that marriage might not have been Brontë's ultimate fulfilment (though she does admit how 'narrow' Nicholls seems[18]), Gaskell is perhaps uneasy on her own account, confronted with questions which struck also at her ambiguous position as an artist/wife.

In her correspondence, Gaskell expresses more openly her ambivalence about women's roles and their inevitable complexities. As has been indicated, she never directly challenges the view that marriage and motherhood represent the highest, most natural female fulfilment. Her note to Charles Eliot Norton on the birth of the Nortons' son in 1863 is a good example of her faith in the blessings of maternity — 'I think she [Mrs Norton] has passed the acme of her life, — when all is over, and the little first born darling lies nuzzling and cooing by one's side'.[19] She is always delighted when her women friends marry, advising against long engagements and recommending that obedience to the dictates of the heart should take precedence over mere financial considerations wherever possible. Gaskell sees perfectly clearly, however, that women have needs and desires which no one state can wholly satisfy. For herself, she realises that she could never have endured Brontë's 'life of monotony and privation of any one to love',[20] yet at the same time she is uneasy about a friend's suggestion that she is ' "too much of a woman" in always wanting to obey somebody'.[21] As she explains to Tottie Fox, she has within her several selves in conflict with each other, but how

> am I to reconcile all these warring members? I try to drown myself (my *first* self,) by saying it's Wm who is to decide on all these things, and his feeling ought to be my rule, And so it is — only that does not quite do.[22]

If only, she continues, half-wistfully, half-ironically, we could return to

> the old times where right and wrong did not seem such complicated matters; and I am sometimes coward enough to wish that we were back in the darkness where obedience was the only seen duty of women.[23]

In more general terms, Gaskell recognises the inadequacy of simplistic idealism about matrimony. Permanent self-dependence for a woman is, she feels, at best a compromise, to be remedied if possible. Sisterhoods demonstrate their 'usefulness' only because they may help to alleviate 'the trials of many single women, who waken up some morning to the sudden feeling of the *purposelessness* . . . of their lives', and who, because they are 'deprived of their natural duties as wives and mothers, must look out for other duties if they wish to be at peace'.[24] As she bluntly admits, 'I think there must be a few years of great difficulty in the life of every woman who foresees and calmly accepts single life'.[25] In a later letter to Norton, she reiterates her belief that spinsterhood — for her, of course, an unexperienced state — is second-best: 'I think an unmarried life may be to the full as happy, *in the process of time* but I think there is a time of trial to be gone through with *women*, who naturally yearn after children'.[26] On the other hand, she is candid about the less rosy side of marital experience. Her energies dissipated in the concurrent exercise of her roles as wife, mother, and writer, she personally suffered the frustration of trying to do justice to all of them. Her letters are full of half-ironic complaints about the continual interruptions to her work caused by domestic crises, frequent visitors, and parish business, and her joky self-mockery about an early lesson of married life — 'as I happen to be a woman instead of a bird, as I have ties at home and duties to perform . . . why I must stay at home'[27] — fails to conceal an underlying regret for sacrificed freedom of movement. The seemingly irreconcilable conflict between domestic responsibilities and artistic urges is a frequent topic of her correspondence. Her remarks to Tottie Fox on the subject reveal, in their hesitancy and shifts of tone, her deep-seated ambivalence:

> One thing is pretty clear, *Women*, must give up living an artist's life, if home duties are to be paramount . . . I am sure it is healthy for them to have the refuge of the hidden world of Art to shelter themselves in when too much pressed upon by daily small Lilliputian arrows of peddling cares; it keeps them from being morbid . . . I have felt this in writing . . . so assuredly a blending of the two is desirable. (Home duties and the development of the Individual I mean) . . . but the difficulty is where and when to make one set of duties subserve and give place to the other.[28]

Echoing Brontë and Sewell, she tries to resolve her dilemma here by arguing that each individual must find out her appointed work and do it, but a later letter indicates her continuing uncertainty about the 'right' exercise of a woman's talent. She advises her correspondent, a would-be writer, to put family duties first, but she also confesses the undeniably attractive lure of absorption in one's art. Interestingly, she bases her attempted reconciliation of the two in this case on the feminists' method of justifying female employment;

a woman will write all the better, she argues, for having '*lived* an active and sympathetic life' through experiencing 'the interests of a wife and mother'.[29]

Gaskell's doubts about the exercise of female energies did not deter her from establishing her own economic independence from the mid-1850s onwards, taking charge of her own earnings and deciding what to do with them. Neither did they prevent her from recommending a tougher version of womanhood than that dear to much of her age. She was concerned that her daughters should develop into sensible, self-reliant young women, and explains to a correspondent that Florence (her third daughter) needs to be wooed into intellectual activity so that she will not 'fall into "young-lady-life" '[30] or stagnate in domesticity. Though cherishing her children's company, she knows the importance of careers for girls; she is prepared to let Meta train as a nurse or even venture into the dubious world of the female artist:

If she really and persistently wished it, I think, at her age, I should think it right to yield, for I believe she has great genius for it; and as, if she had married her life would have been apart and separate from mine, so I think she has a *right* to make it now.[31]

The important point here is her recognition that womanly individuality must be allowed to flourish. Gaskell also joins with Sewell and Eliot, among others, in deploring the inadequacy of current female education. She writes that she has rejected one school for Marianne because its chief areas of instruction are good manners and ladylike deportment;[32] she warns her daughter that if women are to avoid being told that it is absurd for them to 'meddle' with politics, they must make sure that their opinions are grounded on sufficient knowledge.[33] Read in the light of these observations, one of her most apparently anti-feminist statements becomes an oblique commentary on poor educational opportunities for women rather than an admission of her sex's intellectual shortcomings:

I would not trust a mouse to a woman if a man's judgment was to be had. Women have no judgment. They've tact, and sensitiveness and genius, and hundreds of fine and lovely qualities, but are at best angelic geese as to matter requiring serious and long scientific consideration.[34]

Gaskell's response to the more radical of feminist proposals shows the characteristic two-mindedness of her age. She admits that she is '*not* a friend of Female Medical Education',[35] and she confesses her inability to conquer her innate distaste for uncompromising protestors like Barbara Bodichon who pit themselves 'against the established opinions of the world'.[36] Yet, despite her initial reluctance, she agreed to sign Bodichon's petition for a Married Women's Property Act, and one of her closest friends, Tottie Fox, was an enthusiastic champion of women's rights. As ambivalent in this area as on the question of women and marriage, Gaskell most clearly reveals her unresolved doubts in her attitude towards the age's most revered symbol of female heroism, Florence Nightingale. She deeply admires Nightingale for her combination of intellectual powers and almost saint-like single-mindedness. At the same time, she is uneasy about the conditions on which her achievement is based: Nightingale's 'great work' has been made possible only because her sister, Parthenope, has taken on all home duties for her[37] — Nightingale, she implies, has been lucky because she has been released from the kinds of conflict which she herself and so many others have continually to face. Gaskell also demurs at the psychological implications of such a success story. Nightingale's triumph has been at the cost of normal womanly instincts; apparently untouched by romantic yearnings, and unfemininely rigid in character, she embodies for Gaskell the paradox that a woman who dedicates herself to a great cause may be emotionally deficient:

> That text always jarred against me, that 'Who is my mother and my brethren?' — and there is just that jar in F.N. to me. She has no friend — and she wants none. She stands perfectly alone, half-way between God and his creatures.[38]

Significantly, she 'quarrels' with Nightingale's proposal that children be brought up in crêches; that, for Gaskell, 'exactly tells of what seems to me *the* want'.[39] It is perhaps ironic that Gaskell's conservatism actually penetrates below the image of idealised womanhood — saintly, self-sacrificing, serving — which Nightingale embodied for so many of her contemporaries, to point out that only by being unlike other women has this female pioneer been able to implement her aspirations. The penalty, Gaskell feels, is too great, yet she realises that it may have to be paid if women are to free themselves from restrictive ideologies.

* * *

As with most Victorian women novelists, Gaskell's work reveals a division between life and art. She does not integrate into her fiction all the dichotomies of her own experience. There are, for instance, no working wives in her novels who suffer the conflict between domesticity and professionalism; marriage as an institution is never directly challenged; and her heroines rarely indulge in conscious questioning of sexual roles. Nevertheless, almost all of her work touches on the issue of female self-expression, often in the context of romantic relationships which she subjects to penetrating scrutiny. Her refusal to be wholly bound by conventional assumptions, which leads her into certain areas of 'unwomanly' subject-matter, also colours her portrayal of womanhood, thus modifying her apparent conservatism.[40] In order to discuss this aspect of her fiction, it is most helpful to group it thematically. The first group, what have been termed the 'social problem' or 'purpose' novels — *Mary Barton* (1848), *Ruth* (1853), and *North and South* (1855) — though ostensibly devoted to contemporary social and industrial issues, also investigate the possibilities of female self-assertion, with their heroines revealing surprisingly 'unfeminine' energies. The second group is made up of those works, most notably *Sylvia's Lovers* (1863), which portray unhappy marriages and whose depictions of tyrannous or myopic husbands undermine current notions of masculine superiority. The third group consists of those novels and short stories, including 'My Lady Ludlow' (1858), *Cranford* (1853), and *Cousin Phillis* (1864), which deal more directly with the theme of singleness versus marriage, and in which Gaskell looks more closely at the situation of women who for varying reasons exist outside normal romantic relationships. Finally, as a culmination of most of her major concerns, *Wives and Daughters* (1865) weaves her observations about womanhood into a wide canvas which combines social, sexual, and psychological analysis.

We have Gaskell's own word for it that *Mary Barton* was inspired by the state of industrial unrest in the Manchester of her day. Distressed by the 'seeming injustice of inequalities of fortune'[41] which she saw all around her in her husband's working-class parish, Gaskell hoped to open her readers' eyes to the ills of an economy dominated by laissez-faire doctrines. Her predominant 'social purpose' is indicated by her initial title for the novel, which, as she explains the year following its publication, reflected her primary preoccupation:

'John Barton' was the original name, as being the central figure
to my mind . . . and it was a London thought coming through the
publisher that it must be called *Mary* B. So many people overlook
John B.[42]

She decided, however, to adopt the 'suggestions' of her publisher
Edward Chapman, and on his recommendation entitled the work
'Mary Barton, a Manchester Love Story'.[43]

Chapman's preference for the second title was probably due to his
business acumen — the average reader was more likely to be
attracted by prospects of a heroine in a romantic situation — and
clearly Gaskell had reservations about the change. The alteration,
however, does not totally misrepresent the novel; as it progresses,
the focus is increasingly directed towards Mary, and towards the end
she becomes 'the central figure' while her father fades out of the
picture.[44] The themes of working-class suffering and the conflict
between employers and workers gradually give way to those of
romantic relationships and womanly power. These two strands
remain essentially separate, despite some attempt to link them
through plot contrivance; Gaskell does not, like Charlotte Brontë
in *Shirley*, unify her industrial and sexual concerns by suggesting
that women and workers suffer from similar disabilities. But her
treatment of her heroine reveals her attitudes towards women's
roles, and indicates that even while specifically propagandist on one
issue she was also concerned with matters more closely relevant to
her own sex. At the narrative level, Mary is an important figure; as
the daughter of the vengeful workman, and the beloved of the young
engineer who is falsely accused of the murder, she connects the two
parts of the story. She is also socially representative: as a working-
class girl she is the means of introducing such topics as the
desirability of factory employment for women, the seduction of
women workers by their employers, and the nature of male/female
relationships in industrial society. More significantly, she illustrates
Gaskell's interest in female individuality; her increasingly active participation in the story reflects her creator's tentative questioning of
current ideologies about womanly roles.

Perhaps because *Mary Barton* was Gaskell's first full-length
novel, it does not offer any direct challenges to romantic orthodoxies. Unlike some of her other fiction, it does not examine marital
unhappiness, and approves hetereosexual union. In Mary's own
case, the supremacy of love is fully acknowledged. Despite her early

refusal to consider Jem Wilson her sweetheart, and her coldness towards him, she is bascially tied to him emotionally even while eagerly receiving the flattering attentions of the glamorous Harry Carson. Ironically, her dogged rejection of Jem's proposal to her actually teaches her the true state of her feelings: 'it had unveiled her heart to her; it had convinced her that she loved Jem above all persons or things . . . she had discovered the passionate secret of her soul'.[45] Even before she discovers the real nature of Carson's attentions, she privately commits herself to Jem, and after patiently waiting until she can reveal her love, she finally achieves conventional female fulfilment as wife and mother.

Gaskell's orthodoxy is also evident in the novel's traditionally romantic formulations. The heroine, led astray by vanity, is lured by visions of social and material elevation: envisaging marriage to Carson, she 'dwelt upon and enjoyed the idea of some day becoming a lady, and doing all the elegant nothings appertaining to ladyhood' (121). Only after suffering and suspense is she finally united with her worthy lover. Within this conventional framework, Gaskell implements various traditional images of womanhood. Mary is idealised in terms of physical beauty (an interesting aberration in an otherwise admirably uncompromising study of the effects of environmental deprivation) and she frequently displays the noble feminine spirituality so central in Victorian sexual iconography. She supports the grief-stricken Mrs Davenport, comforts Mrs Wilson by 'the influence of those sweet, loving blue eyes, those tears of sympathy, those words of love and hope' (308), and tenderly watches over her father though knowing he is a murderer and the instrument of her lover's arrest. Her angelic qualities compare with those of the blind girl, Margaret, who not only reminds her lover, Will, of an angel but actually brings harmony 'like an angel of peace' (341). Mary herself regrets her departures from feminine virtues. Subdued by the knowledge of 'how much of her sorrow was caused by her having been vain, and foolish' (189), she abases herself for her unwomanly behaviour and seeks to restore her self-esteem through patience, penitence, and self-restraint, obedient to 'the whisperings of her womanly nature that caused her to shrink from any unmaidenly action' (224).

Despite this predominating romanticism, the radicalism which colours the novel's social/industrial themes also touches Gaskell's treatment of womanhood. Her portrayal of her heroine conveys her awareness of the struggles of female individuality in a male-dominated world. She makes it clear that Mary has a stronger sense of self than most girls. Being motherless, she enjoys independence and responsibility:

> She had more of her own way than is common in any rank with girls of her age . . . all the money went through her hands, and the household arrangements were guided by her will and pleasure . . . [Her father] left her, with full trust in her unusual sense and spirit, to choose her own associates, and her own times for seeing her associates. (58–9)

Though Gaskell ostensibly attributes much of Mary's subsequent suffering to the youthful wilfulness which such freedom encouraged, it is plain that like many of the other characters she admires her 'sense and spirit' (64), preferring it to the vapid listlessness of the Carson girls' young ladyhood. Moreover, she implies that Mary's dreams of a materially-enriching marriage are, for all their moral perilousness, the promptings of an ambitious spirit aspiring beyond a restrictive and degrading environment.

Womanly power is linked with emotional fulfilment later in the book, after Jem has been falsely accused of Henry Carson's murder. Strengthened by her realisation of her true feelings, Mary finds a new inner strength, now not to achieve her own selfish wishes but to save her lover. Inspired by her desire to redeem the disaster for which she sees herself responsible, she rejoices in the need to act: 'with the call upon her exertions, and her various qualities of judgement and discretion, came the answering consciousness of innate power to meet the emergency.' (302) The subversive implications of this urge are conveyed a few pages further on in striking metaphors:

> She was like one who finds a jewel of which he cannot all at once ascertain the value, but who hides his treasure until some quiet hour when he may ponder over the capabilities its possession unfolds. She was like one who discovers the silken clue which guides to some bower of bliss, and secure of the power within his grasp, has to wait for a time before he may thread the labyrinth. (311)

The male pronouns here, combined with the suggestion of secret, almost sinister strength, imply Gaskell's keen awareness that female energies must be kept concealed until their full force can be utilised. Mary's self-determination impels her nightmare journey to find Will Wilson, the witness whose testimony is the only means of clearing Jem: spurred on by the action itself, not by the hope of regaining Jem's affection — 'She longed to do all herself; to be his liberator, his deliverer; to win him life, though she might never regain his lost love, by her own exertions' (312) — she symbolises active rebellion not angelic passivity. As Margaret recognises, Mary's 'high, resolved purpose' (302) gives her 'more dignity, self-reliance' (318), so that having succeeded in her mission she has the strength to make public pronouncement in court of her true feelings for Jem. Paradoxically, Mary's guilt about her earlier unwomanly conduct actually leads her to act in a way 'unnatural' to her sex because it involves positive decision-making and defiance of masculine advice.

In this novel, such female power cannot last. Having saved her lover from the gallows, Mary collapses with brain-fever — that illness so popular with Victorian novelists — and retreats to a wholly dependent position. Traditional pieties are restored: content to 'put herself into [her friends'] hands with the trust of a little child' (443), she is ready to worship the man who looks upon her as 'his own, to guard from all shadow of injury with most loving care' (413). Gaskell pictures the happy couple with unashamed sentimentality, with '[Will's] face brightening into proud smiles, Mary Barton hanging on his arm, blushing and dimpling, with eyelids veiling the happy light of her eyes' (431), anticipating the final Utopian vision in Canada at the end of the book. Is this, we may well ask, the tough-minded girl who travelled alone from Manchester to Liverpool and combated dockyard aggressiveness?

Mary Barton, then, makes no great claims for a new view of womanhood or for ultimate female fulfilment other than through love and marriage, any more than it proposes political solutions for the social and economic problems it depicts. But by suggesting that women not only have potential power but may actually enjoy it, it does question Victorian assumptions about acceptable female behaviour. Gaskell's vision is still tentative, but the hints are there waiting to be expanded.

North and South may be considered a bolder and more accomplished version of *Mary Barton*; it deals with similar themes of industrial strife in the context of individual relationships, but its public and private themes are more organically interconnected. Characters are still to some extent representative, but they are also psychologically credible, enabling them to function on two levels. In contrast to Mary Barton, the heroine, Margaret Hale, is not a merely mechanical link between opposing masters and men but actually works to reconcile them; moreover, her personal affairs are intimately related to the wider issues with which she is concerned, so that far more directly than in the earlier novel Gaskell suggests that female power, centred in the responses of the heart, is the real revolutionary force in a male-dominated environment. Her original title for the novel, which up until late 1854 she refers to as 'Margaret',[46] confirms this character's centrality. Though she finally agreed with Dickens that it should be called *North and South* (after he had rejected her own dismal alternative of 'Death and Variations'), Gaskell obviously intended from the first that this heroine, unlike Mary Barton, should be the main dramatic agent in her story.

Margaret's role in *North and South* is complex. On one level, she acts as an observer who learns about industrial life in Manchester and through her investigations into the social and economic situation provides a gloss on contemporary issues. On another level, through her personal involvement with the individuals in these circumstances, she helps to bridge the gap of mutual misunderstanding between employers and employed. On a yet further level, she embodies aspects of womanly development, learning to understand herself and finally achieving emotional satisfaction in marriage. The interrelation between these levels indicates Gaskell's conviction (more optimistic than Eliot's) that the private life affects and is affected by the public life. Her sexual concerns are thus intrinsic elements in the social theme.

The novel centres on the relationship between Margaret and Thornton, the mill-owner, integrating the romance and industrial themes in personal terms. The characters' initial responses to each other are based on assessments deriving from the sphere each represents: Thornton is both angered by Margaret's haughty challenges to his dearly-held beliefs, and disturbed because 'she seemed to assume some kind of rule over him at once';[47] while she finds his materialism and lack of sympathy for the poor the signs of a 'tainted' nature (87). Their slow-growing love contrasts with other romantic attitudes in the novel. Margaret's cousin, Edith, engaged to Captain Lennox at the opening of the book, is a good-natured but rather silly young woman; more concerned with the glamour of her union than with its emotional value, she is content to play at being a soldier's wife, letting her husband treat her like a doll. Fanny Thornton is another somewhat feeble-minded creature whose main pleasure is the anticipation of orange-blossom and white veils. The attraction between Margaret and Thornton is built on very different assumptions, emanating chiefly from Margaret's unconventionality. Margaret represents a marked challenge to many accepted ideals of femininity. Stately rather than 'pretty', she questions where she doubts, chafes at restrictions on her liberty, and always speaks her mind. Refusing to identify with the generality of women, she prefers the 'animated conversation going on among the gentleman' (162) at a dinner-party to the ladies' boring discussions of dress. Her rejection of Henry Lennox's proposal is based partly on his patronising attitude towards women, as well as on her belief that friendship between a man and a woman must be allowed to flourish independently of sexual overtones, a point which is made more forcefully in her reaction to Thornton's proposal.

More than Brontë's and Eliot's independent-minded heroines, and more like Sewell's, Margaret ranges beyond traditional areas of female activity, undertaking responsibilities shirked by others. She tells her mother of her father's decision to move from Helstone to Manchester, because he is too cowardly to do it himself; she controls affairs during her mother's fatal illness; she negotiates the return of her exiled brother, Frederick, to England so that it remains a secret; and at her mother's funeral, she becomes the parent figure, supporting her grief-stricken father in her arms. Margaret's energies are unfeminine in the conventional sense. She not only intervenes in the public male world, but she also derives positive pleasure from such intervention. The most striking example of her extended sexual role is her defence of Thornton in front of the raging mob of hostile workers. Seeing, as he fails to, what has turned the men into maddened beasts, she converts her instinctive concern for individuals into indignation at his apparent cowardice. When, at her command, he goes to 'face them like a man' (177), she herself attempts bodily to protect him:

> She had lifted the great iron bar of the door with an imperious force — had thrown the door open wide — and was there, in face of that angry sea of men, her eyes smiting them with flaming arrows of reproach . . . She threw her arms around him; she made her body into a shield from the fierce people beyond. (178–9)

The battle images here (used without the ironic overtones of the descriptions of 'Amazonian' power among the spinsters of Cranford) suggest masculine strength; though Margaret retreats wounded, she has triumphed both physically (Thornton escapes unhurt) and morally (she has shamed him into confronting the mob).

Significantly, Thornton himself cannot deal with the contradictions Margaret represents. Obsessed by her physical presence, he tries to defuse the force of her challenging selfhood by mentally casting her in a submissively romantic role; he imagines himself meeting her 'with his arms held out in entreaty that she would come and nestle there' (193), while at her mother's funeral he anticipates comforting her like a mother 'when her drooping infant nestles close to her, and is dependent upon her for everything' (269). Thornton feels both threatened and lured by her sexual power later when, as a magistrate, he inadvertently discovers that she has lied to the police about her brother's presence in England. He deals with the disturbing implications of his knowledge by having the case dismissed, thus rescuing Margaret from the shame of public falsehood and keeping her in the private world where he can act as her protector. At the same time, he is helplessly drawn by the idea of her physically. Unwilling to abandon belief in her 'pure and exquisite maidenliness', he suffers 'all sorts of wild fancies [which] chased each other like dreams through his mind' (270) and, believing her to have a secret lover, torments himself with the idea of her passionate sexuality. She becomes for him an image of disturbing duality:

> He dreamt of her; he dreamt she came dancing towards him with outspread arms, and with a lightness and gaiety which made him loathe her, even while it allured him. But the impression of this figure of Margaret — with all Margaret's character taken out of it, as completely as if some evil spirit had got possession of her form — was so deeply stamped upon his imagination, that when he weakened he felt hardly able to separate the Una from the Duessa; and the dislike he had to the latter seemed to envelope and disfigure the former. (331)

His helplessness in the face of this almost demonic female ambiguity is recalled at the end of the novel when he is rendered financially, if not overtly sexually, subordinate to her, needing her inheritance in order to start up his mill again.

Through Thornton's response to Margaret, Gaskell explores the implications of potentially annihilating female power. Through Margaret she expresses more overtly her reservations about certain ideologies of womanhood, and questions some traditional attitudes towards love and marriage. Though Margaret does not directly challenge the ideal of marital fulfilment, her experience of widened responsibilities teaches her that women must take a new view of their roles. Believing that she has lost for ever her chance of regaining Thornton's love, she acknowledges her other commitments, not in a spirit of self-sacrifice but rather in recognition that a woman must take 'her life into her own hands' (416). Like Dorothea Brooke in *Middlemarch*, Margaret undergoes a night of painful self-examination and learns

in those solemn hours of thought, that she herself must one day answer for her own life, and what she had done with it; and she tried to settle that most difficult problem for women, how much was to be utterly merged in obedience to authority, and how much might be set apart for freedom in working. (416)

This of course was a dilemma for Gaskell, as for many other Victorian women writers, and there is authorial approval behind Margaret's determination that, despite her cousin's fears that she will become 'strong-minded', 'as I have neither husband nor child to give me natural duties I must make myself some' (417).

Margaret's reaction to Thornton's proposal of marriage further reveals Gaskell's unorthodoxy. Already annoyed because she realises that her attempt to defend him from the mob will be viewed as an expression of love, whereas she regards it merely as an instinctive and impersonal act, she is deeply resentful of what she considers his offensive presumption. His offer, she knows, is inspired by his belief

'that my conduct of yesterday . . . was a personal act between you and me . . . you seem to have imagined that I was not merely guided by womanly instinct, but . . . that I was prompted by some particular feeling for you.' (195)

Margaret's indignation derives partly from the reconogition that men inevitably interpret women's behaviour in sexual terms, and though Gaskell, with psychological astuteness, implies a degree of self-deception in her heroine — Margaret's anger is a convenient means of disguising to herself the beginnings of her love for Thornton — she shares her heroine's protest. More subtly, Gaskell suggests her sense of the female fear of violation by aggressive masculinity. Margaret shudders at the knowledge of Thornton's passion for her:

> The deep impression made by the interview, was like that of a horror in a dream; that will not leave the room although we waken up, and rub our eyes, and force a stiff rigid smile upon our lips. It is there — there, cowering and gibbering, with fixed ghastly eyes, in some corner of the chamber, listening to hear whether we dare to breathe of its presence to anyone . . . she shuddered away from the threat of his enduring love. (198)

The association of sexual passion here with nightmare and terror evokes the idea of possession, even annihilation, with astonishing insistence; Thornton has 'mastered her inner will' (198) and her innate selfhood is threatened. Margaret's desire to clear herself to Thornton over her lie about Frederick is, too, based partly on her awareness that only in this way can she release herself from the power to intrude on her inner world which his knowledge gives him.

In the end, as with *Mary Barton*, Gaskell returns to the traditional ideologies. Margaret and Thornton are finally reconciled and united in marriage, though having achieved far more mutual understanding than the characters in the earlier novel. The romantic conclusion may seem rather sudden in terms of plotting; Gaskell was forced to compress her story when she discovered she had been allowed only twenty numbers of *Household Words* in which to complete it, instead of twenty-two as she had expected. But she felt that the suddenness was psychologically justifiable:

> I am not sure if, when the barrier gives way between 2 such characters as Mr Thornton and Margaret it would not go all smash in a moment, — and I don't feel quite certain that I dislike the end as it now stands.[48]

The ending is not without sentimentality, either, even though partially prepared for by Margaret's change of image in the second half of the novel. Her aggressive forthrightness gives way to more conventionally 'feminine' traits of hesitancy and nervousness, and she takes the self-deprecating view that she is 'not good enough' (435) for Thornton when he makes his second proposal. This is hard to harmonise with her earlier determined individuality. But the union between the two lovers represents more than mere romantic stereotype. Their interchange has been mutually beneficial: Margaret, in teaching Thornton the need for better communication between men and masters, has learnt to assert herself more effectively; Thornton, in helping Margaret to recognise her emotional needs, has gained understanding of the individual. As in the marriage between Jane Eyre and Rochester, successful matrimony here depends on balance and sympathetic interaction; had Gaskell had more space, she might even have proposed a role for Margaret as manageress of Thornton's new workers' refectories.

Gaskell's other 'social purpose' novel, *Ruth*, deals more specifically than *Mary Barton* or *North and South* with an issue of direct female concern — the fallen woman. Yet, ironically, in contrast to these two whose theme of industrialisation provides a springboard for the wider question of sexual roles, *Ruth*'s particularity confines Gaskell to a relatively narrow treatment of womanhood. Because she is dealing with a topic which, as she was well aware, demanded extremely delicate handling, she is more cautious about approaching the subject of female independence and self-assertion. Understandably, she cannot cast her heroine as an overt rebel, since this would defeat her aim of breaking down sexual prejudices. Her radicalism lies in her choice of subject-matter and in her presentation of Ruth as a basically good woman; but only through traditionalism — portraying her heroine's gradual re-integration into society through motherhood, self-sacrifice, and devotion to others — can she hope to achieve her purpose.

Ruth has to be idealised in conventionally feminine terms because she symbolises victimisation by male exploitation and double standards of morality. She is beautiful, but not vain; her outer perfection is matched by inner purity and innocence; her capacity for love is totally selfless. She is also shown as a creature of heightened moral sensibility. After she has been rescued by the Bensons, she prepares to do penance for her 'sin', with 'soft, yet dignified submission',[49] and she continually queries her own worthiness as a mother and, later, a teacher. Gaskell is careful to point out her continuing humility, even after she has regained some self-respect; though she proves to have considerable intellectual ability, she remains completely unconscious of 'uncommon power, or unusual progress' (185), and has no personal ambition. Gaskell also vindicates her heroine through traditional images of womanly perfection. Elevated and saved by her self-abnegating maternal love, she seems to her son, Leonard, an angel with 'large, soft, white-feathered wings' (256), whose example helps him to accept his bitter lot:

> Her lovely patience, and her humility, was earning its reward . . . her quiet piety, bearing sweetly the denial of her wishes . . . called out his reverence at last . . . and thus softly she was leading him up to God. (380)

At the end of the novel, as a sick-nurse defying the terrors of the typhus epidemic, Ruth becomes a madonna-figure, encircled, in the grateful eyes of her patients, by a saint-like aura. Her final self-sacrificial heroism in nursing her fever-ridden betrayer climaxes her redemption through martyrdom, a consummation considered somewhat extreme even by some of Gaskell's staunchest admirers.[50]

In its prime intent to plead that 'to every woman who, like Ruth, has sinned should be given a chance of self-redemption — and that such a chance should be given in no supercilious or contemptuous manner, but in the spirit of the holy Christ' (347–8) — then, the novel exploits idealised patterns of female behaviour. Paradoxically, Gaskell's orthodoxy is a means of making her unorthodoxy more palatable. But even within this framework, she looks quizzically at other, less obviously contentious, contemporary assumptions about sexual roles. One of these is the notion of male superiority, attacked also by fellow-novelists such as Sewell and Craik. Gaskell's most obvious target is of course the seducer himself, Henry Bellingham, whose shabby behaviour is not only essential to the plot but also highlights the glaring injustice of double-standard sexual morality. Spoilt, self-centred, and shallow, he is both emblematic of masculine insensitivity and represents a creature of a lower order than that symbolised by Ruth's womanhood.[51] The tyrannical and self-righteous Mr Bradshaw, who has forced his wife and children into either deceit or ill-suppressed rebellion, illustrates another kind of masculine deficiency — lack of sympathy or self-perception — while his son, Richard, too weak to resist the temptations of criminal gain, forges the signature of the father who has so brow-beaten him. Even ostensibly good men in this novel reveal limitations: Mr Benson is morally strong, but practically indecisive; and Mr Farquhar, enthusiastically envisaging Ruth, whom he thinks he would like to marry, as 'a calm serene soul, fashioning the body to angelic grace' (305), is, on learning of her past, too bound by social values to feel other than 'thankfulness that he had escaped a disagreeable position, and a painful notoriety' (367), in having had his proposal refused.

Gaskell defies convention, too, in her overt admiration for sturdy female self-reliance. Central here is Ruth's refusal of Bellingham's offer to 'make up' to her, many years later, by marrying her. Ruth's rejection of him, though not an ideological stand against male oppression since it derives largely from the desire to protect her son from such a father, is nevertheless a denial of conventional morality.[52] Though prepared to submit to social ostracism and personal hardship as penance for her 'sin', her self-respect will not accept the code which argues that she should legally unite with her seducer and become 'respectable' . As we have seen, Ruth's final redemption is enacted through pseudo-wifely devotion, but Gaskell's contravention of a social morality in favour of a more sympathetic and individualistic one here shows her independence of mind.

Apart from Sally, the Bensons' doggedly self-determined servant, whose eccentric justifications for her singleness are merely comic interpolations in the narrative, the only other instance of female assertiveness is Jemima, Bradshaw's daughter. Unconventional and rebellious, she defies her father by championing Ruth. Ultimately she is schooled into normality by her marriage to Farquhar, though this does not occur without considerable inner questioning on her part; pride and anger at being 'managed' or disposed of as if she were material property co-exists in her with a desire for protection, and she accepts Farquhar only when quite sure of his love. Though Jemima achieves the traditional womanly satisfaction denied Ruth, Gaskell implies that the relationship will not crush her heroine's individuality — as she remarks *in propria persona*, 'similarity of opinion is not always — I think not often — needed for fulness and perfection of love' (373).

In her more direct examination of marriage in her novels, Gaskell employs a strategy common among those Victorian female novelists who seek to express dissent from current matrimonial ideologies. Of course not only the women writers of the period dig below the glossy surface to uncover the miseries beneath. Dickens mercilessly exposes the mutual torments of marital union effected as a business contract, and Thackeray pinpoints the sufferings of wives subjected to their husbands' selfish egoism. But whereas the male novelists usually criticise a particular distortion of the ideal, the female novelists have a much broader sense of how the hypocrisies of romantic ideologies fall heaviest upon their own sex; as they are well aware, not only do wives suffer more than their spouses from the unromantic actualities of married life, but a man who remains single is rarely accused of eccentricity or unnaturalness like the much-abused spinster. Gaskell, like Anne Brontë, Sewell, Craik, and Eliot, recognises that women's marital experiences are frequently quite different from popular conception. Like theirs, her unhappy wives are victims, partly of exploitation, partly of social attitudes and conditions which have bred in them delusions as fatal to happiness whether nobly idealistic or selfishly materialistic.

Gaskell's short stories which deal with marriage range from those which give an essentially traditional view to those which offer a more positive challenge to it. 'The Manchester Marriage' (1858), for example, contains a meek, docile wife who is wholly prepared to be implicitly obedient to her reliable, kindly husband. In 'Right at Last' (1858), the faithful wife remains loyal to her husband, even after discovering that he has concealed the fact that his father was an exiled convict; here traditional womanly devotion extends into a positive assertion of moral and social courage, as she persuades him to admit publicly his secret and brave the ensuing disgrace. Others of Gaskell's stories strike out more directly at the sufferings of women in disastrous unions. One of the narratives of 'Morton Hall' (1853) tells the story of a proud girl subdued into loving a dominating man 'with all the wild strength of her heart',[53] only to be abandoned by him after marriage and subsequently imprisoned as a madwoman. 'The Grey Woman' (1861) depicts, somewhat melodramatically, the indelible psychological scars of a wronged wife. The heroine (who tells her own story in a manuscript letter) marries an elegant but mysterious Frenchman who flatters her by his attentions; unable to escape the net in which she has been trapped 'through my own timidity and weakness',[54] she is increasingly terrorised by his iron will. Finally discovering that he is a ruthless brigand who is likely to murder her, she and her maid escape disguised as a tailor and his wife — a defiance of male tyranny which, ironically, relies on sexual conventions. But her bitter experience has permanently crushed her; though later she remarries, this time an older father-figure, she lives on as a mere shadow, her personality extinguished:

I lived in . . . deep retirement, never seeing the full light of day

. . . my yellow hair was grey, my complexion was ashen-
coloured, no creature could have recognised the fresh-coloured,
bright-haired young woman of eighteen months before . . . They
called me the Grey Woman.[55]

This is one of Gaskell's most vivid symbolic representations of the
destructiveness of male treachery. In 'Six Weeks at Heppenheim'
(1862), such marital sufferings are averted because the heroine,
Thekla, is persuaded in time that the man she feels she ought to
marry because she can 'be his salvation for earth and heaven'[56] is a
blackguard. Here Gaskell punctures the false ideal of self-sacrifice
which may motivate a woman; Thekla realises 'she would be doing
wrong instead of right if she married a man whom she had entirely
ceased to love'.[57]

Gaskell's stories concerned with marriage rarely penetrate its
complexities, partly because they are slight in plot, and partly
because in many of them the historical setting and simply-drawn,
almost emblematic, characters give a remoteness to the narrative. In
Sylvia's Lovers (1863), her most detailed and uncompromising scrutiny of matrimony, both setting and characterisation contribute to
her achievement. Placed in a period remote from Gaskell's own
peculiarly self-obsessed age, the story deals with simple characters,
of a class unaccustomed to self-analysis, thus starkly outlining the
suffering and disappointment which it portrays. In addition,
because the heroine does not encounter the mid-Victorian woman's
problems of 'redundancy' or the conflict between domesticity and
public activity, her dilemma becomes more representative of the
fundamental disharmonies of sexual relationships.

Gaskell's treatment of the topic in the novel is divided into an
analysis of romantic motivation and response and a portrayal of
marriage itself. With the first, she sets up contrasts between her
main characters. Sylvia herself, combining the simple, instinctive
passions of a child with the innate sexual awareness of a woman, is
at first barely conscious of emotional needs, and, without desiring
any particular alternative, has no positive matrimonial ambitions.
Her natural delicacy finds Molly Corney's unashamedly pragmatic
motives for 'pick[ing] up a measter'[58] distasteful, and disinclines
her for similar self-gratification. Initially, she regards neither her
worthy cousin, Philip Hepburn, nor the glamorously heroic speck-
sioneer, Charley Kinraid, as a prospective husband; she finds Philip
unmanly because he works in a draper's, and is irritated by his

persistent attentions, while her earliest idealisation of Charley centres on the belief that he is Molly's true love. As her emotions deepen, she comes to associate Philip with a somewhat wearisome friendship which imposes undesired obligations on her, whereas Charley's growing attractiveness arouses her almost against her will. Her differing response to the two men is well imaged by her behaviour at the Corneys' New Year's party: she is unable to play the flirt with Charley as the game of forfeits demands, feeling instead 'a new strange state of happiness not to be reasoned about, or accounted for' (150); in contrast, Philip seems to her a kind of dreary conscience, gazing at her with reproachful eyes as she guiltily tries to avoid him.

Sylvia's contrasting reactions signal Gaskell's awareness of the tragic dichotomy, imposed on women by social and moral pressures, between natural responses and obedience to external conditions. Both Sylvia's hero-worship of Charley and her ready dismissal of Philip are, Gaskell implies, deficiencies of judgment, but neither incorporates traditional notions of domestic womanly fulfilment. Her impulsive and passionate capitulation to Charley takes her into a dream world where she can project the two of them 'into a dim, glorious future of life' (208). Her chill indifference to Philip, whom she regards as different 'in every point' from 'her ideal husband' (128), makes her hostile to any suggestion of a long-term relationship. Her final acceptance of him is joyless and unhopeful. Her spirit broken by the rumour which Philip has deceitfully allowed to stand that Charley has disappeared for ever, she is gradually worn down by her own loneliness and her cousin's relentless wooing. Distressed by her mother's querulous urgings, and realising that she needs masculine support, she deliberately denies the instinctive side of her nature and commits herself passively, from a sense of duty:

> she obeyed his expressed wishes with gentle indifference, as if she had no preferences of her own . . . she met him quietly in all the arrangements for the time of their marriage, which she looked upon more as a change of home . . . than in any more directly personal way. (330, 334)

Gaskell focuses less on Sylvia's moral guilt in accepting a man she does not love than on her helplessness; choice for the woman here becomes obedience to overweening circumstances, a condition shared by many of Kavanagh's, Sewell's, and Eliot's heroines. The Hardyesque fatality of plot (Sylvia does not find out about Charley's seizure by the press-gang until he returns after she is married) highlights the dangers of taking duty as an ethical imperative with regard to women's emotional experience.

Gaskell examines the stressful paradoxes of this experience from another angle with Hester Rose, the young shop-assistant who works with Philip.[59] Hester's portrayal in many ways rests on more conventional assumptions about women and romance. In love with the blithely oblivious Philip, she has to subdue her jealousy of Sylvia and channel her unreciprocated emotion into sacrificial martyrdom and self-denying service. Knowing that she is only a friend to Philip, she helps to achieve union between him and the unwilling Sylvia, and 'crav[ing] for the affection which had been withheld from her' (347), she hushes 'her own private rebellion . . . into submission by her gentle piety' (417). Hester is presented in traditional terms, both as a thwarted single woman, denied the normal avocations of wifehood and motherhood, and as an angelic figure, acting as an agent of peace and support, like 'a star, the brightness of which was only recognised in times of darkness' (362). She wins Sylvia over by her selfless devotion to her after Philip has fled in shame on Charley's return, and the barriers between them are finally broken when she confesses her love for Sylvia's husband. Even at the last, having effected a reconciliation between the estranged couple, she remains an isolated figure, denied participation in their last meeting: ' "Oh, Lord God Almighty!'' said she, "was I not even worthy to bring them together at last?'' And she went away slowly and heavily' (498). Hester's saintly but self-abnegating spinsterhood represents a more orthodox attitude towards female roles than does Sylvia's unwilling wifehood. Gaskell does, however, show in her some of the toughness we have already seen in Mary Barton and Margaret Hale. Hester's refusal to compromise her feelings by accepting a lover for whom she has no passion both indicates her emotional strength and contrasts favourably with Sylvia's eventual capitulation to Philip. Set against the vitality 'of those who are led by the passionate ebb and flow of impulse', her nature, 'guided solely by obedience to principle' (488) may seem pitifully thin, yet Gaskell makes us admire her resolution (she refuses to be her ex-suitor's bridesmaid, for instance) and self-respect. Finally, in bringing up Sylvia's child after its mother's death, and in founding almshouses in the town, she makes a more permanent mark on history and the outside world than any other character in the book.

Gaskell's depiction of marriage in this novel not only uncompromisingly analyses marital disharmony but also punctures falsifying images. There are no ideal marriages here: the reported unhappiness of Hester's mother's union with a ne'er-do-well sailor ironically spurs Philip's self-deluding determination to save Sylvia from a similar fate; Sylvia's parents' marriage, based ostensibly on conventional sex-roles, remains stable only because Mrs Robson is prepared constantly to humour her 'domestic Jupiter' (51). The disastrous relationship between Philip and Sylvia most forcefully substantiates the matrimonial anti-idyll. Gaskell comes closest to Eliot here in her depiction of psychological torment and in her inclusion of the male viewpoint, underplayed by novelists such as Anne Brontë and Sewell, who chiefly focus on the wife's suffering. Having already suggested a contrast in male attitudes towards romance — Charley's warm but essentially thoughtless love is set against Philip's constant but selfish devotion — Gaskell looks critically but not coldly at the intolerable dilemma of a man who achieves his heart's desire only at the cost of moral probity. She is fair to Philip: she praises his energy and perseverance in 'a rare and constant love that deserved a better fate than it met with' (129); she shows his worth when he helps Sylvia and her mother after Robson has been committed for his part in the riots; and, like Eliot with Tito in *Romola*, she reveals how easily the sophistical thinking engendered by desire can convert dishonesty into self-justifying necessity. Yet she never blurs over his emotional and moral deficiencies. In contrast to Charley, who, perhaps because he is more patently an instrument in the plot, is not directly marked as culpable, Philip's weaknesses tell heavily against him as suitor and as husband. He deliberately blinds himself to the unsuitability of a match between himself and Sylvia:

> it was the one subject on which he dared not consider, for fear that both conscience and judgment should decide against him, and that he should be convinced against his will that she was an unfit mate for him. (128)

He also, for all his apparent gentleness, betrays a typical masculine myopia with regard to women. He is oblivious to Hester's love, and persists in treating Sylvia as a child rather than a woman capable of deep-rooted feeling. Once married, cheated of his anticipated reward, his guilty secret gnawing at his heart, he becomes both pitiful and despicable, a disappointed husband who has created his own hell.

In presenting Sylvia's side of the case, Gaskell broadens her range of implication. Whereas Philip's self-engendered wretchedness is peculiar to his own situation, Sylvia's misery symbolises that of all her sex entrapped in loveless marriages. Her dual inheritance — an almost fatalistic sense of duty from her mother, a wilful passionateness from her father — represents the dichotomies of female personality which women cannot reconcile. Though Gaskell makes clear both the self-indulgence of Sylvia's obsession with Charley and the inhumanity of her bitter vindictiveness towards Philip, she paints the nightmare of her married life with disturbing acuteness, especially in the chapter ironically entitled 'Happy Days'. Sylvia, fretted by the petty trivialities and proprieties of urban domestic life, and tormented by her husband's desperate attempts to win her affection, longs to return to 'solitude and open air and the sight and sound of the mother-like sea' (350) which image not only her lost freedom but also her lost love. Her, hopelessness and sense of alienation are only exacerbated by her creed of passive obedience:

> She did not know what else she could have done . . . but, at the same time, it was like lead on her morning spirits when she awoke and remembered that the decision was made, the deed was done, the choice taken which comes to most people but once in their lives. (351)

Moreover, though stressing the mutuality of suffering, Gaskell pinpoints the difference between male and female experience in this respect:

> even in the most tender and stable masculine natures, at the supremest season of their lives, there is room for other thoughts and passions than such as are connected with love . . . Philip had other thoughts and other occupations than those connected with his wife during all this time. (357)

Women, Gaskell implies, have no such outlet.

In this novel, then, Gaskell undertakes a much more penetrating analysis of matrimony than in any of her earlier works. On occasions, she speaks in her own voice in order to generalise about the experiences she is describing, further reminding us of Eliot. She argues, for example, that most people discover the gap between the anticipation and the actuality of 'long-desired [marital] happiness' (343), and that 'the resisting forces which make all such harmony and delight impossible are not recognized by the bystanders, hardly by the actors' (395). She is also much more open about her ambivalent attitude to matrimonial ideologies. Maternity, she claims, strengthens and 'saves' Sylvia, but it also further estranges her from Philip; likewise, she shows how a woman's experience of so-called male devotion may embitter her towards the sex as a whole — a form of disillusionment which in fact confers a dignified maturity on her heroine: 'I'm speaking like a woman; like a woman as finds out she's been cheated by men as she's trusted, and has no help for it' (443-4). Ultimately, it is through relinquishing the support of matrimony that Sylvia attains real individuality. Trained by suffering, she develops self-respect and courage; she stands on her own, acting as father and mother to her child, and with her moral sympathies broadened. The ending, like that of *Ruth*, with the woman tending her betrayer on his death-bed, may seem a last-minute reversion to sentimental idealism; but here, though the couple are temporarily reconciled in love, the woman is the survivor. Gaskell takes us no further into Sylvia's self-dependent widowhood, but she has suggested a new pattern of sexual roles. Women, she hints, may well be happier on their own than absorbed by romantic involvement.

Gaskell's treatment of single women — those who either remain romantically uninvolved, or who are betrayed in love and subsequently make their way in life alone — reveals the same ambivalence which we have seen in her general views on female fulfilment. But it is in this area of her writing that her unorthodoxy most strikingly co-exists with her conservatism. In various and often unexpected ways she challenges conventional notions of womanly dependence and 'relativity', and voices her own creed of female self-expression. Her depiction of women on their own in her short stories ranges from the conventional to the radical. Many are narrated by spinsters, usually telling someone else's history. In this, these single women demonstrate the duality of their state: their artistic separation from the main action symbolically enacts their own personal isolation, while their roles as 'tellers' make them active creators and instigators. 'The Doom of the Griffiths' (1858) is presented by a single woman who is an authoress in secret (a pointed comment on the deviousness imposed on female creativity); in

'Morton Hall', two spinster sisters give the account of events; the unmarried narrator of 'My French Master' (1853) lives alone abroad, energised by the characters about whom she writes; 'My Lady Ludlow' (1858) utilises multiple female narrators, most of whom are unmarried and whose story-telling gives a focus to their lives. Though none of these is a professional writer, together they represent Gaskell's awareness of the potential of alternative female occupation.

Gaskell's portrayal of singleness often relies on stereotype. On the one hand, she clings to the traditional image of the old maid as a somewhat absurd figure, odd in appearance and manner; on the other hand, she subscribes to the more sentimental view of the spinster as a pathetic creature, sometimes ennobled by self-abnegation and dedication to others. 'Mr Harrison's Confessions' (1851) shows an uncharacteristic failure of taste in its account of the series of misunderstandings which the central character undergoes, as several desperate women try to lure him into matrimony. The story is amusing but too close to caricature for comfort, from a feminist point of view. The final section of 'Morton Hall' draws on a similar source of humour. The current inhabitants of the hall are three elderly maiden sisters, notable for their contrasting eccentricities: one is haughtily self-important, one is a faded beauty with a penchant for poetic utterance, and one is unpredictable in dress and temper. Their matrimonial ambitions render them additionally absurd. Miss Annabella's looks have led to predictions of a good match, but fate has decided otherwise:

> Her sisters were angry with her for not having married some great rich gentleman; though, as she used to say . . . how could she help it? She was willing enough, but no rich gentleman came to ask her.[60]

Miss Dorothy has also 'done her best' in the marriage market — 'With not half the good looks of Miss Annabella, she had danced with an honourable at Harrogate three times running'[61] — but with the same lack of success.

In contrast to this slightly uneasy satire, Gaskell elsewhere takes a more sentimental approach to singleness. The narrator of 'The Doom of the Griffiths' is a 'poor pale governess'[62] who, unaccustomed to attention, is overwhelmed with nervousness when asked to read her story. The first of the narrators in 'My Lady Ludlow' is an elderly woman crippled from youth by a hip disease; having taught herself to look upon her exclusion from active life as a necessary discipline, she now plays the role of sympathetic sofa-invalid, bringing sweetness and light to others. The sacrificial role of the single woman is stressed again in 'Morton Hall', where the heroine gives up her chances of marriage to devote herself first to her brother, then to her profligate nephew, finally dying of malnutrition so that the younger man may have enough to eat.

'The Well of Pen-Morfa' (1850) and 'Libbie Marsh's Three Eras' (1847) explore more fully this notion of blessed self-denial. In the former, the beautiful young Welsh girl, Nest, crippled for life from a fall, is abandoned by her fiancé; an old Methodist preacher helps her to overcome her bitterness and teaches her to develop a new altruism:

> 'Henceforward you must love like Christ; without thought of self, or wish for return. You must take the sick and the weary to your heart, and love them . . . You do not require pity. You are powerful enough to trample down your own sorrows into a blessing for others; and to others you will be a blessing.'[63]

Here the notion of female strength is directed to self-denying ends; Nest takes a half-witted girl to live with her and is rewarded by the idiot's slavish devotion. In 'Libbie Marsh's Three Eras', the heroine is a self-dependent orphan whose physical unattractiveness cuts her off from the normal expectations of womanhood:

> [she had] hardly even the natural though hidden hope of a young girl's heart, to cheer her on with the bright visions of a home of her own at some future day, where, loving and beloved, she might fulfil a woman's dearest duties.[64]

Holding marriage sacred (like Sylvia, she deplores a friend's casual attitude towards it), she finds a substitute for biological maternity by befriending a crippled boy. After his death, she extends her function as one of the world's 'viewless angels'[65] by going to live with his grief-stricken mother, refuting the charge that she has failed as a woman:

> as God has seen fit to keep me out of woman's natural work, I should try and find work for myself . . . I can see many a one

misses it in this. They will hanker after what is ne'er likely to be theirs, instead of facing it out, and settling down to be old maids; and, as old maids, just looking round for the odd jobs God leaves in the world for such as old maids to do.[66]

Libbie's down-to-earth pragmatism reminds us of Craik's and Sewell's realistic approaches to singleness. But it is weakened by its self-deprecating tone, and Gaskell's concluding vision of Libbie, with 'peace shining on her countenance' as she enacts her 'holy' purpose,[67] embodies all the sentimental idealism of the stereotype.

As has been indicated, Gaskell's belief that women were essentially made for marriage and motherhood prevented her from envisaging a really satisfying alternative, and an apparently unquestioning acceptance of self-sacrificial, morally ennobled spinsterhood is a prominent feature of many of her stories; in this respect, though delicately and warmly handled they are too conventional for notability. But in two tales Gaskell allows her art to speak for a more rigorous version of female self-dependence. 'Half a Lifetime Ago' (1855) tells the story of a strong, capable woman who runs her own farm, having been left isolated by circumstances. The pattern, familiar in outline, is given a new slant. Susan Dixon, loving her fiancé but also feeling responsible for her idiot brother, Willie, sacrifices her own feelings when her lover refuses to be burdened with the boy; she breaks off the engagement and dedicates herself to Willie, in an act which both commits her to loneliness and is a rebellion against male selfishness. Many years later, when by unlikely chance her ex-lover is killed in a snow-storm near her house, she not only carries his body to shelter and informs his family of his death, but takes the widow and her children to live with her. Despite her apparent conventionality as a deprived and self-martyring spinster, Susan is an image of female strength. She becomes the central controller of events, and if her life seems wasted in the normal sense it represents a female triumph in terms of personal choice.

The most memorable spinster in Gaskell's short stories is Miss Galindo, Lady Ludlow's clerk.[68] Though she is lightly satirised for her eccentricities, she is also presented with respect and admiration. She is refreshingly unorthodox about womanly roles, and briskly unromantic about marriage:

'I have long left off trying to conjecture what makes Jack fancy Gill, or Gill Jack. It's best to sit down quiet under the belief that marriages are made for us, somewhere out of this world, and out of the range of this world's reason and laws.'[69]

There are strong echoes of Sewell's Aunt Sarah here. Like the older woman, Miss Galindo not only believes that conventional notions of female fulfilment are cruelly limiting, but refuses to accept false prescriptions about womanly behaviour. She is Gaskell's most thorough-going portrayal of female involvement in a man's world. Employed as a 'professional', she battles to win the respect of Lady Ludlow's steward, and later of her lawyer who is 'inclined to treat her, in this capacity, with polite contempt';[70] having broken down the latter's arrogant prejudice, she enjoys being 'amusingly conscious of her victory over his contempt of a woman-clerk and his preconceived opinion of her unpractical eccentricity'.[71] Astutely aware of the strategies needed for survival in a male-oriented society, like Brontë's Shirley she deliberately adopts a masculine manner, while gloating over her secret female identity:

'I read the man. And, I am thankful to say, he cannot read me. At least, only one side of me. When I see an end to be gained, I can behave myself accordingly.'[72]

Miss Galindo's positive self-regard and exploitation of sexual orthodoxies for her own ends are paralleled in Lady Ludlow herself, who, though socially reactionary, manages her own affairs and maintains a stoutly individual outlook. With both these women, Gaskell shows us that she has faith, albeit cautious faith, in the capacities of female independence.

The retrospective setting of 'My Lady Ludlow' tends to point the reader away from contemporary application of its unorthodoxy; Miss Galindo and Lady Ludlow can safely be admired because they are anomalies in their own age and offer no direct challenge to mid-Victorian ideology. But if Gaskell wished to diffuse her radicalism in this way here, in *Cranford* (1853), her most direct and extensive treatment of women on their own, she comes much closer to her own day (the novel is set in the 1840s) thus achieving a more immediate relevance. Though she originally intended the first two chapters as a single, self-contained contribution to *Household Words*, she and her readers found her topic so attractive that she extended it largely;[73] the final novel-length work is her most detailed analysis of spinsterhood in her own society. Critical opinion is sharply divided as to its social and sexual implications. Some critics claim that the Cranford Amazons are deliberately shown as inadequate because they live in an all-female world, and that the men in the story, challenging this existence, finally triumph in the figure of the returned Peter Jenkyns.[74] In contrast, one recent feminist critic stimulatingly argues that Cranford represents a community of women which has progressed from the sphere of household management to that of government and which appropriates the normality it excludes; the victorious female spirit, embodied in Miss Matty, reigns over the outside economic and masculine universe.[75] Neither of these viewpoints takes adequate account of the pervasively distanced, ironic tone of the novel, Gaskell's means of expressing her essential ambivalence. As we shall see, though she recognises the strengths and integrity of this society, she does not wholly uphold this 'alternative' female lifestyle which runs counter to her own most treasured experiences.

Gaskell shows how much the town has achieved on its own terms. The Cranford ladies, for all their eccentricities, have successfully formulated their own code of living; responsible only to themselves, they can dismiss the arguments about sexual distinctions going on in the outside world. As Miss Jenkyns sniffs, 'she would have despised the modern idea of women being equal to men. Equal, indeed! she knew they were superior'.[76] Their 'very much acknowledged gentility' (41) is not an enfeebling propriety as much as a defence against contemporary materialistic values which threaten the individual. Moreover, their tactics of survival quite shamelessly employ duplicity, a conscious and self-protective role-playing which like all such strategies has its own inviolable rules. In Cranford, traditional female weaknesses are converted into strengths. Miss Matty, for example, vague and unbusiness-like though she appears, becomes a symbol of fine integrity in her unwavering insistence on taking personal responsibility for the bank's collapse:

> 'I don't pretend to understand business; I only know that if it is going to fail, and if honest people are to lose their money because they have taken our notes . . . then it will only have been common honesty in me, as a shareholder, to have given this good man the money.' (177)

Her individual defiance of inhumane commercialism also triumphs when, anxious not to injure the town's other tea-merchant, she consults him before setting up her own business. Her disregard of the principles of competition pay off for 'not only did Mr Johnson kindly put at rest all Miss Matty's scruples . . . but . . . he repeatedly sent customers to her' (200). Such female 'simplicity' (201), as the narrator's father scornfully terms it, succeeds where male efficiency fails.

The men in *Cranford* represent forces which must be weakened or destroyed. Miss Pole's colourful cynicism sums up the prevailing attitude to the male sex:

> 'Well, Miss Matty! men will be men. Every mother's son of them wishes to be considered Samson and Solomon rolled into one — too strong ever to be beaten or discomfited — too wise ever to be outwitted.' (145)

Captain Brown, who, for all his kindness (interestingly, his self-denial towards his daughter is a typically womanly virtue) threatens Cranford with his new literary enthusiasms and open defiance of social etiquette, is killed off in a railway accident; though his end, Gaskell claims, was 'very much against my will',[77] it is nevertheless part of the novel's overall pattern. Mr Holbrook, Miss Matty's lover of former days, is swiftly removed from the story by the hand of death, remaining merely as a shadowy reminder of an unfulfilled romance. Signor Brunoni's magic 'tricks', quite different from Cranford's little self-conscious hypocrisies, disturb the society's stability, and his power has to be overthrown. Where Miss Pole's tactics — 'scientific explanations' culled from the Encyclopaedia and designed 'to explain and detect Signor Brunoni's arts' (132–3) — fail, nature scores; weakened by illness, 'pale and feeble . . . with his heavy filmy eyes', plain Samuel Brown is no longer a force to be reckoned with:

> finding out that he, who had first excited our love of the marvellous by his unprecedented arts, had not sufficient every-day gifts to manage a shying horse, made us feel as if we were ourselves again. (155)

The only two men who remain within the Cranford community are fixed in unthreatening roles. Mr Hoggins's professional medical activities compensate for, though do not excuse, his generic male weaknesses:

As a surgeon we were proud of him; but as a man — or, rather, I should say, as a gentleman — we could only shake our heads over his name and himself, and wished that he had read Lord Chesterfield's Letters in the days when his manners were susceptible of improvement. (154)

Moreover, by his marriage to Lady Glenmires, he is absorbed into a safely separate matrimonial sphere. Peter, Miss Matty's long-lost brother, comes back to Cranford only when he has redeemed his youthful transgression; his boyish prank of dressing up in his elder sister's clothes and pretending to be nursing a baby hardly warrants his father's severity, but it suggests a typically masculine obliviousness to female sensibilities which is never fully overcome. Though he 'saves' Miss Matty and restores her to her private world, his unconscious tactlessness about her failed romance with Holbrook ('You must have played your cards badly, my little Matty, somehow or another' 213) betrays his inherent deficiencies. And despite the fact that he is the ultimate agent of social harmony among the ladies, as a bachelor brother he is, like the clerical mentors of many Victorian women's novels, 'not exactly' male or female.[78]

Gaskell's women, then, most of whom are spinsters, with a sprinkling of widows, not only survive but flourish in their queendom. Her portrayal of a society which functions independently of the normal womanly occupations of wifehood and motherhood, and enjoys itself, calls in question the conventional notion of female singleness as penitentially self-abnegating. *Cranford* is, however, not a novel of radical protest, and it queries rather than opposes traditional assumptions. Its dualities of subject-matter and style — satire and sympathy, conservatism and challenge — reveal Gaskell's ambivalence about the conditions necessary for female fulfilment. The opening paragraph establishes the tone which Gaskell, through her narrational persona, Mary Smith, adopts towards her material:

For keeping the trim gardens full of choice flowers without a weed to speck them; for frightening away little boys who look wistfully at the said flowers through the railings; for rushing out at the geese that occasionally venture into the gardens if the gates are left open; for deciding all questions of literature and politics without troubling themselves with unnecessary reasons or arguments; for obtaining clear and correct knowledge of everybody's affairs in the parish; for keeping their neat maid-servants in admirable order; for kindness (somewhat dictatorial) to the poor, and real tender good offices to each other whenever they are in distress, the ladies of Cranford are quite sufficient. (39)

The combination of benevolently patronising irony and appreciative warmth here encapsulates Gaskell's two-sided attitude. These spinsters are both absurd and admirable; their self-determined preoccupations are trivial, ridiculous, and narrow-minded (as we have seen from her advice to Meta, Gaskell knew that women who tried to discuss literature and politics without reasons or arguments only added fuel to anti-feminist assertions of female brainlessness[79]), but they are also effective and commendable. Women can exist without male support, Gaskell implies, though in so doing they run the risk of becoming caricatures of themselves.

This balance between traditional and less conventional approaches characterises the novel as a whole. Gaskell's spinsters, communally formidable as they are, are not revolutionary dissenters. Most are single from circumstances, not from choice. While Miss Deborah Jenkyns's fierceness has put off all prospective suitors, Miss Matty's unresisting capitulation to her family's opinion that Holbrook was not good enough for her has doomed her to perpetual spinsterhood. Even the dragon-like Miss Pole, who expresses the most dogmatic anti-matrimonial sentiments in the novel, once, it is rumoured, gave 'very vigorous chase' (136) to the newly-arrived Rector, suggesting a less than whole-hearted self-containment. Gaskell makes it clear that this society represents accommodation to contemporary conditions rather than resistance to them.

Gaskell's characterisation also indicates her divergent responses to her theme. Though avoiding the extremes of caricature or sentimentality to be found in her short stories, she still implements some of the stereotypical images of the spinster. The younger Miss Brown, for example, before her marriage appears as an angelic figure, patiently bearing her sister's ill-temper and sacrificing her own interests to care for her. Miss Matty, gentle and absent-minded, combines the benevolence and peculiarities of the conventional old maid. In contrast, Gaskell further defuses the subversive implications of this self-reliant female world by focusing on its comic elements. In particular, she exploits one of the traditional spinsterly characteristics — its pseudo-masculinity. So Miss Deborah Jenkyns, the archetypal 'strong-minded' single woman, asserts her selfhood through 'maleness'. She not only dresses to look like a man, with her 'bonnet like a jockey-cap' (51) or a helmet, but has male accomplishments — knowledge of the classics and a Johnsonian style. Her steely individuality is expressed through a quasi-paternal authority which even after her death can reduce Miss Matty to submission, and which, Gaskell stresses, has almost totally destroyed her natural womanliness. The description of the Cranford ladies as 'Amazons' is in itself both mocking and eulogistic. The Amazons were a race of warrior females whose power lay in their assumption of masculine behaviour and denial of womanhood. The Cranford spinsters are not only very much mini-warriors, but actually display their inherent femaleness in episodes such as 'The Panic' where Gaskell's ironic deflation of their attempted bravery about the robbers shows how vulnerable they are.

Gaskell reveals her own dualistic attitudes, too, in indicating the discrepancies between doctrine and desire within Cranford society, in particular suggesting that its defensive strategies represent a suppression of normal emotional needs, not triumphant transcendence over them. The Amazons both overtly reject and secretly desire male intrusion. Captain Brown wins their reluctant admiration; Peter's social diplomacy has to be recognised. In addition, beneath their 'distaste of mankind' (45) and 'mysterious dread of men and matrimony' (64) they share universal female feelings. Both Miss Deborah Jenkyns and Miss Matty indicate their inherent womanliness by acknowledging the importance of sexual relationships, the former by finally withdrawing her opposition to the union between Major Gordon and Jessie Brown, the latter by allowing her servant Martha to have a 'follower'. The narrator's satirically ingenuous comments about the general excitement caused by the engagement between Mr Hoggins and Lady Glenmire carry the weight of general authorial observation:

> I have noticed that, just after the announcement of an engagement in any set, the unmarried ladies in that set flutter out in an unusual gaiety and newness of dress, as much as to say, in a tacit and unconscious manner, 'We also are spinsters'. (169)

Miss Matty is the most notable embodiment of the mood of regret which, alongside its social comedy, pervades the novel. She never recovers from the pain of her lost romance, wistfully recollecting 'the time when she had looked forward to being married as much as any one' (157). It is Matty's honesty about her unfulfilled hopes which makes her, in her creator's eyes, superior to the other Cranford ladies. Her recurrent dream of a child, a formulation of her 'strange yearning at my heart whenever I see a mother with her baby in her arms' (158) symbolises, albeit somewhat sentimentally, her frustrated maternity. And if she is the enduringly triumphant female spirit in the book, it is significant that her influence depends on a transference of normal womanly functions; Martha, Jem, and their child, the traditional family unit, transform her disappointment into the fulfilment of the next generation.

The dualities inherent in Gaskell's approach are highlighted by the role of the narrator, Mary Smith, who to a large extent represents the authorial position. She functions primarily as a device by which Gaskell can articulate her own two-sided attitudes. Mary is both within and without this society; as a frequent visitor to Cranford she values its customs and creeds, yet as a native of Drumble, the centre of a male-oriented commercial world, she can see the deficiencies of the female enclave. She shares many of the inhabitants' responses to events — their fear of the robbers and their incredulity at the Hoggins/Glenmires engagement, for instance — but her general tone of kindly satire shows up their absurdities and limitations. Her ambiguous role may hint at a possible future; as a young old maid who unites the dying all-female race of Cranford Amazons, with its roots in the past, and the next generation of women represented by Matilda Hearn and Flora Gordon, she may represent a new kind of female singleness, more outward-looking and less self-conscious. If Gaskell cannot contemplate a truly radical breed of Amazons who will overtly challenge the orthodoxies of wifehood and motherhood, through Mary she does at least make us consider the potential of 'going it alone'.

Like *Cranford, Cousin Phillis* is concerned with female self-identification and fulfilment, but here Gaskell focuses on the immediate effects of emotional isolation instead of on singleness as an established condition. Despite its apparent slightness, it is a much maturer work than the former, treating its subject with delicacy and understanding from which the earlier vein of comic satire is largely absent. It is also a more psychologically penetrating study of romantic betrayal and loss, in which Gaskell directly confronts the implications of female sexual maturity and the development from innocence to experience. Her central theme is more tightly woven into the whole than in *Cranford*, partly because it deals with a single episode, and partly because it is essentially one character's story.

Phillis embodies the dichotomies of early Victorian womanhood. She is first seen in terms of current angel/child iconography. To the narrator, Paul Manning, she seems almost saint-like, invested with a quasi-religious glory — 'The westering sun shone full upon her, and made a slanting stream of light into the room within'.[80] She is also infantine, dressing in girlish clothes, and prefectly obedient to her parents, unquestioningly accepting their authority. Her innocence is suggested by her association with the natural world. She is an intrinsic element in the idyllic Eden of Hope Farm (whose name is to prove so ironic), blending with the lives of animals and plants:

> standing under the budding branches of the gray trees, over which a tinge of green seemed to be deepening day after day, her sun-bonnet fallen back on her neck, her hands full of delicate wood-flowers . . . intent on sweet mockery of some bird in neighbouring bush or tree. (289)

Phillis is also, however, part of the more complex modern world. She is 'learned', not only reading Greek and Latin but capable of understanding the technicalities of scientific inventions. Her intellectual abilities, combined with her longing for further knowledge, place her beyond conventional notions of femininity, represented by her parents' narrowly protective attitudes and Paul's unease at her cleverness — 'She's more like a man than a woman' (252), he comments with prim naivety. As with Maggie Tulliver, the average masculine mind regards her as a kind of *lusus naturae* who will only be restored to normality by matrimony. As Paul's father condescendingly puts it, she is

> 'a scholar — but that can't be helped, and is more her misfortune than her fault, seeing she is the only child of a scholar — and as I said afore, once she's a wife and a mother she'll forget it all, I'll be bound.' (252)

Significantly, these abilities play a part in her subsequent suffering. Her mental energies, which make her 'a fitter companion' (249) for her father than is her domestically-oriented mother, draw her to Holdsworth because he not only shows signs of love but also encourages her intellectual aspirations: 'he directed her studies into new paths, he patiently drew out the expression of many of her thoughts, and perplexities, and unformed theories' (271). Phillis, then, is caught between two worlds, the traditional and the more progressive, and she represents her creator's uncertainty about women's roles in a changing society.

Gaskell's treatment of Phillis's romantic awakening, too, reveals her ambivalence about the emotional needs of women. Phillis's vulnerability is marked by her natural response to Holdsworth's attentions and by the physical manifestations of her increasing psychological turmoil — her fall into a decline when Holdsworth suddenly leaves for Canada, her brief period of blissful 'renewed life and vigour' (287) when Paul tells her that his friend loves her, and her near-fatal brain-fever on learning of his marriage. The implications of this experience are deliberately ambiguous. Phillis loses her innocent faith in the sacredness of love, her close relationship with her parents is destroyed, and she learns the untrustworthiness of men. Yet in order for her to reach full womanhood, she must go through the pain of sexual enlightenment; unlike Rebekah, to whom Paul, with unconscious irony, compares her, Phillis cannot remain in the Old Testament world of implicit obedience and female subservience. As with Sylvia, the anguish of disillusion is a necessary step towards human understanding as well as conferring new dignity and self-respect. At her moment of sharpest suffering, she defends Paul against her father's accusation that the young man has destroyed her 'peaceful maidenhood' (307), and she takes responsibility for her own sexual commitment. In so doing, she finally abdicates her filial role, thus achieving the individuality of adulthood. Her story embodies the paradox that the cost of emotional maturity may be emotional loss.

The ambiguity is reinforced by the ending. Directed by Betty, the family servant, to shake off her self-pitying lethargy — 'we ha' done a' we can for you . . . and more than you deserve, too, if you don't do something for yourself' (316) — Phillis resolves to overcome the stupor of her grief. Yet her renewal depends on a self-deluding belief in an idyllic past: her last words, with which the novel concludes, ring hollowly with unsubstantiated and regressive optimism:

'we will go back to the peace of the old days. I know we shall; I can, and I will!' (317)

Like Gwendolen at the end of *Daniel Deronda*, Phillis is offered no prospect of a future self-reliant existence, only a vague hope of spiritual regeneration. More honest than many of Gaskell's short stories in its refusal to propose a self-abnegating substitute for personal fulfilment, *Cousin Phillis* leaves us with a bleaker picture of female isolation.

In *Cranford*, Gaskell covers her ambivalence to a large extent by the comic tone, combined with a slightly patronising benevolence. She attempts to convey her belief that women can live and flourish without men, but she is not wholly convincing; she hedges about the emotional cost of independent womanhood, and, because of the nature of her artistic material, is neither able nor willing to carry us into a clearly-defined, less solipsistic future. In *Cousin Phillis*, she is more open about her ambivalence. Recognising that women can and may have to function without men, she acknowledges the pain and regret which may accompany such an existence. Phillis, like the sleeping beauty to which Holdsworth compares her, has to be awakened by a kiss which leads her not into the romantic world of marriage and sexual fulfilment but into a new, harsher world of personal responsibility. Gaskell asks pertinent questions in this book — does all-engrossing romantic love destroy the female spirit? are independence and sexual fulfilment incompatible? is emotional betrayal a necessary step to the achievement of womanly individuality? — but she admits that there are no easy answers. At the end, Phillis has no future; Holdsworth and Paul, the men of science, may go forward into a new age, but she stays in limbo between lost Edenic innocence and painful experience. The negative openness may seem chilling, but it faithfully represents Gaskell's admission of dualities.

Wives and Daughters (1865), Gaskell's last novel, is generally agreed to be her richest and most accomplished work, in scope and artistic maturity having much in common with Eliot's *Middlemarch*. It moves between the four main centres of The Towers (the aristocracy), Hamley Hall (the squirearchy), the Gibsons' (the professional middle class) and the Misses Brownings' (town society), thus encompassing social and geographical diversity; its references to contemporary political and scientific developments further extend its range. The plot unfolds against this background which influences but does not ostensibly predetermine character activity, so achieving a sense of realism. Events are intrinsic elements of the naturalistic chronicling and not evidently superimposed on it.

Whereas in *North and South*, for example, Gaskell brings the Hales to Manchester so that she can involve Margaret in the social and industrial confrontations, Molly Gibson's stay at Hamley Hall, while introducing her to new patterns of human behaviour as well as to her future husband, does not strike us as a piece of plot engineering, but is a perfectly plausible occurrence. The narrative technique, too, is more skilful here than in Gaskell's earlier fiction: she makes considerable use of 'point of view' and keeps direct authorial intrusion to a minimum, helping to create the impression of her characters' freedom.

As the title suggests, women-related topics are an important aspect of the novel. It incorporates many of the themes which Gaskell has already treated, such as disharmonious marriages, romantic delusions, spinsterhood, and female individuality. But there is now less sense that such topics are 'issues'. As we have seen, many of her novels and stories which cannot be classified as 'purpose' fiction are nevertheless predominantly concerned with matters of particular concern to women: marriage in *Sylvia's Lovers*, singleness in *Cranford*, for instance. In *Wives and Daughters*, Gaskell presents her 'women's themes' in the context of and closely woven into her whole fictional milieu, so that they call less attention to themselves. As, too, perhaps seems likely with a novel written when the author was in her mid-fifties, it is tinged with the conservatism of middle-age and in some ways seems less ideologically questioning than her earlier works. Gaskell appears more contented with the status quo, more tolerant of human fallibility, and more benevolently disposed towards social creeds and institutions. In many respects, her characters, especially the women, are fixed in defined roles and do not challenge sexual orthodoxies. The central heroine, Molly Gibson, remains in the domestic sphere, never venturing into the public world encountered by Mary Barton, Margaret Hale, Ruth (as the town's sick-nurse) or even Miss Matty in her shop. The novel traces her growth from childhood, her relationships with her father, stepmother, and step-sister, and her moral and emotional maturity which develops from involvement with family and close acquaintances, so her confinement to a small, private arena is appropriate. It does, however, seem to represent a diminution of female potential. In herself, Molly is less assertive than many of Gaskell's other heroines; though she learns to act and make decisions, her inner dilemmas do not express themselves in her outward behaviour. Much of her experience, too, is vicarious; one of her most important

roles is listener and carrier of messages. Her early reliance on paternal support is understandable, given her motherless state, but even
when she is no longer a child, she still seeks for her father's wisdom,
as when she is confronted with the Hamley family troubles — 'Her
father . . . would solve the difficulty — her father, whom she
always looked to as so clear-seeing and experienced'.[81] Significantly,
her eventual suitor is a man whom she has not only known since
childhood but to whom she is first drawn because he befriends and
advises her, and who remains for her a Mentor figure, 'a staff and a
stay in the troublous times which appeared to lie not far ahead'
(549). Far more than in other romantic unions in Gaskell's fiction,
their relationship is reminiscent of those in Jane Austen's work,
where husbands are often substitute fathers or brothers.

Wives and Daughters portrays many types of womanhood, but
none who offers notable resistance to conventional ideologies,
either with regard to female occupation or romantic relationships.
There are no women here such as Margaret Hale, Susan Dixon, or
Miss Galindo, enjoying the positive benefits of social and economic
independence. Gaskell, it seems, is not interested in pursuing the
theme of female self-reliance, in terms of community or of individuals, and indeed when she touches on the question of singleness she
hardly moves away from the stereotypical, whether the absurd or
the pathetic. Miss Eyre, Molly's governess, does little more than
introduce the predicament of the single woman forced by circumstances to seek employment; fleshed out just enough to give a picture of long-suffering patience, she soon disappears from the novel.
The drudgery of the teaching profession, one of the few openings
for self-supporting women, is dealt with again in a more comic vein
with Mrs Gibson, who is unusually honest with herself about her
motives for a second marriage:

> it was such a wonderful relief to feel that she need not struggle
> any more for a livelihood . . . (140) She looked to it [marriage] as
> a release from the thraldom of keeping school — keeping an
> unprofitable school with barely pupils enough to pay for house
> rent and taxes, food, washing, and the requisite masters. (156)

The subject, however, is not taken up further. Lady Harriet
Cumnor, an apparently self-determined spinster, is, for all her
strong-mindedness, confined to the responsibilities of her familial
and social position, and makes no forays into more feminist activity.

The most extensive depiction of spinsterhood in the novel is that of the Misses Browning, and this represents no advance on the gently satiric caricature of *Cranford*. The contrast between the two sisters is familiar, the elder assertive and somewhat formidable, the younger nervous and anxious. The distorting effects of their singleness are indicated by oddities of speech and dress, and their attitudes towards matrimony are always presented humorously. Miss Phoebe's misconceptions about Mr Gibson's 'intentions', for example, which inspire 'a little hope' (178) in her breast, are treated to rather cumbersome authorial mockery, while Miss Browning's crisp definition of marriage as 'a weakness to which some very worthy people are prone' (551) calls merely for a smile, not psychological understanding. In a novel which upholds the essential normality and overall satisfactions of marital union, there is no place for any more challenging version of female autonomy.

In some ways, then, *Wives and Daughters* seems Gaskell's culminating vindication of nearly thirty years of married happiness. It would, however, be misleading to suggest that it takes a wholly unquestioning approach to sexual relationships. The marriage theme in the novel is of structural as well as thematic significance, again reminding us of *Middlemarch*; Gaskell's juxtaposition of contrasting unions contributes to the complexities of plot as well as highlighting the diversities of marital experience. The apparent happiness of the Hamleys' union does not belie the damaging effect of conventional sex-roles. Though Mrs Hamley's husband adores her, and she is content to be the traditional female peacemaker and moral arbiter, Gaskell suggests that she 'would not have sunk into the condition of a chronic invalid, if her husband had cared a little more for her various tastes, or allowed her the companionship of those who did' (73); her unresisting adoption of compromise and self-sacrifice has created a stable marriage, but has also broken her spirit. The most penetrating depiction of matrimonial unease is that of the Gibsons'. Mrs Gibson, as we have seen, marries for her own satisfaction and has no scruples about disrupting the previous pattern of household life; despite Gaskell's satirical treatment of her social pretensions and moral elasticity, she makes us feel the devastating power of her smooth obstinacy which causes her husband so much unanticipated discomfort. Yet characteristically Gaskell shows us the faults on both sides. Mr Gibson's remarriage is primarily to provide himself with a housekeeper and Molly with a mother, and, while unable to remedy his error of judgment, he is uneasily aware of it.

Mr Gibson illustrates a typical masculine deficiency — the inability to understand women properly — which once more Gaskell makes a key element in her sexual debate. Though he loves Molly dearly, he fails to comprehend her emotional or her mental needs; as his creator shrewdly remarks, 'surgeon though he was, [he] had never learnt to anatomize a woman's heart' (442). In the same way, his bitter irritation at his domestic disharmony vents itself in sarcastic outbursts against his wife which penetrate even her thick skin and make her a temporarily pathetic figure:

> she saw she was often in some kind of disfavour with her husband, and it made her uneasy . . . she wanted to regain the esteem which she did not perceive she had lost for ever. (457)

Other men in the novel reveal similar limitations. We have already seen how Squire Hamley unwittingly crushes his wife's individuality. His son, Osborne, also displays insensitivity; his feminine manner and appearance do not incorporate conventional female virtues. Osborne cowardly refuses to tell his father of his secret marriage, thus condemning his wife to social and geographical isolation, and he is blind to the likelihood that his visits to the Gibson household will awaken delusive romantic expectations in its female hearts. Even Roger Hamley, the novel's ostensible hero, has his weaknesses; he is kind to Molly as a girl, but fails to recognise her worth as a woman who loves him, deluding himself instead with a sentimental vision of Cynthia Kirkpatrick, imaged by Gaskell with finely sardonic precision: 'with all a lover's quickness of imagination and triteness of fancy, he called her a star, a flower, a nymph, a witch, an angel, or a mermaid' (415). The irony is, of course, that for some time he fails to realise the power of Cynthia's witch- and mermaid-like qualities, and only after she herself has shattered his idealism is he ready to turn to Molly. Most of the male characters are treated sympathetically, and apart from Preston, whose role as villain is too patently mechanistic, they are not shown as solely responsible for lack of harmony in sexual relationships. The Cumnors' marriage, for instance, survives its vicissitudes only because of Lord Cumnor's compliance to his wife's more forceful personality. But even in this, Gaskell's most mellow work, her cool scrutiny penetrates the façades of sexual patterning to reveal the underlying anomalies.

Gaskell's examination of the romantic experience of young women is also formulated through structural contrast. The step-sisters, Cynthia and Molly, represent different kinds of female selfhood and differing responses to sexual commitment. Cynthia is, as she herself realises, a girl who has gone wrong because of bad upbringing. Conscious that her beauty is her only asset, and neglected by a mother whose example encourages her frivolous attitude towards love, she treats men as playthings created for her amusement — when she wants to be amused. Molly's ideal of an omniscient, guiding husband is anathema to her; her spirited individuality cannot bear the thought of restraint. Gaskell concedes admiration for her self-protective instincts and determined independence of mind — Cynthia represents a species which, in the vocabulary of Roger's scientific interests, is fitted to survive. She also acknowledges her vulnerability in a world of predatory men. Though Preston is unconvincing as a character, we understand Cynthia's fear of his power; for all her self-confidence, she is not strong enough to disentangle herself from the net of deception and exploitation into which her youthful folly has cast her. Further, Gaskell makes perfectly plausible her almost fierce resistance to deep emotion; her experience of betrayal and hypocrisy in sexual affairs have taught her to distrust 'too much love' (619).

Cynthia's ultimate situation seems ambiguous. Her rebellious energy is deflected into a conventional marriage with the socially desirable Mr Henderson, for whom she has no strong feeling and who is, as she expresses it, the '*juste milieu*' (657) between Roger and Preston. The union is appropriate and we can believe that she will be an adequate wife, but there is something suspect about her fate. Are we to see traditional 'relativity' as her reward or her punishment? Is there any intentional irony in the fact that the woman who affected to despise the romantic orthodoxies ends up in the most respectable of alliances? The openness here perhaps indicates Gaskell's unwillingness to make definitive judgment on Cynthia's attractive but unreliable vitality.

There is certainly nothing suspect about Gaskell's treatment of Molly's emotional experiences. Molly's character is in marked contrast to Cynthia's; shyer and less self-assertive, she is morally far stronger, and her developing womanhood is marked by spiritual as well as social growth. She can be outspoken and act decisively when necessary, though her energies are less stimulated by challenge than those of Gaskell's more lively heroines. She is, however, Gaskell's most psychologically credible and engaging heroine, and the hints of autobiography in her characterisation perhaps account for her lack of 'strong-mindedness'.[82] Molly embodies many of the conventional womanly virtues. She schools herself to accept her stepmother's bossy interference in her life, she abandons her own interests in order to further Roger's happiness with Cynthia, and she takes on the role of peacemaker left vacant at Mrs Hamley's death. And if in all this Molly is a true heroine of her time, she is rewarded in an equally traditional manner. Unlike Phillis, she is granted the fulfilment of her romantic desires; though the novel has no concluding chapter, we can be sure that Gaskell intended Molly and Roger to marry. In some respects this will be a 'modern' marriage: Molly's new self-reliance will make her a respected companion, not a downtrodden slave, and her husband, moving in a progressive world of exploration and changing values will, we feel, be less blinkered than his father or brother by restricting notions about female behaviour. The romantic closure is nevertheless Gaskell's final commitment to conventional womanhood. There is no suggestion that it represents reluctant accession to literary demands nor that she wishes to suggest anything other than future happiness for the couple. Paradoxically, Gaskell's maturest artistic achievement culminates in her most unequivocal statement of orthodoxy.

Notes

1. Letter to Lady Kaye-Shuttleworth, 14 May [1850]. *The Letters of Mrs. Gaskell*, ed. J.A.V. Chapple and Arthur Pollard (Manchester, 1966), p. 118.
2. The most thorough-going proponent of this thesis is Aina Rubenius, who in her *The Woman Question in Mrs. Gaskell's Life and Works* (Uppsala, 1950) claims that Gaskell found marriage irksome and detrimental to her personal development. Rubenius's arguments are, however, unconvincing.
3. Letter to Eliza Fox, 26 April 1850. Gaskell, *Letters*, p. 113.
4. *Memorials of Two Sisters: Susanna and Catherine Winkworth*, ed. Margaret J. Shaen (London, 1908), p. 23.
5. Eliza Lynn Linton, *My Literary Life* (London, 1899), p. 93.
6. Letter to Carlyle, 12 September 1851. *New Letters and Memorials of Jane Welsh Carlyle*, ed. Alexander Carlyle (London, 1903), vol. II, p. 29.
7. *Letters of Geraldine Endsor Jewsbury to Jane Welsh Carlyle*, ed. Mrs Alexander Ireland (London, 1892), p. 383.
8. Letter to Lady Kaye-Shuttleworth, 7 April [1853]. Gaskell, *Letters*, p. 228.
9. Letter to F.J. Furnivall, [6 December 1853]. Gaskell, *Letters*, p. 255.
10. Letter to Eliza Fox, 24 December 1854. Gaskell, *Letters*, p. 325.
11. Letter to George Smith, [? 1 October 1859]. Gaskell, *Letters*, p. 577.
12. E.C. Gaskell, *The Life of Charlotte Brontë* (2nd edn, London, 1857), vol. I, p. 151.

13. Ibid., vol. I, p. 319.
14. Ibid., vol. II, pp. 135-6.
15. Ibid., vol. II, pp. 273, 317.
16. Ibid., vol. II, pp. 317-19.
17. Ibid., vol. II, p. 317. Gaskell was so keen for Brontë to marry that she secretly negotiated with Lord Houghton to secure Nicholls a small pension so that his suit would be more acceptable to Mr Brontë. Her determined emphasis on Brontë's conventional femininity also reveals itself in the high praise she gives to Frances Henri in *The Professor*, Brontë's 'most *charming* woman . . . and a glimpse of that woman as a mother'. (Letter to Emily Shaen, [7 and 8 September 1856]. *Letters*, p. 410).
18. Letter to John Forster, [? 8-14 May 1854]. Gaskell, *Letters*, p. 282.
19. Letter to Charles Eliot Norton, 28 July [1863]. Gaskell, *Letters*, p. 709.
20. Letter to Lady Kaye-Shuttleworth, 7 April [1853]. Gaskell, *Letters*, p. 229.
21. Letter to John Forster, [23 April 1854]. Gaskell, *Letters*, p. 280.
22. Letter to Eliza Fox, [? April 1850]. Gaskell, *Letters*, p. 108.
23. Ibid., p. 109.
24. Letter to Lady Kaye-Shuttleworth, 14 May [1850]. Gaskell, *Letters*, p. 117.
25. Ibid., p. 118.
26. Letter to Charles Eliot Norton, 19 January [1860]. Gaskell, *Letters*, p. 598.
27. Letter to William and Mary Howitt, [May 1838]. Gaskell, *Letters*, p. 14.
28. Letter to Eliza Fox, [c. Feb. 1850]. Gaskell, *Letters*, p. 106. This foreshadows her comments on the similar dualities of Brontë's life as woman and author: 'a woman's principal work in life is hardly left to her own choice; nor can she drop the domestic charges devolving on her as an individual, for the exercise of the most splendid talents that were ever bestowed'. Gaskell, *Life of Charlotte Brontë*, vol. II, p. 50.
29. Letter [to unknown correspondent], 25 September [?1862]. Gaskell, *Letters*, p. 695.
30. Letter to Charles Eliot Norton, 27 August [1860]. Gaskell, *Letters*, p. 632.
31. Ibid.
32. Letter to Lady Kaye-Shuttleworth, 12 December [1850]. Gaskell, *Letters*, p. 138.
33. Letter to Marianne Gaskell, [7 April 1851]. Gaskell, *Letters*, p. 148.
34. Letter [to unknown correspondent], 31 October 1856. Gaskell, *Letters*, p. 419.
35. Ibid.
36. Letter to Charles Eliot Norton, 5 April [1860]. Gaskell, *Letters*, p. 607.
37. Letter to Emily Shaen, 27 October 1854. Gaskell, *Letters*, p. 317.
38. Ibid., p. 319.
39. Ibid., p. 320.
40. For a survey of 'patriarchal' critical attitudes towards Gaskell which belie her real achievement as a novelist and ignore her subversive attacks on Victorian ideals of femininity and marriage, see Dale Spender, *Man Made Language* (London, 1980), pp. 206-11.
41. Letter to Mrs Greg, [? early 1849]. Gaskell, *Letters*, p. 74.
42. Letter to Miss Lamont, 5 January 1849. Gaskell, *Letters*, p. 70.
43. Letter to Edward Chapman, 17 April 1848. Gaskell, *Letters*, p. 56.
44. Gaskell's outline for the novel makes it clear that Mary was always intended to have a prominent role in the plot. See Edgar Wright, *Mrs. Gaskell: the Basis for Re-Assessment* (London, 1965) for a discussion of the changes between the first draft and the final version.
45. Elizabeth Gaskell, *Mary Barton* (Penguin English Library, Harmondsworth, 1982), pp. 176-7. Subsequent page references are to this edition and will be included in the text.

46. It began serialisation in *Household Words* on 2 September 1854 and appeared in book form in early 1855. Gaskell refers to 'Margaret' in a letter of 1854.

47. Elizabeth Gaskell, *North and South* (Oxford, 1977), p. 62. Subsequent page references are to this edition and will be included in the text.

48. Letter to Anna Jameson, [January 1855]. Gaskell, *Letters*, p. 329.

49. Elizabeth Gaskell, *Ruth* (Everyman edn, London, 1967), p. 144. Subsequent page references are to this edition and will be included in the text.

50. Typical of this objection is that made by Elizabeth Barrett Browning, who, perhaps already projecting her own *Aurora Leigh* (1857), was particularly enthusiastic about Gaskell's bold choice of subject-matter — 'I am grateful to you as a woman for having so treated such a subject — was it quite impossible but that your Ruth should *die*? I had that thought of regret in closing the book.' Letter to Mrs Gaskell, 16 July 1853. In Ross D. Waller (ed.), *Letters addressed to Mrs. Gaskell by Celebrated Contemporaries* (Manchester, 1935), p. 42.

51. One of Gaskell's closest friends, Catherine Winkworth, felt that the authoress had been thoroughly successful with her portrait of Bellingham — 'one of Mrs. Gaskell's objects was to make her readers feel how much worse he was in every way than Ruth, although the world visited her conduct with so much heavier a penalty than his.' Letter to Eliza Patterson, 9 February 1853. In M.J. Shaen (ed.), *Memorials of Two Sisters* p. 101.

52. One of the earliest critics of *Ruth*, while praising Gaskell's depiction of the regenerative influence of 'hallowed motherhood', felt that it was Ruth's moral responsibility to marry Bellingham, since in so doing she could have stirred up the seeds of goodness in him ([J.M. Ludlow], '*Ruth*', *North British Review*, vol. XIX [May 1853], pp. 151–74).

53. Elizabeth Gaskell, *Lizzie Leigh and Other Tales* (London, 1913), p. 150.

54. Ibid., p. 249.

55. Ibid., pp. 296–7.

56. Ibid., p. 348.

57. Ibid., p. 349. This story, like several of the others which offer a rather soured view of marriage, was actually written *c.* 1858–9, at a time when Gaskell's eldest daughter, Meta, had just broken off her engagement to a man who had become 'no good', in her and her family's opinion. The incident probably heightened Gaskell's awareness of the pitfalls of matrimonial commitment.

58. Elizabeth Gaskell, *Sylvia's Lovers* (Oxford, 1982), p. 115. Subsequent page references are to this edition and will be included in the text.

59. As has often been pointed out, the contrast between Hester and Sylvia in this novel is remarkably similar to that between Dinah Morris and Hetty Sorrel in *Adam Bede*, published four years earlier. Like Hetty, Sylvia is childishly fond of admiration and charmingly wilful; she also resents the prudish sobriety of the grave, self-effacing Hester. She does, however, develop a maturity which Hetty never achieves. Gaskell never acknowledged Eliot's influence here, but she must have had the latter's work somewhat in mind when writing *Sylvia's Lovers*.

60. Gaskell, *Lizzie Leigh*, p. 172.

61. Ibid., p. 173.

62. Mrs Gaskell, *My Lady Ludlow and Other Tales* (London, n.d.), p. 244.

63. Gaskell, *Lizzie Leigh*, pp. 59–60.

64. Ibid., p. 370.

65. Ibid., p. 375.

66. Ibid., p. 394.

67. Ibid., pp. 398–9.

68. It is curious that Miss Galindo is the only instance in Gaskell's fiction of a woman doing 'male' work. Clerkship was in fact one of the possible spheres of female employment suggested by the early feminists. One wonders if Gaskell felt no hesitation in depicting such a figure in a story with a retrospective setting, because she

would not seem to be overtly championing contemporary feminist protest.

69. Gaskell, *My Lady Ludlow*, p. 184.

70. Ibid., p. 155.

71. Ibid., p. 155.

72. Ibid., p. 155.

73. It was to have appeared just in the December 1851 number of *Household Words* but actually ran until 1853.

74. See Peter Keating's Introduction to *Cranford* (Penguin English Library, 1978) pp. 7–26, and Martin Dodsworth, 'Women without Men at Cranford', *Essays in Criticism*, vol. 13 (1963) pp. 132–45.

75. Nina Auerbach, *Communities of Women: An Idea in Fiction* (Cambridge, Mass., 1978), 'Beyond the Family', pp. 77–97.

76. Elizabeth Gaskell, *Cranford* and *Cousin Phillis* (Penguin English Library, Harmondsworth, 1978), p. 51. Subsequent page references are to this edition and will be included in the text.

77. Letter to John Ruskin, [? late February 1865], Gaskell, *Letters*, p. 748.

78. This phrase is used by the forthright and unconventional Mrs Bradshaw in Sewell's *Journal of a Home Life* (1867), who somewhat shocks the narrator, Mrs Anstruther, by describing the local rector, a narrow-minded and stiff young cleric, as 'belonging to a race . . . [which] is "not exactly" ' male or female (52–3).

79. Letter to Marianne Gaskell, [7 April 1851]. Gaskell, *Letters*, p. 148.

80. Elizabeth Gaskell, *Cranford* and *Cousin Phillis* (Penguin English Library, Harmondsworth, 1978), p. 226. Subsequent page references are to this edition and will be included in the text.

81. Elizabeth Gaskell, *Wives and Daughters* (Penguin English Library, Harmondsworth, 1969), p. 630. Subsequent page references are to this edition and will be included in the text.

82. It has been suggested that Molly's distress at her father's second marriage represents Gaskell's recall of her own similar feelings when her father remarried, but since she never lived for long with him and his new wife, and there are no hints of resentment beneath her ostensibly happy childhood with her aunt, it is hard to substantiate this interpretation.

6 GEORGE ELIOT: CONSERVATIVE UNORTHODOXY

George Eliot is regarded as one of the 'giants' of Victorian literature, a critical evaluation which marks her out from the other
women novelists in this study. Her placement in the 'great tradition'
of nineteenth-century fiction has until lately tended to isolate her
from specifically gender-oriented treatment. Without obscuring the
importance of her formal artistry, recent critical discussions of her
work have, however, stressed her significance as a woman writer
concerned with issues of major concern to her own sex, an approach
which has proved very fruitful.[1] Not only do her novels suggest a
deep interest in the conditions of womanhood, but her own life
reflects this interest, itself challenging many of the social and sexual
creeds of her day. Her questioning of contemporary ideologies
about women, while set in a wider social, political, and historical
context than that of most Victorian women novelists, establishes her
within the literary group which they represent, sharing assumptions
and modes of articulation.

Overtly, Eliot seems more of a rebel than most of her fellow
women writers. Her unorthodoxy took various directions. Though
she always recognised the necessity for some kind of faith, her break
with established Christianity made her less susceptible to supra-
human imperatives than those who, like Sewell, Brontë, or Gaskell,
sought to transcend their doubts by reference to a higher spiritual
authority. Her rejection of what she considered the restrictiveness
of mere forms had a profound influence on her personal life. Her
intellectual abilities, galvanised partly by her friends the Brays and
the Hennells who introduced her to German scholarship, gained her
entry into the male world of ideas. Defying the contemporary view
that extensive mental cultivation and self-assertion were unsuitable
for women, Eliot moved in a sphere in which one of her sex was
something of an anomaly. Established in London in the sexually
liberated Chapman household, she met and was influenced by a
variety of radical thinkers, including energetic workers for women's

rights such as Barbara Leigh Smith (later Bodichon) and Bessie Parkes. Her situation as a young single woman, independent of her family and holding a position of considerable responsibility as co-editor of Chapman's *Westminster Review*, represented far more of a challenge to social and sexual convention than the careers of most literary women of her day, with the possible exception of Eliza Lynn. Even Craik's sturdily self-reliant existence looks tame in comparison. The most ostensibly unorthodox element in Eliot's life is of course her 'irregular' liaison with George Henry Lewes which made her in the majority of her contemporaries' eyes an overt rebel,[2] a view which was never wholly erased even after her literary eminence had gained her social respect.

It would seem likely that Eliot's personal unconventionality would exhibit itself in her creative writing. Examination of her fiction, however, reveals an unexpectedly conservative attitude towards female roles. Indeed, in some ways her work is built more firmly on sexual orthodoxies than that of many other Victorian women novelists. She responded artistically to the paradoxes of her life by asserting traditional values, rather than demanding new patterns of female behaviour, perhaps because her own experience acutely heightened her awareness of the conflicting impulses of conventionalism and revolt and she was only too aware of the penalties, as well as the rewards, of active unorthodoxy. Her life contained more obvious tensions than those of the other novelists discussed here, since she endured the practical repercussions of dichotomies which they never directly had to face. The product of a conservative environment which inculcated the traditional pieties of kinship and respectability, she was torn by the opposing claims of family duty and responsibility to the self; the sense that she could not be both the dutiful daughter and sister, and the independent woman, originating in her alienation from her father over her apostasy and culminating in her estrangement from her brother over her union with Lewes, was fully obliterated only after her marriage to Cross had restored her 'normality'.

Furthermore, her career in the masculine-dominated literary world especially alerted her to the problematic dualities of female roles. Intellectually superior to Chapman, in her editorial capacity she advised, supervised, and criticised his work, having no hesitation in reprimanding him for what she regarded as business shabbiness.[3] Yet her dealings with him also reveal typically feminine qualities deriving from her constant inability to separate professional and emotional commitment.⁴ Though she did most of the real work on the *Westminster*, she was content to remain in the background behind his titular editorship, eager to disavow the idea that she was the real force behind the concern — 'I must protest against being regarded as responsible for anything in the management of his affairs beyond the mere letter-press of the Review'.⁵ It is also fairly certain that, with romantically-inspired self-abnegation, she allowed herself to be paid nothing for her editorial work apart from her own articles. A similar duality operated in her relationship with Lewes. Having helped him with his own work, she soon outstripped him in both financial and creative achievement, yet continued to shelter behind his protection, allowing him to handle her business affairs and to guard her from unwelcome publicity. Her position is strikingly paradoxical: as Virginia Woolf puts it, she

shudd[ered] back into the arms of love as if there alone were satisfaction and, it might be, justification, at the same time reaching out with 'a fastidious yet hungry ambition' for all that life could offer the free and inquiring mind and confronting her feminine aspirations with the real world of men.⁶

Eliot's relationship with Lewes, ironically enough, helped to strengthen her conservatism towards women's social and sexual roles. Convinced of the solemnity of the marriage tie, she regarded her own union as 'a sacred bond',⁷ even while well aware that in public eyes she was acting in deliberate defiance of conventional morality. Consciousness of the apparently revolutionary nature of her chosen path made her almost morbidly anxious to counter implications of iconoclasm. As she wrote to Cara Bray, 'Light and easily broken ties are what I neither desire theoretically nor could live for practically. Women who are satisfied with such ties do not act as I have done — they obtain what they desire and are still invited to dinner'.⁸ It is also important that her union offered her all the traditional matrimonial satisfactions; in contrast to Brontë's doubts about accepting Nicholls, or Gaskell's wry admissions of William's deficiencies, Eliot's expressions of her happiness with Lewes seem to conceal no murmurs of discontent. Indeed, despite the resultant social ostracism — in most instances temporary — Eliot's liaison brought her wider fulfilment than the marriages of many Victorian professional women. Unlike Brontë, Craik, and Gaskell, who encountered husbandly opposition or indifference to their literary endeavours, she was positively assisted by her consort; she would probably never have written fiction at all without Lewes's initial encouragement and consequent dedication to her success, over-protective though it may seem. Her anomalous position also gave her unusual scope for individual self-expression. Not only freed from the kind of family duties imposed on single women like Sewell, Brontë, and the young Mulock, Eliot was also liberated from the more irksome elements of wifehood. Fretted by the more mundane aspects of domesticity, such as worries about curtains and carpeting,[9] she was only too glad to escape these responsibilities, partly by relegating them to the ever-willing Lewes, partly by lengthy sojourns abroad. Her childlessness, too — probably deliberate — exempted her from the continual interruptions to creative activity which Gaskell, as minister's wife and mother, experienced. At the same time, of course, as legally a spinster, she could enjoy the advantages of that state; she could have left Lewes at any moment, and though she gave unstintingly to help him support his family, she had complete control over her earnings. In many ways, in fact, she gained the best of both worlds.

The paradoxes and dualities of Eliot's life were both the fruits of her personal uncertainties and themselves reinforced the ambivalence about female roles revealed in her letters, journals, and essays. Like many of the early feminists, Eliot was cautious about taking too radical a stance on the 'woman question'. To some extent she supported the call for reform. She recognised the hardships faced by self-supporting women, sympathising with her old school-teacher, Maria Lewis, now an over-worked governess, and with fellow-writer, Eliza Lynn, who 'has great difficulty in obtaining any literary employment'.[10] She saw the need for improved education and employment opportunities for women, admiring the energetic campaigns of friends and acquaintances such as Barbara Bodichon, Octavia Hill, Florence Nightingale, and Bessie Parkes to achieve those ends. She signed, albeit without great enthusiasm, Barbara's petition to Parliament about married women's property rights, regarding it as an important step in a long ladder of reform 'stretching far beyond our lives'.[11] She approved of Bessie's *English-woman's Journal* because it '*must* be doing good substantially — stimulating women to useful work, and rousing people generally to some consideration of women's needs',[12] and she supported the foundation of Girton College, because 'the better Education of Women is one of the objects about which I have *no doubt*',[13] and because 'women ought to have the same fund of truth placed within their reach as men have . . . the same store of fundamental knowledge'.[14] Eliot, however, always avoided a revolutionary position. She kept her sights on practical issues and specific measures; refusing to be drawn into more ideological partisanship, she declared herself unable to give 'a judgment on the Woman Question',[15] partly because of its complexities and partly because she regarded innovations like Women's Suffrage as 'an extremely doubtful good'.[16] Indeed the ironic tone of her mocking references to women lawyers in Russia and women professors in Italy[17] indicates a basic scepticism about the desirability of radical change — a hesitancy which we have already seen in all the other women novelists.

At the root of Eliot's cautiousness lies a profound ambivalence towards womanly functions. She herself veered between commitment to and withdrawal from a specifically female orientation. As a writer, she identified herself with male culture, not only adopting a male pseudonym (a means of artistic freedom as well as a strategy of sexual concealment) but often speaking with a 'masculine' voice. She felt more at ease with men than with women, and sought to separate herself from the obvious limitations of her own sex; in her well-known essay, 'Silly Novels by Lady Novelists', for example, she is relentlessly ironic about the varieties of 'feminine fatuity'[18] of which lesser female writers than she are capable. Her lack of enthusiasm for radical feminist programmes derives from a belief that women are incapable of dealing with social and political ideas; with brisk decisiveness, she declares to a feminist friend that ' "Enfranchisement of women" only makes creeping progress; and that is best, for woman does not yet deserve a much better lot than man gives her'.[19] Her focus on what is 'good for human nature generally' rather than 'what is specially good for women'[20] may indicate a breadth of mind capable of transcending sexual parochialism, but it also suggests a deep need to evade identification with womanhood in general, emanating from a curious mixture of self-hatred and intellectual arrogance.

At the same time, Eliot gave conscious allegiance to the traditional female virtues. She sought the approbation of other women for her union with Lewes, as if to assure herself of her own womanliness, and her willingness to alleviate the torments of artistic self-doubt by sheltering behind Lewes seems a typically 'feminine' reaction. While she rejected differentiation between the sexes in terms of practical function, she unhesitatingly acceded to a moral and psychological distinction. She based this distinction on traditional womanly qualities such as domesticity, self-abnegation, and feeling. In a letter to Emily Davies, she points out 'the spiritual wealth acquired for mankind by the difference of function' and the benefits of women's 'special moral influence':

> We can no more afford to part with that exquisite type of gentleness, tenderness, possible maternity suffusing a woman's being with affectionateness, which makes what we mean by the feminine character, than we can afford to part with the human lore, the mutual subjection of soul between a man and a woman.[21]

Several of her early essays stress the 'distinctively feminine condition'[22] — its maternal emotions, its involvement in 'the smallest offices of domestic care or kindliness',[23] and its power to stimulate men to higher things. Eliot's panegyric to Mme de Sablé, for representing the 'rare combination' of 'ease and grace . . . an intellect that men thought worth consulting . . . warm affections, untiring activity for others, no ambition as an authoress, and an insight into *confitures* and *ragouts*',[24] could almost have come from the lips of the esteemed Mrs Ellis. It would be tempting to see a parodic masculinity in some of this, but it clearly reflects Eliot's own vindication of 'normal' womanhood now that she was herself enjoying such a role for the first time. According to Cross, too, Eliot 'was, and as a woman she wished to be, above all things feminine'.[25] Her increasing respectability within established society only strengthened her adherence to such ideals.

Eliot's acceptance of the womanly ideal, associated with domestic virtues and a subordinate or supportive function, is linked to her conviction that wifehood represents the noblest type of femininity. Her own life proved the accuracy of the character-reading made by the phrenologist, George Combe:

> She was of a most affectionate disposition, always requiring some one to lean upon, preferring what has hitherto been considered the stronger sex, to the other and more impressible. She was not fitted to stand alone.[26]

Even her earliest and piously self-righteous dismissals of romance and matrimony fail to sound wholly convincing:

For my part, when I hear of the marrying and giving in marriage that is constantly being transacted, I can only sigh for those who are multiplying earthly ties which, though powerful enough to detach their hearts and thoughts from heaven, are so brittle as to be liable to be snapped asunder at every breeze.[27]

Throughout these youthful letters, we find strong hints of Eliot's need for emotional fulfilment — fears of loneliness and isolation, an awareness of her own unattractiveness, and 'a consciousness that I am a negation of all that finds love and esteem that makes me anticipate for myself — no matter what'.[28] She cannot listen to 'the voice of foreboding that has long been telling me, "the bliss of reciprocated affection is not allotted to you under any form" '[29] with quite the calm contentment of her own Dinah Morris in *Adam Bede*; more characteristic is her empathy with Margaret Fuller's deep desire for a sweetness in life which no intellectual conquests can give her.[30] An offer of marriage in 1845, refused because of the young man's suspected insanity, caused Eliot distress as much from feelings of guilt as from emotional disappointment (interestingly, this is one of the grounds on which she wholly approved of the duty of 'abstinence from marriage'[31]), but a year later the joke letter which she sent to Sara Hennell, pretending to be a German professor recently arrived in Coventry in search of a learned, rich and ugly wife, contains a ruefulness beneath its self-mockery; "Miss Evans" 's acceptance of the professor, 'thinking that it may be her last chance',[32] may well have signalled the real Miss Evans's anxieties.

Long before she became involved with Lewes, Eliot was constantly demonstrating her desire for romantic fulfilment. Her passionate outpourings to Herbert Spencer about the 'hopeless wretchedness' he has caused her, for example, reveal — with penetrating self honesty — her state of mind:

I want to know if you can assure me that you will not forsake me . . . I could gather courage to work and make life valuable, if only I had you near me . . . Those who have known me best have always said, that if ever I loved any one thoroughly my whole life must turn upon that feeling, and I find they said truly.[33]

Her eventual union with Lewes confirmed the predictions of her old friend Charles Bray that she was 'likely to devote herself to some *one* other, in preference to all the world, and without reference either to the regularity or legality of the connection'.[34]

Eliot found in marriage the answer to her emotional needs; after four months of living with Lewes, she writes, 'I think it is impossible for two human beings to be more happy in each other',[35] and her subsequent letters and journal entries contain frequent references to the increasing blessedness of her 'sort of Siamese-twin condition' with her husband.[36] It is not surprising, then, that she extolled the state which was so fulfilling for her. Her half-ironic, half-wistful envy of Sara Hennell's independent life expresses a rarely-heard nostalgia for her previous freedom:

> She has been making the most of the advantages that belong to a single state over a married one (there really are some such advantages over and above what St. Paul saw) — the power of opening the window at any hour of the night without dread of giving a husband a sore throat, and the power of sitting up as long as she likes without danger of disturbing his rest.[37]

She was conscious that being single could harden a woman; after her marriage to Cross, she writes, 'I shall be a better, more loving creature than I could have been in solitude'.[38] Her own happiness created in her a reverence for matrimony — 'if there be any one subject on which I feel no levity it is that of marriage and the relation of the sexes',[39] she declares solemnly — and she was always delighted when others found the same happiness, desiring, like Gaskell, that young people should have the ideal of marriage 'in their minds as a goal'.[40] For her, 'the love of men and women for each other must always be more and better than any other';[41] the 'marriage state . . . holds the highest possibilities of our mortal lot'.[42] Eliot's union with Cross marks the final demonstration of her inability 'to stand alone'; though she at last gained social and family approval through it, this was not her main motivation, and if she ever had doubts about her second commitment, made after prolonged dedication to another, we have no evidence of them. Having vindicated her romantic idealism, she lived it out to the end.

*　　*　　*

Despite the centrality of courtship and marriage in Eliot's fiction, romantic relationships play a rather different role in her work than in that of most of her fellow women writers. Whereas in the novels of Brontë and Craik, for instance, examination of the significance of emotional fulfilment in women's lives is a self-contained theme, Eliot sets her discussion of the topic in a wider social and philosophical context. In her novels, marriage is both a key to and a touchstone for modes of human behaviour. While sexual commitment is an intrinsic element of her characters' aspirations, it is also a moral testing-ground, a means of exploring the individual's relationship to the outside world and to more universal issues. Her treatment of marriage also frequently transcends distinctions of gender, presenting men and women as equal units in a more general pattern of interconnectedness. Her characters' moral growth depends on their recognition of this pattern; by broadening their sympathies and becoming aware of the needs of humanity at large, they merge their personal and sexual identities in a vision of fellowship. Marriage in Eliot, then, takes on a symbolic significance: as an emblem of social cohesion it represents an order which must be respected and upheld; as an embodiment of moral response it represents a measure of individual worth.

The extended thematic function of marriage in Eliot's fiction reinforces the impression of her orthodoxy; indeed, it would be both inappropriate and counter-productive for her to challenge radically the institution which she implements and sanctifies as an instrument of ethical evaluation. Her treatment of female roles also reflects her growing conservatism, and is coloured more by her thankful commitment to a state of sexual relativity than by the dichotomies of her earlier experience. There is in fact less sense of tension or duality in her work than in that of many other Victorian women novelists who led more ostensibly conventional lives. For one thing, Eliot seems little interested in the specific question of female singleness either as a social problem or a psychological state. Few of her women characters function in the outer world of employment. We gain a fleeting glimpse of the governess's life with the meekly self-effacing Miss Merry in *Daniel Deronda* (1876), over whom Gwendolen so unashamedly tyrannises, and Eliot touches on the artistic profession with Deronda's mother, and with Armgart in the poem of that name, but the struggles of women in her own time to achieve social, financial, and legal independence are never given prominence in her work. In this respect, she is reflecting her cautiousness towards contemporary feminist activity rather than drawing on her own pre-marital experiences. It is significant that one important ramification of the mainly retrospective settings of her novels is that the heroines are even more socially and economically restricted than the

women of her own day. One of her most active female contemporaries, Florence Nightingale, draws attention to this feature
of her work; ignoring *Middlemarch*'s historicity, she crisply attacks
Eliot for the smallness of opportunity which she grants Dorothea:

> This author now can find no better outlet for the heroine . . .
> *because* she cannot be a 'St. Theresa' or an 'Antigone', than to
> marry an elderly sort of impostor . . . Yet close at hand, in actual
> life, was a woman . . . and if we mistake not, a connection of the
> author's, who has managed to make her ideal very real indeed.[43]

This woman was Octavia Hill, whose sister had married Lewes's
eldest son, and whose admirable work in London's East End was
well known to Eliot. Nightingale's sense that Eliot was not being
quite honest in her depiction of her character's thwarted aspirations
— 'Could not the heroine, the "sweet sad enthusiast", have been
set to some such work as this?'[44] — would have been even more
strongly aroused by *Daniel Deronda*, Eliot's only contemporaneous
work. In this novel, Gwendolen, left isolated and emotionally shattered, is offered no positive sphere at all in which to enact the
newly-developed desire to do good which Deronda has instilled in
her.

If Eliot fails to take full cognisance of female singleness as a
problematic current phenomenon, she is at least sparing in her use of
stereotype when depicting spinsterhood. There are few comic caricatures of old maids in her novels, and while figures such as the
Misses Irwine in *Adam Bede* (1859) and Miss Noble in *Middlemarch*
(1871–2) are treated with warm sympathy, the kind of heavy irony
directed towards the elderly spinsters in 'Janet's Repentance' (1857)
makes us thankful that Eliot resorted to this kind of writing so
rarely:

> The Misses Linnet were in that temperate zone of old-maidism,
> when a woman will not say but that if a man of suitable years and
> character were to offer himself, she might be induced to tread the
> remainder of life's vale in company with him; Miss Pratt was in
> that arctic region where a woman is confident that at no time of
> life would she have consented to give up her liberty, and that she
> has never seen the man whom she would engage to honour and
> obey.[45]

Eliot also eschews the sentimental image of the woman disappointed in love, living a self-denying, substitute existence, which, as we have seen, was popular with several of her fellow women novelists. What is an artistic gain in terms of psychological realism, however, may be seen as a distortion of social fact; Eliot was clearly reluctant to suggest the rewards of the single life, and was not disposed to explore in any detail the opportunities open to women set apart from sexual relationships.

While placing marriage at the centre of her vision of social harmony and emotional fulfilment, Eliot maintains a coolly critical awareness of its perils and shortcomings. Like many Victorian female novelists, she shows how women may be trapped by the false promises it offers. Rosamond Vincy in *Middlemarch*, for instance, taught that matrimony will bring her her much-coveted social success, is sister to Sewell's Agatha Percival and Anne Brontë's Helen Huntingdon; all believe, and are disabused of their belief too late, that they can control their own destinies through tactically-negotiated marital unions. Eliot does not suggest that society is wholly to blame for the ensuing suffering; even her most socially conditioned female characters are partly responsible for their own tragedies. But she lays bare the alluring ideologies which make marriage seem such a glamorous proposition for women and by which even the most intelligent are influenced. She also points unerringly to the economic conditions which, as much as romantic idealism, may force women into matrimonial imprisonment. Several of her heroines turn with relief to the chance of being provided for. In 'Janet's Repentance', Janet marries Dempster not only because she thinks he is superior to her but because he will save her from having to become a governess. The most chilling depiction of this situation occurs in *Daniel Deronda*. Encouraged to think of herself as 'exceptional',[46] Gwendolen cannot contemplate the humiliations of economic dependency; after her grand schemes of an artistic career have been rudely shattered by Klesmer, the prospect of teaching other people's children fills her with gloom. Dimly aware of her own helplessness and inadequacy, she is impelled towards the romantic alternative by an almost unconscious revulsion from Sawyer's Cottage and dull respectability with the bishop's family. Though Eliot is far from uncritical of her 'spoiled child' at this juncture, her sympathetic portrayal of Gwendolen's new and painful awareness that she has been tossed into 'a hurrying roaring crowd in which she had got astray, no more cared for and protected than a myriad of other girls' (278) gives poignant credibility, if not moral justification, to her eventual acceptance of Grandcourt.

Eliot does not see matrimonial entrapment as a peculiarly female condition; both Lydgate and Adam Bede, for example, are lured by images of womanhood which bear little relation to true domestic comfort. But she implies that the conditions of marriage can be far harsher for women than for men. Her male characters do not have to depend solely upon marriage for economic survival; furthermore, their occupations in the outside world enable them to override the bitterness of emotional disappointment. Seth Bede derives comfort from his carpentry when he loses Dinah to Adam; Farebrother can give up Mary to Fred with a sense that at least he has other demands on him; Rex, Gwendolen's cousin, overcomes his adolescent infatuation by making a new life abroad. Eliot's ill-matched husbands, too, have outlets for their energies which mitigate the worst of their suffering. Tito blots out his unease about his deteriorating relationship with Romola by involving himself in the stimulating sphere of Florentine politics; both Lydgate and Casaubon gain some protection from the smarts of marital disillusionment through their professional activities, inglorious though these prove. In contrast, Eliot's unhappy wives are stifled and thwarted by the lot they chose with such hopefulness. Lacking the means of fulfilment outside marriage, they are driven in upon themselves and their grievances. Mrs Transome in *Felix Holt* (1866) experiences a 'woman's hunger of the heart forever unsatisfied';[47] with no inner resources or solid accomplishments to console her, she is imprisoned by her own irreversible act. For Dorothea, the 'labyrinth of petty courses'[48] of her aimless pre-marital existence is replaced by the 'anterooms and winding passages which seemed to lead nowhither' (228) of life with Casaubon; denied the chance of self-expansion through helping him, she has to face the hopelessness of her sterile isolation.

Though Eliot thus calls into question the romantic codes and social conditions which deny women alternatives to matrimonial fulfilment, she nevertheless maintains her basic conviction that marriage represents the heart of female experience, often a means of moral regeneration as well as of emotional satisfaction. Almost none of her heroines tries seriously to challenge the supremacy of marriage in women's lives. Eliot herself idealises the qualities most closely linked with women's traditional roles of wifehood and motherhood, glorifying the virtues of service, devotion to others, and self-abnegation. This idealisation of womanhood seems partly to derive from her own ambivalent attitude towards femaleness. As we have seen, while rejecting close identification with her own sex, she sought to establish herself as the most womanly of women. Having become 'Mutter' and 'Madonna' to Lewes and his sons, she compensated for her sense of insecurity by playing an archetypal feminine role, at the same time enjoying the personal prominence conferred by literary success. Her heroines attain individual pre-eminence by achieving traditional standards of womanliness — they become exceptional not by defying conventional roles but by excelling in them, and defaulters are punished according to the extent of their departure from them. As with her non-fictional vindications of female 'distinctiveness', Eliot's idealism contains no hint of irony. From Milly Barton in 'The Sad Fortunes of the Reverend Amos Barton' (1857), whose 'soothing, unspeakable charm of gentle womanhood' (54) and 'sublime capacity of loving' (55) are the marks of an almost saint-like femininity, to Romola who becomes an angel of mercy to the plague-stricken village, and Dorothea who is Virgin-like in her self-dedication to others, Eliot's successive portrayals of Madonna figures confirms her acceptance of the high spiritual potential of her own sex.

The most fruitful approach to Eliot's assumptions about marriage and sexual relationships is through her heroines. Though she may be said to have an androgynous imagination which is able to penetrate the male as well as the female mind and sees human behaviour in terms of moral individuality as much as of sexual differentiation, she puts most of herself into her central female characters, using them as the focal point for her exploration of marital roles. In establishing her epitome of womanhood, Eliot contrasts different versions of female behaviour. In most of her novels, there are 'models' against which other characters are measured. In *Middlemarch*, for example, the selflessness and true wifely supportiveness of Mrs Bulstrode and Mrs Garth make Rosamond's selfish disloyalty look even more despicable, while Mary Garth's level-headed affected for Fred, based on knowledge of his limitations, highlights Dorothea's and Rosamond's ignorance of their respective partners. In *Daniel Deronda*, too, Mirah's humble devotion to Deronda makes a striking contrast to Gwendolen's egocentric attitude to marriage, even though the somewhat sickly portraiture of the former makes her a far less interesting character than Gwendolen. Most of Eliot's major heroines have to learn the highest female virtues, taught by others and by experience. They can be divided into two main types. First are those women who seek to defy orthodox womanhood, or to separate themselves from traditional womanly functions; for this, they may undergo harsh chastisement or a more gentle restoration to the normality of female experience. Second are those women who abuse the matrimonial pieties, either as wives or as the objects of devotion; those who err from self-delusion or misplaced idealism are redeemed by a process of spiritual regeneration, while those who act more wilfully, to gratify themselves, endure deeper suffering.

Eliot is curiously judgmental towards those of her heroines who seek, as she did, to escape from the frustrations of domesticity and family responsibility. There may be an element of self-chastisement in her attitude, since later in life she claimed that her own rebelliousness was the result of youthful intellectual arrogance,[49] needing the curbs of greater maturity. Her most striking portrayal of a woman's attempt to escape the conditions of matrimony and exercise individual self-expression is found in *Daniel Deronda*. Deronda's mother, the Princess Halm-Eberstein, has sought autonomony through her acting career. Her rejection of the normal functions of womanhood is clearly shown as both misguided and unnatural. On his first meeting with her, Deronda is struck by her coldness as she justifies her early abandonment of him: 'I did not want affection. I had been stifled with it. I wanted to live out the life that was in me, and not be hampered with other lives' (688). As she explains, she married not for emotional fulfilment, but in order to free herself from paternal bondage and to assert her own will; she desired neither love nor children. With acute perceptiveness, Eliot points to the agonising dilemma of a woman who feels 'different'; the Princess voices the feminist protest of her creator's own age:

'Every woman is supposed to have the same set of motives, or else to be a monster. I am not a monster, but I have not felt exactly what other women feel — or say they feel, for fear of being thought unlike others.' (691).

But though her rebellion is justifiable on rational grounds, her inability to respond from the heart and her hardened sensibilities condemn her. Like Eliot, the Princess knows 'what it is to have a man's force of genius in you, and yet to suffer the slavery of being a girl' (694), but because she has exploited the wifely role and used her artistic genius for unwomanly ends, she is punished. All she has striven for has turned to nothing, her voice gone and her son embracing the very destiny from which she tried to separate herself and him. Eliot acknowledges the Princess's insistence that she had 'a rightful claim to be something more than a mere daughter and mother . . . a right to be an artist . . . My nature gave me a charter' (728); for her, however, even the noblest creative impulse cannot validate betrayal of the most sacred female responsibilities. As with Craik's Olive and Jewsbury's Bianca, artistic self-expression is too threatening to true femininity to be ultimately vindicated, though their fate is a retreat into normality rather than the bitterness of failed aspiration. In contrast to the Princess, who represents the tragic dimensions of female duality, Mirah, a woman cast in a less heroic mould who has not lost her womanliness in the enactment of her art, triumphs in the private sphere of domesticity; humbly subservient to the man she loves and reveres, she embodies the feminine spirit which survives in the apocalyptic vision at the end of the novel.

Eliot treats the same conflict in 'Armgart' (1871), a remarkably lifeless dramatic poem whose only merit is that it is her most extensive exploration of aspiring female selfhood. Armgart, a successful opera-singer, has channelled her passionate impulses through her creative talents. In the eyes of Graf, her suitor though, 'Too much ambition has unwomaned her'[50]; with the confidence of masculine superiority, he asserts that

> . . . A woman's rank
> Lies in the fulness of her womanhood:
> Therein alone she is royal. (95)

Echoing the sentiments of Patmore and Ruskin, he argues that

> . . . Pain had been saved,
> Nay, purer glory reached, had you been throned
> As woman only, holding all your art
> As attribute to that dear sovereignty —
> Concentering your power in home delights
> Which penetrate and purify the world. (97)

Unimpressed by such opinions, Armgart clings to her belief that Nature has decreed her role as an artist; fulfilling her 'supreme vocation', she feels free from restricting theories about womanhood (98). Like Craik's Olive, she recognises that the exercise of the creative spirit is incompatible with traditional womanly functions. She sees that marriage would involve concessions, and that inevitably the greater share would have to come from her. Her rejection of Graf's offer is based on a passionate sense of self:

> . . . I will live alone and pour my pain
> With passion into Music, where it turns
> To what is best within my better self.
> I will not take for husband one who deems
> The thing my soul acknowledges as good —
> The thing I hold worth striving, suffering for,
> To be a thing dispensed with easily,
> Or else the idol of a mind infirm . . . (102–3)
> The man who marries me must wed my Art —
> Honour and cherish it, not tolerate. (104)

Yet Eliot does not allow her heroine to triumph in her glorious unorthodoxy, though her fate is more ambiguous than that of the Princess. After an illness, Armgart's voice is ruined and she is forced to abandon her career. Despite her recognition that she is now one of those women who feel their lives 'Beating upon the world without response' (127), she still refuses either to contemplate becoming a 'pensioner in marriage' (120) or to take on the drearily vicarious existence of spinsters like her crippled cousin, Walpurga, who only

> . . . know joy by negatives,
> And all their deepest passion is a pang
> Till they accept their pauper's heritage,
> And meekly live from out the general store
> Of joy they were born stripped of. (129)

Armgart rejects the traditional image of self-sacrificing womanhood, though she has no illusions about her future — 'For all life now I am a broken thing' (138). Eliot herself remains ambivalent; at the end she neither vindicates her heroine's brave creative spirit nor sanctifies her resignation, as she leaves her unenthusiastically preparing to become a music teacher in Freiburg. This work, leaden and artificial though it seems, perhaps represents Eliot's most honest admission that wifehood or its substitute in service to others may not be the highest female role, even if she does not suggest alternative modes of satisfaction.

Both the Princess and Armgart are deprived of their means of fulfilment because their strategies of self-expression were deliberate contraventions of womanly pieties. Less sternly, but still unhesitatingly, Eliot disciplines those of her heroines who try to deny their innate femaleness not out of wilfulness but out of some high idealism. In these cases, Eliot, drawing on her belief — expressed succinctly in her well-known criticism of *Jane Eyre*[51] — that there is a limit to wholesome self-sacrifice, restores her erring characters to a recognition of normality. The two most notable examples are Dinah Morris in *Adam Bede* and Fedalma in *The Spanish Gypsy* (1868), and the contrast in their treatment highlights the change from Eliot's basic optimism of the late 1850s to her more gloomy outlook a decade later. Dinah Morris, far from being a rebel against traditional womanliness, represents in many ways the perfection of her sex. Her 'feminine delicacy',[52] modest demeanour, and 'simple . . . candid . . . gravely loving' expression (67) make her saint-like, and she is regarded as an angel or a Madonna by those whom she helps. But her femininity is deficient in one important respect; believing that she has been divinely called, she has put aside her innermost needs as a woman in favour of serving others. As she explains to Seth Bede:

'God has called me to minister to others, not to have any joys or sorrows of my own, but to rejoice with them that do rejoice, and to weep with those that weep . . . I desire to live and die without husband or children. I seem to have no room in my soul for wants and fears of my own, it has pleased God to fill my heart so full with the wants and sufferings of his poor people.' (79–80)

Even near the end of the novel, when she is made aware of Adam's feelings for her, Dinah continues to express her conviction that the love of God takes precedence over that of man, though now there is more sense that she feels the temptation of earthly affection:

'I know marriage is a holy state for those who are truly called to it and have no other drawing; but from my childhood upward I have been led towards another path; all my peace and joy have come from having no life of my own, no wants, no wishes for myself, and living only in God and those of his creatures whose sorrows and joys he has given me to know.' (552)

Eliot's treatment of the Methodist preacher demonstrates the inherent conservatism underlying all her thinking about women. Dinah seems the complete antithesis to Armgart and the Princess. Her divergence from womanly normality, unlike theirs, is not inspired by self-assertiveness or protest at the restrictiveness of female roles but by a spiritual creed which transcends the personal and embodies the highest ethical standards. Yet Eliot makes clear that despite her saintliness Dinah is not a faultless model of womanhood. As several characters remark, there is an element of obstinate eccentricity in her rejection of female sexuality. Seth, with the understandable ruefulness of a disappointed lover, feels that 'She's too good and holy for any man' (77), while Mrs Poyser, with her customary pragmatic bluntness, expresses her disapproval of her niece's behaviour:

> . . . you might get married to some decent man, and there'd be plenty ready to have you . . . But where's the use o' talking, if ye wonna be persuaded, and settle down like any other woman in her senses, instead o' wearing yourself out with walking and preaching, and giving away every penny you get'. (122)

With Dinah, Eliot also strikes at the deficiencies of angelic images of femininity. Though Dinah has some maternal qualities, her high spiritual idealism does not give her insight into others of her sex. Her well-intentioned rebuke to Chad's Bess at the preaching terrifies the young girl, making her feel her natural female responses as sinful. She also fails to comprehend Hetty; her 'higher nature' (206) cannot empathise with a lower one, and her vague warnings about the future merely bewilder her empty-headed cousin. The scene where Hetty dresses up in Dinah's clothes actually suggests a shared flaw, despite their overt dissimilarities: both, in denying the centrality of emotional commitment in women's lives, are guilty of distorting the innate female nature.

But though Eliot refutes misleading sexual ideologies, she replaces them with a vision which is, in its own way, equally conventional. Because her aberration has not destroyed her inherent warmth of spirit, Dinah is not chastised like the Princess. Instead she is brought to the perfection of complete womanhood. Her repressed sexuality — hinted at by her blushes when she first encounters Adam at home — finally flowers when her selfhood triumphs in the roles of wife and mother. As we have been made to recognise the life-denying character of her creed of self-renunciation, so Dinah herself at last acknowledges that she is not called to 'lay [my] natural, lawful affections on the altar' (554). Eliot, then, offers no new image of womanhood to counter the inadequacies of the angelic one. Dinah renounces the career which gave her an asexual individuality (an act validated by historical actuality,[53] but wholly appropriate to Eliot's purpose here), and by adding 'naturalness' to her already awesome set of virtues becomes the symbol of a truly ideal femininity. There is an ironic significance in the fact that marriage to Adam was not part of Eliot's original plan for Dinah but was suggested by Lewes.[54] Without the weight of conventional masculine opinion behind her, would Eliot have perhaps left her heroine to enjoy an active, fulfilling single life?

To some extent, Fedalma, the heroine of *The Spanish Gypsy*, is a complementary figure to Dinah. Both women are called by an external authority which demands the rejection of normal female roles. But Fedalma's denial of natural womanhood is not, like Dinah's, inspired by a religious conviction which Eliot herself feels unable to verify, but by a specific cause. When Fedalma discovers that Zarca, the gypsy leader, is her father, she responds to her inherited condition by giving up her affianced lover, Silva, in order to be 'the angel of a homeless tribe'[55] and lead them to a promised land. As Eliot's 'Notes to *The Spanish Gypsy*' indicate, she was attracted not so much by the subject of renunciation of marriage as by the grand tragic theme of the Greek dramatists — the unremitting operation of destiny. Fedalma has to meet 'the hereditary claim' on her, and the story enacts the 'adjustment of our individual needs to the dire necessities of our lot'.[56] Her rejection of 'the ordinary lot of womanhood' in favour of 'a terribly different experience'[57] is far more heroic than Dinah's. Her early yearnings for freedom from the usual restrictions of being a woman foreshadow her readiness to embrace a new kind of selfhood:

A longing . . . haunts me in my dreams —
Dreams where I seem to spring from off the walls,
And fly far, far away, until at last
I find myself alone among the rocks. (109)

Once called, she knows she must now act in traditionally unfeminine ways. She is to be a leader in battle, undertaking 'work as pregnant as the acts of men' (151) and sanctified as a far more potent goddess

than the angel on the hearth. Such heroism is, as her father bluntly
points out, remote from normal female domestic activity:

> . . . the woman who would save her tribe
> Must help its heroes — not by wordy breath,
> By easy prayers strong in a lover's ear,
> By showering wreaths and sweets and wafted kisses . . .
> Not to such petty mercies as can fall
> 'Twixt stitch and stitch of silken broidery . . . (149–50)

Fedalma's renunciation is not revolt. It involves self-sacrifice and
deep suffering:

> . . . I will take
> This yearning self of mine and strangle it . . .
> Die, my young joy — die, all my hungry hopes. (163)
> . . . I forsook him [Silva] for no joy, but sorrow,
> For sorrow chosen rather than a joy
> That destiny made base! (258)

Though she herself argues that love is a 'fresher law' of nature than
laws of birth (156), her abandonment of personal romantic satisfaction in response to wider loyalties has its own courageous vitality:

> If it were needed, this poor trembling hand
> Should grasp the torch — strive not to let it fall
> Though it were burning down close to my flesh . . .
> Father, I will be true! (271)

Yet though Fedalma's unwomanliness is more glorious than
Dinah's, she too is denied the fulfilment of her chosen role. In her
case, the inadequacy of her transcended sexuality is forced upon her
when, after her father's death, she fails to prove strong enough to
unify and lead the tribe. She remains faithful to the cause, in the
knowledge that she has lost a woman's greatest blessing:

> . . . I will plant
> His sacred hope within the sanctuary
> And die its priestess — though I die alone,
> Cold 'mid cold ashes. (370)

Eliot's final vision of Fedalma as the Gypsy Queen and Silva as a 'grey[-]clad pilgrim' (363), dedicating themselves to a higher kind of spiritual union than earthly love, reveals her disinclination to deal further with her heroine's dilemma. Eliot told Blackwood that she had altered the ending in order to make it less tragic,[58] but we are in fact left with a resolution which, though of a piece with the sombre mood of her fiction at this time, fails to examine fully the dichotomies of female experience which her story has presented. Fedalma remains single but personally unfulfilled; the theme of conflict between the desire for emotional commitment and the urge towards a more individualistic self-expression is overcast by Eliot's deterministic vision which prevents deeper exploration of the sexual issues.

The Mill on the Floss (1860) treats the dualities of womanhood in a different way from the works just referred to. Maggie's dilemmas arise from the environmental and familial conditions of childhood and adolescence rather than from the conflict between womanly normality and commitment to a vocation. Awareness of the incompatability of conventional femininity and less orthodox self-assertion is early forced on Maggie, herself torn between the desire to be loved and the desire to express her individuality. Her predicament centres on the two versions of femaleness offered her. On the one hand is womanly conformity which will secure her the affection she longs for. This kind of orthodoxy means propitiating men (even in the childhood jam-puff episode, Maggie is willing to abase herself before quite unjustifiable male displeasure) and curbing self-will, and is most unequivocally symbolised in Maggie's cousin Lucy, a pretty, good girl who is constantly admired as a model child. Maggie both wants to destroy this perfection which provides such a threatening contrast to her own selfhood, and wishes to emulate it, imagining a world containing a crowned queen 'just like Lucy . . . only the queen was Maggie herself in Lucy's form'.[59] On the other hand is the possibility of rebellion. Maggie as a child is always being made to feel 'different', not only because of her naughtiness but also because of her evident intelligence. Her most bold assertions of individuality, such as cutting her hair, represent revolt and alienation from her own sex, yet as she finds out they win only social disapproval.

As she moves into adolescence, Maggie's yearnings to find a meaning in her 'hard, real life' (379) are similarly linked to opposing images of womanhood. Thomas à Kempis's creed, with its stress on resignation and rejection of self-will, is a spiritualised version of traditional female behaviour; Maggie's dedication to its tenets actually makes her more womanly, giving her face 'a tender soft light' (387). Philip Wakem and Stephen Guest, in contrast, offer her the tempting doctrines of unrestricted self-gratification. Despite their personal dissimilarities they both encourage Maggie to revolt against the self-abnegating discipline to which she tries to cling, and to open herself to her inner impulses. Philip teaches her the importance of mental enlargement, and shows her the distortions of her hard-won resignation:

> '. . . you are shutting yourself up in a narrow self-delusive fanaticism, which is only a way of escaping pain by starving into dulness all the highest powers of your nature . . . It is mere cowardice to seek safety in negations.' (427, 428–9)

Stephen teaches her the power of sexual passion, the less ethereal side of her incipient womanhood. Both men, too, use arguments of feeling and natural law to try to persuade her of the validity of their views. Yet ultimately each appeal to nature is revealed as a betrayal of the most sacred female responsibilities. Stephen's doctrine is morally more perilous than Philip's. Maggie's involvement with him is associated with her earlier acts of rebellion, and commitment to him would mean the destruction of friendships and family loyalties. Even to marry him would be an offence against all the pieties of womanhood, because it would be pure self-pleasing and a denial of the wider human sympathies on which such a relationship must be founded. Though Philip's kind of love initially seems more acceptable because he offers Maggie a deeper and worthier devotion as well as a refuge from her more dangerous emotions, he too calls for rejection of family pledges and offers fulfilment at the expense of inherited duties.

Maggie, then, must choose between womanhood as conformity — now not to social orthodoxies but to a higher self-denial — and womanhood as the expression of individual impulses. Here, unlike in *Adam Bede* and *Daniel Deronda*, female naturalness is associated with moral lawlessness; as in *The Spanish Gypsy*, rejection of normal sexuality (though in the later work this sexuality has no implications of sinfulness) is sanctified as noble self-sacrifice. Eliot, however, remains characteristically ambivalent about womanly fulfilment. Unwilling to adjudicate between self-denying isolation and passionate self-satisfaction, she resolves her heroine's dilemma by removing her altogether from the sphere of conflict. Maggie finally assumes a distinctive female role as an angelic figure functioning in a pre-sexual childhood state. She does not achieve the normality of marital happiness like Dinah nor is she granted some purpose as a single woman, albeit disillusioned, like Fedalma or Armgart. Instead she is martyred as a Madonna, rescuing herself and Tom from the ravages of the adult world and embodying a quasi-maternal and spiritual power which transcends but does not come to terms with the problems of her womanly experience.

The second group of heroines in Eliot's work consists of those women who instead of questioning or defying traditional female roles, accept but exploit or misuse them. They also may be subdivided according to the nature and grounds of their failings. Eliot is harsher towards those who deliberately disregard the sanctities of marriage and sexual relationships than towards those who are impelled by misconceived idealism. Her earliest extended study of the former kind — apart from the unconvincing portrayal of the obsessively jealous Caterina in 'Mr Gilfil's Love Story' (1857), whose 'diseased susceptibility' (198) breeds murderous desires towards her faithless lover — is Hetty Sorrel in *Adam Bede*. Throughout the novel, Hetty's limitations are stressed; her beauty is babyish, her 'little silly imagination' (145) is entirely solipsistic, and her intellectual feebleness cannot deal with the blow of parting from Arthur:

> Reasons why he could not marry her had no existence for her mind; how could she believe in any misery that could come to her from the fulfilment of all she had been longing for and dreaming of? She had not the ideas that could make up the notion of that misery. (379)

Eliot combines scorn and sympathy towards Hetty, but she does not release her entirely from moral responsibility. Hetty offends against the pieties of womanhood in both its loving and maternal aspects. Her acceptance of male adoration is based not on feeling but on the satisfaction of her vanity. She will not contemplate Adam as a husband because he cannot make her 'a lady in silks and satins' (358); the fact that he loves her is nothing to her. Conversely, she allows herself to be courted by Arthur because of his glamour and because he flatters and spoils her. Basically hard-hearted, Hetty regards marriage merely as a stepping-stone to personal ascendancy, not as an expression of sympathy and devoted service. Her eventual listless acceptance of Adam after she has been abandoned by Arthur is a betrayal of all the matrimonial sanctities — 'Why should she not marry Adam? She did not care what she did, so that it made some change in her life . . . any further thought about Adam's happiness in the matter had never yet visited her' (385).

Hetty also sins against the maternal element of womanhood. Early on, her lack of motherly qualities is made clear. Her indifference to the charms or needs of Totty Poyser is an indication of this deficiency. Ironically, it is Adam, not she, who feels 'the mother's yearning, that completest type of the life in another life which is the essence of real human love' (477). Hetty's gravest crime is finally to deny a mother's love by causing the death of her child. In physical terms, her punishment (transportation and eventual death) is crueller than that accorded any other of Eliot's heroines, though her spiritual shallowness, momentarily touched by Dinah's insistent pleadings for repentance, prevents her from suffering the psychological tortures of the Princess or Mrs Transome in *Felix Holt*. Eliot's severity derives partly from a deep conviction that wifehood and motherhood must be regarded as the most valued aspects of female experience. Her treatment of Hetty reveals not only her ideological conservatism but also her antipathy towards denaturing female selfishness.

Mrs Transome in *Felix Holt* (1866) is a more complex illustration of the betrayal of matrimonial pieties. She plays a far more notable part in the novel than the earnestly pedantic Felix or the undistinguishedly romantic Esther Lyon, and her predicament most strikingly represents Eliot's concern with female suffering. Vainly attempting to compensate for the wretchedness of her married life by tyrannising over husband and neighbourhood, Mrs Transome is perpetually haunted by her secret past. With her, we see the fruits of this past, rather than the acts themselves which have woven their own web of Nemesis around her. She has offended against motherhood by wishing for the death of her hated elder son, trying to deny that a 'mother's love . . . can only continue to be joy on the same terms as other long-lived love — that is, by much suppression of self, and power of living in the experience of another' (98); and she has betrayed the sanctity of love itself by capitulating to a worthless man because 'she had thought there was a poetry in such passion beyond any to be found in every-day domesticity' (515). Like the

Princess, Mrs Transome is punished with internal anguish and the bitter knowledge that all her aspirations have turned to dust. Her own son, whose return was to bring her compensation for past misery, becomes the unconscious instrument of chastisement, and she is forced to face the consequences of her wrong-doing. Though her self-determination reflects none of the high idealism of the Princess's — her deeds were motivated by self-gratification not by the promptings of a creative spirit — she is in many ways a more tragic figure than the latter. Her dismal fate as an unloved, disappointed old woman helps to darken the overall mood of the novel, despite the conventionally romantic conclusion of marriage between Felix and Esther. It also reflects both Eliot's severity and psychological perception with regard to sexual transgression; wilful flouting of the finer aspects of womanhood is, she insists, moral dereliction and incorporates its own retribution.

Rosamond Vincy is guilty as a woman in a different way. Her prototype is Hetty Sorrel rather than Mrs Transome. In her small-minded egocentricity she is too obsessed with the conditions of her own world to be aware of the wider ranges of human existence; her awakening, such as it is, has none of the tragic implications of the elderly woman's. With this perfectly-finished creature, Eliot punctures the contemporary image of ideal womanhood more devastatingly than in *Adam Bede*. Rosamond looks like an angel, but her self-possessed refinement masks a remorseless egoism which eventually destroys her husband. Created for marriage by her upbringing and environment, she uses it as the means of social elevation; in her the female virtues of devotion and service are converted into uncompromising dedication to her own interests. Indeed, she marries not an individual man but the hero of a 'preconceived romance' (195), who she imagines will bring her all the gratification she desires. Though, as with Hetty, we are in part made to pity her as the victim of a false ideology and of masculine exploitation, Eliot subjects her to some of her most acid irony. Even her apparent generosity towards her has a biting edge: 'Think no unfair evil of her pray: she had no wicked plots, nothing sordid or mercenary; in fact, she never thought of money except as something necessary which other people would always provide' (301). For her, Rosamond's unforgivable shortcoming as a woman is not so much her purely hedonistic attitude towards marriage as her total negation of the distinctively female qualities of sympathy and self-denial which, as she makes clear, lie at the heart of 'the conditions of marriage itself . . . its demand for self-suppression and tolerance' (810).

As has already been suggested, the sufferings of this shallow 'waternixie' (700) for whom 'the terribly inflexible relation of marriage had lost its charm of encouraging delightful dreams' (711), are less poignant than those of Eliot's more passionately rebellious heroines, though she experiences one supreme moment of anguished disillusionment when Ladislaw brutally shatters the romantic drama she has been weaving around him and tells her his true feelings:

> all her sensibility was turned into a bewildering novelty of pain . . . the terrible collapse of the illusion towards which all her hope had been strained was a stroke which had too thoroughly shaken her: her little world was in ruins, and she felt herself tottering in the midst as a lonely bewildered consciousness. (836–7)

One of the ironies of the novel in fact is that the false angel triumphs in her deviousness. Apart from her flash of impulsive honesty when she tells Dorothea the true nature of her relationship with Ladislaw, she remains cold-hearted and morally blinkered; she is neither punished by real adversity nor reborn into true womanliness. Victorious in her self-containment, she ends as she began, 'mild in her temper, inflexible in her judgment, disposed to admonish her husband, and able to frustrate him by stratagem' (893), finally achieving through a second marriage to 'an elderly and wealthy physician' (893) the social and financial standing she always coveted. Curiously enough, it is with Rosamond that Eliot reveals her most realistic attitude towards women in this novel. As we shall see, Dorothea becomes an angel-wife; even the down-to-earth Mary Garth is a model of uprightness and dependability. Rosamond, the antithesis of female virtue, is allowed to survive, and though her unshakable egocentricity is made more despicable because juxtaposed with the images of ideal womanhood, it is not quenched by them.

Gwendolen Harleth in *Daniel Deronda* is Eliot's finest portrayal of female selfhood seeking to assert itself by exploiting traditional roles. While the depiction of marital relations in this novel is less wide-ranging than in *Middlemarch* and Grandcourt himself has less interior reality than the husbands in the earlier work, Eliot's presentation of an unhappy wife whose wretchedness is exacerbated by her own guilty conscience is masterly. Gwendolen's attitude towards marriage is highly complex. She is astute enough to recognise the vacuousness of most of society's matrimonial truisms. She sees no evidence to support her mother's claim that 'Marriage is the only happy state for a woman' (58), and her uncle's complacent creed that marriage will provide 'a new fountain of duty and affection. It is the only true and satisfactory sphere of a woman' (180) seems to represent the very diminution of her personality which she is determined to avoid.

Gwendolen is, however, no second Shirley boldly striking out against restricting matrimonial ideologies. She is quite conventional — 'her horizon was that of the genteel romance' (83), her creator comments acidly — and her overt unorthodoxy is not only superficial but also based on self-gratification. Like the Princess, she regards marriage as 'the gate into a larger freedom' (183), not one in which she can exercise a creative spirit but where she can do what she likes. Marriage in itself has no attractions for her except as a necessary instrument in her plans for self-elevation:

> her thoughts never dwelt on marriage as the fulfilment of her ambition; the dramas in which she imagined herself a heroine were not wrought up to that close . . . Of course marriage was social promotion; she could not look forward to a single life . . . (68–9)

Later, when she begins seriously to consider Grandcourt as a possible husband, she still looks on matrimonial commitment with cool pragmatism:

> the question of love on her own part had occupied her scarcely at all in relation to Grandcourt. The desirability of marriage for her had always seemed due to other feelings than love (343)

If Gwendolen's confidently self-centred vision lacks heroic dimensions it is also determinedly unsentimental. Eliot indeed gives unmistakable hints of sexual revulsion in Gwendolen; not only is she emotionally cold, but she finds all passionate love-making deeply distasteful. Like Margaret in *North and South*, who feels momentary horror when Thornton proposes to her, Gwendolen both fears and resists the personal violation represented by sexual relationships. One of the reasons for her eventual acceptance of Grandcourt is that he seems to make no physical or emotional demands on her.

Gwendolen's contempt of matrimonial sanctities is psychologically far more intricate than that of Hetty or Rosamond because, unlike the other two women, she accepts marital union in the full knowledge that in so doing she is not only betraying her finer sensibilities but is also injuring someone else. By uniting herself 'with an outworn life, full of backward secrets' (343) she is deliberately 'mak[ing] my gain out of another's loss' (500), and her marriage, far from enacting the wider human sympathies, aims at promoting self-interest at the expense of one of her own sex, already a victim of masculine exploitation. Lacking Fedalma's heroic alternative, Gwendolen is too weak to meet the call of renunciation which comes from Mrs Glasher; her capitulation to Grandcourt, though ostensibly necessitated by her sudden reversal of fortune, is more powerfully impelled by an unacknowledged reckless determination to gamble with her own future: 'She seemed to herself to be, after all, only drifted towards the tremendous decision: — but drifting depends on something besides the currents, when the sails have been set beforehand' (348).

Eliot's depiction of Gwendolen's tangled response to marriage demands recognition of her as a morally aware agent in her own fate. Because of this, the consequences of her actions are particularly traumatic. Gwendolen is racked by the knowledge that her guilty secret is the prime weapon by which Grandcourt can terrorise her into submission while retaining the chilling propriety of their public relationship. Her greatest agony, however, stems from 'that unwilling penance which conscience imposed' (373), eating into her in her nightmarish isolation. Since she recognises and respects the challenge of her own moral sense, Gwendolen can be redeemed. Taught by Deronda, to whom she is linked by their mutual experience of betrayal, she is introduced to a wider view of selfhood:

> 'Look on other lives besides your own . . . Try to care about something in this vast world besides the gratification of small selfish desires . . . ' (501–2)
> 'Take the present suffering as a painful letting in of light.' (508)

Having brought Gwendolen to a new spiritual awareness, Eliot does not reward her with the comforts of womanly fulfilment, reserving her idealism for the conventionally romantic union between Deronda and Mirah. With Gwendolen and Grandcourt, she focuses on personal relations more as a means of exploring the nature of moral development than of isolating specific sexual patterns within marriage, though of course the two themes are closely linked since Gwendolen's revulsion from her husband is compounded by his retributive hold over her. Gwendolen's mounting desperation in the face of relentless male domination — her 'habitual stifling consciousness of having an immovable obstruction in her life, like the nightmare of beholding a single form that serves to arrest all passage though the wide country lies open'[60] (744) — is accompanied by a slow growth of inner enlightenment for which her marital experience is the catalyst. As the novel proceeds, its earlier emphasis on the social and economic motivation behind Gwendolen's 'choice' moves to the psychological effects of her self-destructive and traitorous act. She has sinned against the ideals of womanhood, but, more profoundly, she has also sinned against the wider laws of human sympathy and interrelatedness, and because her offence thus transcends gender-oriented significance, her ultimate fate is to be made aware of herself as an erring soul, not just as an unfulfilled woman.

In the end, Eliot seems uncertain about what to do with her heroine. As has been indicated, she does not restore her to the womanly normality of wifehood and motherhood, nor does she leave her at a climax of redemptive action such as Maggie's at the end of *The Mill on the Floss*. She does not even accord her the quasi-matrimonial roles of female service enacted by Janet and Romola. Despite Gwendolen's tremulous obedience to Deronda's idealistically vague exhortations — 'I shall live. I shall be better . . . I may live to be one of the best of women who make others glad that they were born' (879, 882) — she is left without clear purpose and with no definite channel for her new sense of self. Eliot's unwillingness to impose artificial parameters on the potential of this individual awakening may seem more honest than obviously manipulated romantic closure, but it also gives a sense of incompleteness. Her reluctance to formulate a wider, less traditional future for female individuality, either in terms of sexual roles or of more general human involvement (and Deronda's glorious Jewish mission is no model of possible action for those left in England) makes the open-endedness oddly unsatisfactory. It is also perhaps an unintentional irony on Eliot's part that Gwendolen's new awareness leads her back to the familiar vision of the single woman's resigned and sacrificial existence, of which she was before so contemptuous. Gwendolen has learnt more about herself as a woman and as a unit in a moral universe than any other of Eliot's heroines, but she has no more means of enacting her awareness in new spheres than they have.

If Eliot's conservatism is evident in her treatment of those heroines who wilfully offend against womanly ideals in sexual relationships by exploiting them for their own interests, it expresses itself even more firmly with those who misapprehend the conditions of marriage through naïve idealism. Towards such women, whom she regards as less morally guilty, Eliot is both more generous and more conventional in approach. These are her favoured heroines, and paradoxically, while the distortions of their visions are revealed, they are finally elevated to the highest womanhood in roles which embody many elements of their idealism.

Esther Lyon in *Felix Holt* represents a mid-way position in this respect, coming between the most reprehensible offenders and those who err from ignorance. When we first see her, she is — like Hetty and Rosamond — vain and discontented, envisaging a lover who will gratify her desire for a life of ease and elegance. But, Eliot assures us, Esther possesses an inner warmth which, under the right influence, will overcome her egocentricity and flower into blessed womanliness. Esther is in fact one of Eliot's most boring heroines because she so soon and so easily reaches ideal womanhood, her spiritual regeneration rewarded with a pompous, paternalistic husband who has taught her to respond to her nobler impulses. Felix has an important ideological role in the novel. He recognises that women must redeem themselves from the trite images of their sex promulgated by society, and actively prove their right to worthier evaluation:

'If a woman really believes herself to be a lower kind of being, she should place herself in subjection: she should be ruled by the thoughts of her father or husband. If not, let her show her power of choosing something better.' (210)

He shakes Esther's self-contentment and makes her see the 'growing into the possession of higher powers' (327) as an intrinsic element in romantic commitment. He also teaches her how the conventional female attributes, such as beauty, can become the visible evidence of a woman's 'best self' (366). Unfortunately, his humourless self-righteousness casts a leaden weight on this romantic relationship and increases the sense of its contrivance.

Esther's transformation relies wholly on stereotypical notions of female virtue. As she improves under Felix's influence, she becomes a model of her sex:

> The consciousness of her own superiority amongst the people around her was superseded, and even a few brief weeks had given a softened expression to her eyes, a more feminine beseeching-ness and self-doubt to her manners. (338)

Femininity here is associated with reliance on external authority and self-deprecation. Felix, who for all his concern for Esther, is actually highly patronising about women, reminds her that she is no St Theresa or Elizabeth Fry; and her creator herself tells us that she is 'intensely of the feminine type, verging neither towards the saint nor the angel . . . "a fair divided excellence, whose fulness of per-fection" must be in marriage' (551), who will remain in touch with the 'wider life' (468) only through a superior husband. We may suspect that Eliot is really not very interested in this exemplum of regenerated womanhood who has so little capacity to move or sur-prise us. Even where she suggests psychological struggle in Esther, torn between the allurement of becoming Harold Transome's rich, petted wife and the satisfaction of maintaining her new-found moral elevation through union with Felix, this never makes an impact as serious internal conflict. Esther's choice of Felix, though it involves the renunciation of personal comfort, hardly strikes us as heroic, since Eliot is so committed here to the doctrine that the highest womanly fulfilment can be achieved only through ennobling love. Esther has none of the majesty of Eliot's Madonnas; her conven-tional womanliness lacks the more awesome angelic qualities. In contrast to Mrs Transome, whose tragic dilemma is far more fasci-nating to Eliot, she represents the limpness of idealism divorced from any real engagement with character.

Eliot vindicates the traditional ideologies of womanhood most positively with those heroines who having initially made 'bad' mar-riages re-enact their wifely dedication either in second marriages or in quasi-matrimonial roles. Janet Dempster is Eliot's earliest por-trayal of a woman who, despite flaws of pride and wilfulness, retains an idealistic belief in 'sweet wedded love and hope' (334). Even in her worst rages against her husband's brutality, she never wholly loses her innate goodness; she is 'the wife, beginning her initiation into sorrow, wounded, resenting, yet still hoping and forgiving' (344). Like Gwendolen, she is saved from spiritual self-annihilation by a male mentor who teaches her to live for others. Rescued from the danger of becoming unsexed, not only through the dereliction of wifely duty but also through the incipient alcoholism which threatens to turn her into an animal, Janet returns to her dying husband with angelic intentions: 'She would wait on him with such tenderness, such all-forgiving love, that the old harshness and cruelty must melt away forever under the heart-sunshine she would pour round him' (384). Eliot's realism in depicting a man in the last stages of delirium tremens (a description much objected to by some contemporary readers)[61] does not undercut the idealism, verging on sentimentality, of her image of the redeemed wife. After Dempster's death, Janet continues her role of dedicated service, leading a sanctified and sober life, her affectionate impulses now exercised in acts of benevolence. She is not granted the fulfilment of second marriage (her mentor, Tryan, dies a saintly death), but is elevated into a symbol of blessed self-abnegation which combines the spirituality of a Madonna and the calm resignation of a separate existence from which all emotion has passed away: 'She saw the years to come stretch before her like an autumn afternoon, filled with resigned memory. Life to her could never more have any eagerness; it was a solemn service of gratitude and patient effort' (411–12).

The image of idealised womanhood is developed more fully in *Romola* (1863). Romola is a majestic, statuesque figure, 'like a tall lily',[62] her incipient pride and passion transfigured by loving pity 'to the most lovable womanliness' (95). She is a historical amalgam, her Renaissance nobility combined with Victorian virtues of tenderness and devoted service — a nineteenth-century angel in fifteenth-century Florence. Because Eliot wants her to symbolise the highest female potential, she implies that naïvety is the chief cause of her subsequent suffering. Romola is 'in a state of girlish simplicity and ignorance concerning the world outside her father's books' (104), so that when Tito appears it is almost inevitable that he will stir her muffled consciousness with 'all images of joy . . . all objects and all sounds that tell of Nature revelling in her force' (238). She is also sexually naïve, and blind to the intricate emotional aspects of matrimonial relationships; her predominant motive for marrying is her wish to continue serving her father, she explains to him — 'I love Tito — I wish to marry him, that we may both be your children and never part' (181). Significantly, she finally rejects her husband not because she feels personally injured but because he has broken trust with her father by selling the latter's library. Her own deeper spiritual alienation from him is caused by his similar betrayals of Savonarola and her godfather, who have both been mentor figures to her.

Eliot intends us to see that Romola is still in a state of childlike immaturity, as yet unaware of her own womanly needs. 'The proud stoical heroism' with which, as a wronged wife, she proposes to ennoble her 'solitary loveless life' (394) is the creed of naïve idealism, like the stern asceticism which Maggie Tulliver picks up from Thomas à Kempis, and which takes no account of individual circumstances. Eliot also makes clear that the wide-eyed goodness of this goddess is actually an instrument of matrimonial disharmony, as it turns out to be with Dorothea and Casaubon. On first meeting her, Tito is awed by Romola's saintliness, and after his marriage he becomes increasingly disturbed by her instinctive fine uprightness which mercilessly probes his moral shabbiness. He feels 'a certain repulsion towards a woman from whose mind he was in danger' (314), recognising that his wife embodies 'a nobleness which might prove an alarming touchstone' (371). Eliot in no way wishes to exonerate Tito from his despicable acts of treachery which his conscience is too cowardly to prevent, but she makes us sharply aware of how the most ostensibly admirable female virtues can, in their absolutism, enact their own limitations in matrimonial relations. A perfection which cannot apprehend the weaknesses of others is, Eliot suggests, not only a contributing factor in marital breakdown, but is itself a weakness which must be remedied.

Despite these perceptions, however, Romola's function as a supreme example of ideal womanhood is never seriously challenged in the novel. The theme of matrimonial conflict, itself increasingly overtaken by Eliot's preoccupation with the crippling determinism of deeds, is transcended by her depiction of female saintliness. She introduces the theme of conflict between wifely obedience and rebellion, but leaves it unresolved. Savonarola, who, despite his dehumanising fanaticism, is Romola's guide to moral perfection, tells her to remain loyal to 'the holy mystery of matrimony' (430), while bearing her marital cross as a step in spiritual growth:

'Make your marriage-sorrows an offering . . . an offering to the great work by which sin and sorrow are being made to cease.' (436)

Romola comes to recognise Savonarola's deficiencies, but is sanctified by his teaching. On her return from her first flight from Florence, she has achieved a greater sanctity:

> All that ardour of her nature which could no longer spend itself in the woman's tenderness for her father and husband, had transformed itself into an enthusiasm of sympathy with the general life. (463)

Taught like Gwendolen to convert her own sorrow into works of womanly sympathy, she is, unlike the latter, given an arena for her extended consciousness. On her second flight she becomes a Madonna, performing saint-like acts of mercy in the plague-stricken village, her earlier anguish and wifely dilemmas eclipsed by a glorious vision of charitable duties. Having brought to our attention the misconceptions underlying marital commitment, and, like Craik and Anne Brontë, suggested that separation may be the best answer to a tortuous union built on false ideologies, Eliot puts aside the complex question of sexual relationships. She gets rid of the retrograde husband and presents her heroine with a new kind of commitment in which she can express her selfhood.

Romola, then, stops being a wife, but continues to enact the beatitudes of wifehood. As an 'Unseen' and a 'Visible' Madonna tending the distressed in famine-ridden Florence, she embodies service to others; as the supporter of Tessa, Tito's childlike mistress, and her children, in a female-dominated family unit, she embodies noble quasi-maternal devotion. Release from 'the special ties of marriage' (650), moreover, though making Romola's relations with other people simpler and more effective, does not lead her towards more aggressive or unconventional self-assertion. Most notably here, of course, the historical setting exempts Eliot from considering more overtly feminist alternatives, but her final depiction of Romola, radiating her influence from a domestic centre and living out her belief that 'we can only have the highest happiness . . . by having wide thoughts, and much feeling for the rest of the world as well as ourselves' (674) represents her own traditional conception of womanhood. Romola's earlier naïvety about marriage is transformed into a higher idealism through which, without a husband or children of her own, she can function as a perfect woman; Eliot, it seems, has chosen to ignore the inherent ironies of her situation.

Dorothea Brooke in *Middlemarch* is less consistently idealised than Romola, but Eliot still assesses her heroine's femininity in essentially traditional terms. If Dorothea is, as Leavis claims, Eliot's 'day-dream ideal self'[63] her perfection lies in the kind of high womanliness which her creator herself was anxious to represent. Eliot subjects her heroine to a critical scrutiny which does not threaten this ideality. Dorothea's sexual childishness is satirised — 'the really delightful marriage must be that where your husband was a sort of father, and could teach you even Hebrew, if you wished it' (32) — and we see clearly the strong element of wilfulness in her determination to marry Casaubon, in the face of less flattering appraisals of his qualifications as a husband. At the same time, Eliot indicates that Dorothea is hardly to blame for her naïvety, which is shown as the product of circumstances as much as of inherent weakness; her convention-ridden social background, and the 'girlish instruction comparable to the nibblings and judgements of a discursive mouse' (50) which has passed for her education have certainly not equipped her to recognise the fallacies of her own enthusiasms. Even more importantly, Eliot never suggests that Dorothea's centring of her ardent aspirations in the idea of marriage to a superior man is in itself a cause for regret. At the end of the novel, as we shall see, she hints that matrimonial fulfilment may be something of a compromise, but her account of her heroine's goal is relayed in language whose elevation transcends its own incipient irony:

> the union which attracted her was one that would deliver her from her girlish subjection to her own ignorance, and give her the freedom of voluntary submission to a guide who would take her along the grandest path. (5)

Dorothea chooses the wrong man, but her concept of marriage as 'a state of higher duties' (64) will be vindicated by her subsequent experience; like Janet and Romola, she suffers from the results of misplaced idealism, not because she has attempted to escape from womanly responsibilities.

Dorothea's matrimonial unhappiness becomes, as for Gwendolen, the means of greater self-knowledge and moral enlargement, but, unlike the latter, her nobility of character which seeks to transcend its own egoism is evident even in the earliest days of her marriage. 'I have known so few ways of making my life good for anything . . . I must learn new ways of helping people' (103), she comments wistfully to Casaubon. Though unconsciously alienating her husband by her ardent aspirations, she never seeks positively to separate herself from him; her fine spirit tries to break down his resistance, not to counter it with resistance of her own. Eliot is in fact more generous towards Dorothea than towards most of her other heroines. The young wife aches with disappointment and frustration, but she is spared the pains of moral guilt, and her spiritual enlargement, of which her suffering is the instrument, is a gradual organic process rather than a traumatic awakening. Eliot's generosity towards her heroine also saves her from the agonising choice between rebellion and obedience. Dorothea is caught between respect for her own freedom and acknowledgement of wifely duty, but, unable to deny 'the ideal . . . yoke of marriage' (523), she is released from her dilemma by Casaubon's death, her moral nobility unimpugned. Moreover, while escaping from the destructiveness of misconceived self-sacrifice, she enacts the most traditional aspects of virtuous wifehood in responding to the widened awareness to the needs of others which living with him has taught her.

Dorothea's second marriage has always been difficult for readers to accept, partly because Will Ladislaw himself seems such an inadequate partner for this large-souled heroine, and partly because their union is surrounded by a kind of romanticism from which the other marriages in the novel are exempt. To see it wholly as conventionalism, however, is to ignore the fact that Eliot has set the stage from the beginning for her heroine's ultimate fulfilment through wifehood and motherhood. The Prelude clearly establishes the impossibility of a more outwardly glorious role for Dorothea:[64]

> Many Theresas have been born who found for themselves no epic life wherein there was a constant unfolding of far-resonant action . . . Here and there is born a Saint Theresa, foundress of nothing, whose loving heart-beats and sobs after an unattained goodness tremble off and are dispersed among hindrances, instead of centring in some long-recognizable deed. (25–6)

Despite Nightingale's cavil,[65] the thematic significance of Dorothea's story depends on the predication that her self-expression will be confined to the private sphere of personal relations. In this era of social change and political reform, Eliot argues, women can exert their influence only through their husbands; even the highly intelligent Mary Garth has her literary success attributed to Fred's scholarly assistance. Moreover, it is quite evident from Eliot's very earliest plans for the novel that she always intended Dorothea to remarry,[66] her distinctively feminine qualities finally celebrated in the normality of female relativity.

We may reasonably look for hints of authorial regret at this apparent diminution of female energies. Eliot certainly points to Dorothea's own sense of failure. The young widow says sadly to Celia, 'I never could do anything that I liked. I have never carried out any plan yet' (878), and in the closing pages of the novel we are told that 'Dorothea herself had no dreams of being praised above other women, feeling that there was always something better which she might have done, if she had only been better and known better' (893). The narrative voice here, too, defines Dorothea's final position in terms of compromise:

Many who knew her, thought it a pity that so substantive and rare a creature should have been absorbed into the life of another, and be only known in a certain circle as a wife and mother. But no one stated exactly what else that was in her power she ought rather to have done . . . (894)

Eliot leaves us with no very strong sense of protest, however. Even in the above quotation, her characteristic method of separating herself from opinions which she does not wish personally to validate ('Many who knew . . .') makes her attitude ambiguous. It is also significant that in the 1874 edition of *Middlemarch* which Eliot herself corrected, she cast a vagueness over the causes of her heroine's 'not ideally beautiful' (896) acts. In the first edition, 'the conditions of [the] imperfect social state' (896) which determine Dorothea's role are spelled out:

Among the many remarks passed on her mistakes, it was never said in the neighbourhood of Middlemarch that such mistakes could not have happened if the society into which she was born had not smiled on propositions of marriage from a sickly man to a girl less than half his own age.[67]

In the later edition, she removes the suggestion that attitudes towards marriage need to be changed,[68] thus highlighting the blessings of Dorothea's union with Will which, having earlier presented with almost embarrassing sentimentality, she now describes in traditional images of beneficent nature:

Her finely touched spirit had still its fine issues, though they were not widely visible. Her full nature, like that river of which Cyrus broke the strength, spent itself in channels which had no great name on the earth. But the effect of her being on those around her was incalculably diffusive . . . (896)

If marriage with Will is the best that Dorothea can achieve in the circumstances, it is also the best ideologically in terms of her womanly needs. With her selfhood consummated in wifehood and motherhood, she represents her creator's most considered vindication of the ultimate sanctity of matrimony. Alternatives are inconceivable; as we have seen, even in *Daniel Deronda*, Eliot's last look at marriage, Gwendolen's final isolation is made the more poignant in the context of the emotional satisfaction which Mirah and Deronda find in their union. Secure in her own happiness, Eliot the unconventional woman speaks with the voice of female orthodoxy.

Notes

1. Eliot is discussed as a woman writer in Sandra M. Gilbert and Susan Gubar, *The Madwoman in the Attic* (New Haven and London, 1979), Part V, in Ellen Moers, *Literary Women* (London, 1977), in Elaine Showalter, *A Literature of Their Own* (London, 1978), and in Patricia Meyer Spacks, *The Female Imagination* (London, 1976). Articles by Kathleen Blake, Muriel Bradbrook and Lloyd Fernando also discuss Eliot as a feminist writer: see Bibliography.
2. Even her fellow women novelists, while admiring her artistry, found it hard to accept the irregularity of Eliot's life: Gaskell regretted that she was not really Mrs Lewes (see *Letters*, ed. Chapple and Pollard pp. 566–7, 575, 582, 586–7); Yonge, predictably, both cavilled at and mourned not only her religious scepticism but also her practical disregard of moral obligations ('George Eliot and her Critics', *Monthly Packet*, 3rd ser., vol. IX, May 1885, pp. 471–94); Eliza Lynn Linton objected to the fact that while 'all her teaching went to the side of self-sacrifice for the general good, of conformity with established moral standards . . . her life was in direct opposition to her words' ('George Eliot', *Women Novelists of Queen Victoria's Reign*, London, 1897, p. 88).
3. See letter to Chapman, [2 December 1853]. *The George Eliot Letters* ed. Gordon S. Haight (New Haven and London, 1955–78), vol. II, pp. 130–1.
4. Eliot constantly got emotionally involved with the men whom she first met in literary or professional contexts. This was not only the case with Chapman, but also with Dr Robert Brabant and Herbert Spencer.
5. Letter to Charles Bray, [25 January 1853]. *Letters*, vol. II, p. 83.
6. Virginia Woolf, 'George Eliot', *Women and Writing* (London, 1979), p. 160.
7. Letter to Vincent Holbeche, 13 June 1857, *Letters*, vol. II, p. 349.
8. Letter to Cara Bray, 4 September [1855]. *Letters*, vol. II, p. 214.
9. See, for example, letter to Sara Hennell, 20 December 1860. *Letters*, vol. III, p. 364.
10. Letter to Charles Bray, [24 January 1853]. *Letters*, vol. II, p. 83.

11. Letter to Sara Hennell, [28 January 1856]. *Letters*, vol. II, p. 227.

12. Letter to Mme Eugène Bodichon, 5 December 1859. *Letters*, vol. III, p. 225.

13. Letter to Mme Eugène Bodichon, [16? November 1867]. *Letters*, vol. IV, p. 339.

14. Letter to Mrs Nassau John Senior, 4 October 1869. *Letters*, vol. V, p. 58.

15. Letter to Sara Hennell, 21 September 1857. *Letters*, vol. II, p. 383.

16. Letter to Sara Hennell, [12 October 1867]. *Letters*, vol. IV, p. 390.

17. See letter to Oscar Browning, 14 October 1869. *Letters*, vol. V, p. 59, and her essay 'Woman in France: Mme de Sablé', *Westminister Review*, vol. LXII (October 1854), pp. 448–73.

18. 'Silly Novels by Lady Novelists', *Westminister Review*, vol. LXVI (October 1856), reprinted in Thomas Pinney (ed.), *Essays of George Eliot* (London, 1963), p. 301.

19. Letter to Mrs Peter Taylor, 1 February 1853. *Letters*, vol. II, p. 86.

20. Letter to Mrs Nassau John Senior, 4 October 1869. *Letters*, vol. V, p. 58.

21. Letter to Emily Davies, 8 August 1868. *Letters*, vol. IV, p. 468.

22. 'Woman in France', Pinney, *Essays*, p. 53.

23. 'Margaret Fuller and Mary Wollstonecraft', *Leader*, vol. VI (13 October 1855), Pinney, *Essays*, p. 201.

24. Pinney, *Essays*, p. 73.

25. J.W. Cross (ed.), *George Eliot's Life as Related in her Letters and Journals* (new edn, Edinburgh and London, n.d.), p. 624.

26. Quoted in Gordon S. Haight, *George Eliot. A Biography* (Oxford, 1968), p. 51.

27. Letter to Maria Lewis, [18 August 1838]. *Letters*, vol. I, p. 6.

28. Letter to Maria Lewis, 2[8] May 1840. *Letters*, vol. I, p. 51.

29. Letter to Martha Jackson, 20 October, 1840. *Letters*, vol. I, p. 70.

30. Letter to Mrs Peter Taylor, 27 March 1852. *Letters*, vol. II, p. 15.

31. [*Westward Ho!* and *Constance Herbert*], *Westminister Review*, vol. LXIV (July 1855), Pinney, *Essays*, p. 134.

32. Quoted from Mathilde Blind, *George Eliot* (1883), pp. 46–7, in *Letters*, vol. I, p. 226.

33. Letter to Herbert Spencer, [16? July 1852]. *Letters*, vol. VIII, pp. 56–7.

34. Letter from Charles Bray to George Combe, 28 October 1854. *Letters*, vol. VIII, p. 128.

35. Letter to Charles Bray, 12 November 1854. *Letters*, vol. II, p. 186.

36. Letter to Charles Bray, [28] February [1859]. *Letters*, vol. III, p. 27.

37. Letter to Mrs Charles Bray, 8 July 1861. *Letters*, vol. III, p. 437.

38. Letter to Mme Eugène Bodichon, 29 May-1 June 1880. *Letters*, vol. VII, p. 291.

39. Letter to Mrs Charles Bray, 4 September [1855]. *Letters*, vol. II, p. 213.

40. Letter to Mrs William Smith, 1 March 1873. *Letters*, vol. V, p. 381.

41. Edith Simcox, *Autobiography*, entry of 9 March 1880. Quoted in *Letters*, vol. IX, p. 299.

42. Letter to Catherine Paget, 17 May 1877. *Letters*, vol. IX, p. 192.

43. Florence Nightingale, 'A Note of Interrogation', *Fraser's Magazine*, vol. LXXXVII (May 1873), p. 567. Eliot herself admired Nightingale (see *Letters*, vol. II, p. 45 and vol. III, p. 15) and perhaps had her Crimean activities in mind when portraying the dedicated service of her Madonna-like heroines such as Dinah Morris or Romola.

44. Ibid.

45. George Eliot, *Scenes of Clerical Life* (Penguin English Library, Harmondsworth, 1982), p. 268. The three stories which make up this collection, 'The Sad Fortunes of the Reverend Amos Barton', 'Mr Gilfil's Love Story' and 'Janet's

Repentance', were first published in monthly parts in *Blackwood's Magazine* in 1857, and were subsequently published in book form, in two volumes, by Blackwood in January 1858. Subsequent page references to these stories are to this edition and will be included in the text.

46. George Eliot, *Daniel Deronda* (Penguin English Library, Harmondsworth, 1976), p. 83. Subsequent page references are to this edition and will be included in the text.

47. George Eliot, *Felix Holt* (Penguin English Library, Harmondsworth, 1977), p. 104. Subsequent page references are to this edition and will be included in the text.

48. George Eliot, *Middlemarch* (Penguin English Library, Harmondsworth, 1981), p. 51. Subsequent page references are to this edition and will be included in the text.

49. See *Letters*, vol. VIII, p. 465.

50. George Eliot, *The Legend of Jubal and Other Poems* (Cabinet edn, Edinburgh and London, 1879), p. 76. Subsequent quotations from 'Armgart' are taken from this edition and page references will be included in the text.

51. 'All self-sacrifice is good — but one would like it to be in a somewhat nobler cause than that of a diabolical law which chains a man body and soul to a putrefying carcase' (Letter to Charles Bray, [11 June 1848], *Letters*, vol. I, p. 268).

52. George Eliot, *Adam Bede* (Penguin English Library, Harmondsworth, 1982), p. 66. Subsequent page references are to this edition and will be included in the text.

53. The Methodist Conference banned women preachers in 1803.

54. See her 'History of *Adam Bede*' in her Journal, 30 November 1858. Cross, *Life*, p. 255.

55. George Eliot, *The Spanish Gypsy* (Cabinet edn, Edinburgh and London, n.d.), p. 147. Subsequent page references are to this edition and will be included in the text.

56. 'Notes to *The Spanish Gypsy*', Cross, *Life*, p. 425.

57. Ibid., p. 424.

58. See *Letters*, vol. IV, p. 431.

59. George Eliot, *The Mill on the Floss* (Penguin English Library, Harmondsworth, 1979), p. 117. Subsequent page references are to this edition and will be included in the text.

60. The contrasting images used to describe the heroine's sense of matrimonial entrapment in *Middlemarch* and *Daniel Deronda* indicate Eliot's more overt recognition of its horrors in the later novel; whereas Dorothea feels the mental frustration of a directionless existence (winding passages that lead nowhere), Gwendolen is threatened by a terrible figure of bodily resistance.

61. Eliot justified this distasteful realism, explaining moreover that the actual facts on which the story was based were much worse than the fictional version and that she had deliberately glorified her heroine's final position — 'the real Janet alas! had a far sadder end than mine, who will melt away from the reader's sight in purity, happiness and beauty' (Letter to Blackwood, 11 June 1857. *Letters*, vol. II, p. 347).

62. George Eliot, *Romola* (Penguin English Library, Harmondsworth, 1984), p. 258. Subsequent page references are to this edition and will be included in the text.

63. F.R. Leavis, *The Great Tradition* (Peregrine edn, Harmondsworth, 1966), p. 89.

64. Eliot told Sara Hennell, 'Expect to be immensely disappointed with the close of Middlemarch. But look back to the Prelude' (Letter to Sara Hennell, 22 November 1872. *Letters*, vol. V, p. 330).

65. See above, p. 194.

66. 'Dorothea's second marriage' is listed in Eliot's first notes for the novel. See Jerome Beaty, *Middlemarch from Notebook to Novel: a Study of George Eliot's Creative Method* (Urbana, 1960), pp. 87–98.

67. Quoted in George Eliot, *Middlemarch*, Bert G. Hornback (ed.) (Norton Critical edn, New York, 1977), p. 577.

68. The later version omits this passage, merely referring to 'the mixed result of a young and noble impulse struggling amidst the conditions of an imperfect social state' (896).

SELECT BIBLIOGRAPHY

A. Bibliographies

Houghton, Walter E. (ed.). *The Wellesley Index to Victorian Periodicals, 1824–1900.* 3 vols (University of Toronto Press, 1966–79)

Kanner, S. Barbara. 'The Women of England in a Century of Social Change, 1815–1914: A Select Bibliography', *Suffer and Be Still: Women in the Victorian Age*, ed. Martha Vicinus (Indiana University Press, Bloomington, 1972)

Kanner, S. Barbara. 'The Women of England in a Century of Social Change, 1815–1914: A Select Bibliography, Part II', *A Widening Sphere: Changing Roles of Victorian Women* (Indiana University Press, Bloomington, 1977)

Kanner, Barbara (ed.). *The Women of England from Anglo-Saxon Times to the Present: Interpretive Bibliographical Essays* (Archon Books, Hamden, Connecticut, 1979)

Sadleir, Michael. *XIX Century Fiction: a Bibliographical Record* (University of California Press, Berkeley, 1951)

Watson, George (ed.). *The New Cambridge Bibliography of English Literature*, vol. III, 1800–1900 (Cambridge University Press, Cambridge, 1969)

B. Background Studies

Contemporary Sources

[Adams]. 'Woman's Mission', *Westminster Review*, vol. LII (January 1850), pp. 352–78

[Anon]. 'The Lady Novelists of Great Britain', *Gentleman's Magazine*, vol. XL n.s. (July-December 1853), pp. 18–25

Butler, Josephine E. *Woman's Work and Woman's Culture* (Macmillan, London, 1869)

Carlyle, Alexander. *New Letters and Memorials of Jane Welsh Carlyle*, 2 vols (John Lane, London and New York, 1903)

Chapman, Elizabeth. *Marriage Questions in Modern Fiction and Other Essays on Kindred Subjects* (John Lane, London and New York, 1897)

Cobbe, Frances Power. 'What Shall We Do with Our Old Maids?', *Fraser's Magazine*, vol. LXVI (November 1862), pp. 594–610

——. 'Celibacy v. Marriage', *Fraser's Magazine*, vol. LXV (February 1862), pp. 228–35

——. 'Female Charity — Lay and Monastic', *Fraser's Magazine*, vol. LXVI (December 1862), pp. 774–88

——. 'Criminals, Idiots, Women, and Minors', *Fraser's Magazine*, vol. LXXVIII (December 1868), pp. 777–94

Select Bibliography 227

——. *Essays on the Pursuits of Women* (Emily Faithfull, London, 1863)

Coghill, Mrs Harry. *The Autobiography and Letters of Mrs M.O.W. Oliphant* (Blackwood, Edinburgh and London, 1899)

Ellis, Sarah Stickney. *The Women of England: their Social Duties, and Domestic Habits* (Fisher, Son & Co., London, 1838)

——. *The Wives of England, Their Relative Duties, Domestic Influence, and Social Obligations* (Fisher, Son & Co., London, 1843)

Froude, James Anthony. *Letters and Memorials of Jane Welsh Carlyle*, 3 vols (Longmans, London, 1883)

[Greenwell, Dora]. 'Our Single Women', *North British Review*, vol. XXXVI (February 1862), pp. 62–87

[Greg, W.R.]. 'False Morality of Lady Novelists', *National Review*, vol. VIII (January 1859), pp. 144–67

——. 'Why Are Women Redundant?', *National Review*, vol. XIV (April 1862), pp. 434–60

Huxley, Leonard (ed.). *Jane Welsh Carlyle: Letters to her Family, 1839-1863* (John Murray, London, 1924)

[Kaye, J.M.]. 'The Employment of Women', *North British Review*, vol. XXVI (February 1857), pp. 291–338

[Lewes, G.H.]. 'Currer Bell's *Shirley*', *Edinburgh Review*, vol. XCI (January 1850), pp. 153–73

——. 'The Lady Novelists', *Westminster Review*, vol. LVIII (July 1852) pp. 129–41

Linton, Eliza Lynn. *My Literary Life* (Hodder & Stoughton, London, 1899).

——. *The Girl of the Period and Other Social Essays*, 2 vols (Bentley, London, 1883)

[Ludlow, J.M.]. 'Gaskell's *Ruth*', *North British Review*, vol. XIX (May 1853), pp. 151–74

[Martineau, Harriet]. 'Female Industry', *Edinburgh Review*, vol. CIX (April 1859), pp. 293–336

Mill, John Stuart. *The Subjection of Women*, and Mill, Harriet Taylor. *Enfranchisement of Women* (Virago Press, London, 1983)

[Mozley, Anne]. 'Clever Women', *Blackwood's Edinburgh Magazine*, vol. CIV (October 1868), pp. 410–27

[Mylne, Margaret]. 'Woman and her Social Position', *Westminster Review*, vol. XXXV (January 1841), pp. 24–52

[Oliphant, Margaret]. 'Modern Novelists — Great and Small', *Blackwood's Edinburgh Magazine*, vol. LXXVII (May 1855), pp. 554–68

——. 'The Condition of Women', *Blackwood's Edinburgh Magazine*, vol. LXXXIII (February 1858), pp. 139–54

——. 'Novels' (I), *Blackwood's Edinburgh Magazine*, vol. XCIV (August 1863), pp. 168–83

——. 'Novels' (II), *Blackwood's Edinburgh Magazine*, vol. CII (September 1867), pp. 257–80

Oliphant, Margaret, *et al. Women Novelists of Queen Victoria's Reign: a Book of Appreciations* (Hurst and Blackett, London, 1897)

[Patmore, Coventry]. 'The Social Position of Women', *North British Review*, vol. XIV (February 1851), pp. 515–40

Sandford, Mrs John. *Woman in her Social and Domestic Character* (Longman, London, 1831)

Shaen, Margaret J. *Memorials of Two Sisters: Susanna and Catherine Winkworth*

(Longmans, London, 1908)

Smith, Barbara Leigh. *Women and Work* (Bosworth and Harrison, London, 1857)

Twentieth-century Studies

Anderson, Michael. 'Marriage Patterns in Victorian Britain', *Journal of Family History*, vol. I (1976)

Auerbach, Nina. *Communities of Women: an Idea in Fiction* (Harvard University Press, Cambridge, Mass., 1978)

——. *Woman and the Demon: the Life of a Victorian Myth* (Harvard University Press, Cambridge, Mass., 1982)

Banks, J.A. and Olive. *Feminism and Family Planning in Victorian England* (Liverpool University Press, Liverpool, 1964)

Banks, Olive. *Faces of Feminism: A Study of Feminism as a Social Movement* (Martin Robertson, Oxford, 1981)

Basch, Françoise. *Relative Creatures. Victorian Women in Society and the Novel* (Schocken Books, New York, 1974)

Branca, Patricia. *Silent Sisterhood: Middle-Class Women in the Victorian Home* (Croom Helm, London, 1975)

Calder, Jenni. *Women and Marriage in Victorian Fiction* (Thames and Hudson, London, 1976)

Colby, Robert A. *Fiction with a Purpose. Major and Minor Nineteenth-Century Novels* (Indiana University Press, Bloomington, 1967)

Cruse, Amy. *The Victorians and Their Books* (Allen and Unwin, London, 1935)

Davidoff, Leonore. *The Best Circles: Society, Etiquette and the Season* (Croom Helm, London, 1973)

Elwin, Malcolm. *Victorian Wallflowers* (Jonathan Cape, London, 1934)

Ewbank, Inga-Stina. *Their Proper Sphere: A Study of the Brontë Sisters as Early-Victorian Novelists* (Edward Arnold, London, 1966)

Gilbert, Sandra M. and Gubar, Susan. *The Madwoman in the Attic: The Woman Writer and the Nineteenth-Century Literary Imagination* (Yale University Press, New Haven and London, 1979)

Gorham, Deborah. *The Victorian Girl and the Feminine Ideal* (Croom Helm, London, 1982)

Gorsky, Susan. 'Old Maids and New Women: Alternatives to marriage in Englishwomen's Novels, 1847-1915', *Journal of Popular Culture*, vol. 7 (Summer 1973), pp. 68-85

Harrison, Fraser. *The Dark Angel: Aspects of Victorian Sexuality* (Sheldon Press, London, 1977)

Hayter, Alathea. *A Sultry Month: Scenes of London Literary Life in 1846* (Faber, London, 1965)

Helsinger, E.K., Sheets, R.L., and Veeder, W. *The Woman Question: Society and Literature in Britain and America, 1837-1883*. 3 vols (Garland, New York, 1983)

Holcombe, Lee. *Victorian Ladies at Work: Middle-Class Working Women in England and Wales 1850-1914* (David and Charles, Newton Abbot, 1973)

Houghton, Walter E. *The Victorian Frame of Mind, 1830-1870* (Yale University Press, New Haven and London, 1957)

Johnson, Wendell Stacy. *Living in Sin: the Victorian Sexual Revolution* (Nelson Hall, Chicago, 1979)

Millett, Kate. *Sexual Politics* (Virago Press, London, 1977)

Mitchell, Sally. *The Fallen Angel: Chastity, Class and Women's Reading, 1835–1880* (Bowling Green University Popular Press, Bowling Green, Ohio, 1981)

Moers, Ellen. *Literary Women* (W.H. Allen, London, 1977)

Moore, Katherine. *Victorian Wives* (Allison and Busby, London, 1974)

Rees, Barbara. *The Victorian Lady* (Gordon and Cremonsi, London and New York, 1977)

Rogers, Katherine M. *The Troublesome Helpmate: A History of Misogyny in Literature* (University of Washington Press, Seattle and London, 1966)

Showalter, Elaine. *A Literature of Their Own. British Women Novelists from Brontë to Lessing* (Princeton University Press, Princeton, 1977)

Spacks, Patricia Meyer. *The Female Imagination: a Literary and Psychological Investigation of Women's Writing* (George Allen and Unwin, London, 1976)

Stebbins, Lucy Poate. *A Victorian Album. Some Lady Novelists of the Period* (Columbia University Press, New York, 1946)

Stone, Donald D. 'Victorian Feminism and the Nineteenth-century Novel', *Women's Studies*, vol. I (1972), pp. 65–91

Stone, Lawrence. *The Family, Sex and Marriage in England 1500–1800* (Weidenfeld and Nicolson, London 1977)

Strachey, Ray. *The Cause. A Short History of the Women's Movement in Great Britain* (Virago Press, London, 1978)

Stubbs, Patricia. *Women and Fiction: Feminism and the Novel 1880–1920* (Harvester, Brighton, 1979)

Thomson, Patricia. *The Victorian Heroine. A Changing Ideal, 1837–1873* (Oxford University Press, London, 1956)

——. *George Sand and the Victorians* (Macmillan, London, 1977)

Tillotson, Kathleen. *Novels of the Eighteen Forties* (Oxford University Press, London, 1956)

Trudgill, Eric. *Madonnas and Magdalens: the Origins and Development of Victorian Sexual Attitudes* (Heinemann, London, 1976)

Vicinus, Martha (ed.). *A Widening Sphere: Changing Roles of Victorian Women* (Indiana University Press, Bloomington, 1977)

——. *Suffer and Be Still, Women in the Victorian Age* (Indiana University Press, Bloomington, 1972)

Welsh, Alexander. *The City of Dickens* (Oxford University Press, London, 1971)

Woolf, Virginia. *A Room of One's Own* (Hogarth Press, London, 1929)

——. *Women and Writing* (The Women's Press, London, 1979)

C. Individual Authors

The works listed are those cited in the text; where two dates are given, the first indicates the original year of publication and the second indicates the edition used. The biographical and critical studies listed are those that have proved most useful; it is not intended to give a fully comprehensive bibliography, particularly for the better-known writers, bibliographical information about whom is extensive and easily obtainable.

Julia Kavanagh (1824–1877)

(i) *Works*
Nathalie: a Tale. 3 vols (Henry Colburn, London, 1850)
Daisy Burns: a Tale. 3 vols (Bentley, London, 1853)
Rachel Gray. A Tale Founded on Fact. (Hurst and Blackett, London, 1856)
Adele: A Tale. 3 vols (Hurst and Blackett, London, 1858)
Beatrice. 3 vols (Hurst and Blackett, London, 1865)
John Dorrien. 3 vols. (Hurst and Blackett, London, 1875)
French Women of Letters: Biographical Sketches. 2 vols (Hurst and Blackett, London, 1862)
English Women of Letters: Biographical Sketches. 1862 (Tauchnitz, Leipzig, 1862)
(ii) *Critical and Biographical Studies*
Foster, Shirley, ' "A Suggestive Book": a Source for *Villette*', *Études Anglaises*, tome XXXV (Avril-Juin 1982), pp. 177–84
Macquoid, Katherine S. 'Julia Kavanagh' in Margaret Oliphant, *et al.*, *Women Novelists of Queen Victoria's Reign: a Book of Appreciations* (Hurst and Blackett, London, 1897), pp. 251–62
Martin, Mrs Charles. 'The Late Julia Kavanagh', *Irish Monthly Magazine*, vol. VI (1878), pp. 96–100

Charlotte Mary Yonge (1823–1901)

(i) *Works*
The Heir of Redclyffe. 1853 (Macmillan, London, 1897)
Heartsease, or, the Brother's Wife. 1854 (Macmillan, London, 1880)
The Daisy Chain, or, Aspirations. 1856 (10th edn, Macmillan, London, 1870)
Hopes and Fears, or, Scenes from the Life of a Spinster. 1860 (Macmillan, London, 1879)
The Trial: More Links of the Daisy Chain. (Macmillan, London and Cambridge, 1864)
The Clever Woman of the Family. 1865 (Macmillan, London, 1884)
The Pillars of the House, or, Under Wode, Under Rode. 1873 (2 vols, Macmillan, London, 1889)
The Three Brides. 1876 (Macmillan, London, 1904)
Magnum Bonum, or, Mother Carey's Brood. 1879 (Macmillan, London, 1882)
The Long Vacation. (Macmillan, London, 1895)
Womankind. 1887 (new edn, Walter Smith and Innes, London, 1889)
(ii) *Critical and Biographical Studies*
Battiscombe, G. and Laski, M. *A Chaplet for Charlotte Yonge* (Cresset Press, London, 1965)
Battiscombe, Georgina. *Charlotte Mary Yonge. The Story of an Uneventful Life* (Constable, London, 1943)
Coleridge, Christabel. *Charlotte Mary Yonge. Her Life and Letters* (Macmillan, London, 1903)
Mare, M. and Percival, A. *Victorian Best-seller: the World of Charlotte M. Yonge* (Harrap, London, 1948)
Romanes, Ethel. *Charlotte Mary Yonge: an Appreciation* (Mowbray, London and Oxford, 1908)
Sandbach-Dahlstrom, Catherine. *Be Good Sweet Maid. Charlotte Yonge's Domestic*

Fiction: a Study in Dogmatic Purpose and Fictional Form, Stockholm Studies in
English, vol. LIX (1984)

Geraldine Endsor Jewsbury (1812–1880)

(i) *Works*
Zoë: the History of Two Lives. 3 vols (Chapman, London, 1845)
The Half Sisters: a Tale. 2 vols (Chapman and Hall, London, 1848)
Marian Withers. 3 vols (Colburn, London, 1851)
Constance Herbert. 3 vols (Hurst and Blackett, London, 1855)
Selections from the Letters of Geraldine Endsor Jewsbury to Jane Welsh Carlyle, ed.
Mrs Alexander Ireland, (Longmans, London, 1892)
(ii) *Critical and Biographical Studies*
Fahnestock, Jeanne R. 'Geraldine Jewsbury: the Power of the Publisher's Reader',
Nineteenth-Century Fiction, vol. 28 (December 1973), pp. 253–72
Hartley, J.M. 'Geraldine Jewsbury and the Problems of the Woman Novelist',
Women's Studies International Quarterly, vol. 2 (1979), pp. 137–53
Howe, Susanne. *Geraldine Jewsbury, Her Life and Errors* (G. Allen and Unwin,
London, 1935)
Woolf, Virginia. 'Geraldine and Jane', *The Common Reader, Second Series*
(Hogarth Press, London, 1932), pp. 186–201

Dinah Mulock Craik (1826–1887)

(i) *Works*
The Ogilvies. 1849 (Richard Edward King, London, n.d.)
Olive. 1850 (Richard Edward King, London, n.d.)
Bread Upon the Waters: a Governess's Life. 1852 (Harper's, New York, 1887)
The Head of the Family. 1852 (Walter Scott, London and Newcastle, n.d.)
Agatha's Husband. 1853 (W. Nicholson and Sons, London, n.d.)
John Halifax, Gentleman. 1856 (Everyman's Library, Dent, London, 1961)
A Life for a Life. 1859 (new rev. edn, Hurst and Blackett, n.d.)
Christian's Mistake. 1865 (new edn, Hurst and Blackett, London, n.d.)
The Woman's Kingdom. A Love Story. 1869 (Hurst and Blackett, London, 1870)
A Brave Lady. 1870 (Hurst and Blackett, London, 1871)
Hannah. (Hurst and Blackett, London, 1872)
A Woman's Thoughts About Women. (Hurst and Blackett, London, 1858)
Studies from Life. (Hurst and Blackett, London, 1861)
Sermons Out of Church. (Daldy, Isbister and Co., London, 1875)
Plain Speaking. (Hurst and Blackett, London, 1882)
About Money and Other Things. (Macmillan, London, 1886)
Concerning Men and Other Papers. (Macmillan, London, 1888)
Skerl, Margaret. *The Writings of Mrs Craik: a Select Bibliography* (unpublished
thesis, Dipl. Libra., University of London, 1949)
(ii) *Critical and Biographical Studies*
[Anon]. 'The Author of *John Halifax*', *British Quarterly Review,* vol. XLIV (July-
October 1866), pp. 32–58
——. 'A Novel of the Season', *Chambers Edinburgh Journal,* n.s. vol. XV (January-
June 1851), pp. 4–7
——. 'Our Female Novelists', *Christian Remembrancer,* vol. XXXVIII (October

1859), pp. 305-21

———. 'Miss Muloch (Mrs Craik)', *Victoria Magazine*, vol. XXVIII (April 1877) pp. 479-83

Forgues, E. 'Le Roman de Femme en Angleterre: Miss Mulock', *Revue des Deux Mondes*, tome XXV (février 1860), pp. 797-831

[Greg, W.R.]. 'Recent Novels: "Agatha's Husband" ', *Edinburgh Review*, vol. XCVII (April 1853), pp. 380-90

[Hutton, R.H.]. 'Novels by the Authoress of "John Halifax" ', *North British Review*, vol. XXIX (November 1858), pp. 466-81

Oliphant, Mrs M.O.W. 'Mrs Craik', *Macmillan's Magazine*, vol. LVII (December 1887), pp. 81-5

Pape, Thomas. 'The Birth Centenary of the Author of "John Halifax, Gentleman" '. Reprinted from *Transactions of the North Staffs Field Club* (vol. 60, 1925-6), pp. 1-14

———. 'Mrs Craik's Birth Centenary'. Reprinted from *Transactions of the North Staffs. Field Club* (vol. 61, 1926-7), pp. 1-4

Parr, Louisa. 'Dinah Mulock (Mrs Craik)' in Margaret Oliphant, *et al.*, *Women Novelists of Queen Victoria's Reign: a Book of Appreciations* (Hurst and Blackett, London, 1897), pp. 219-48

Reade, Aleyn Lyell. *The Mellards and Their Descendants* (privately printed at Arden Press, London, 1915)

Showalter, Elaine. 'Dinah Mulock Craik and the Tactics of Sentiment: a Case Study in Victorian Female Authorship', *Feminist Studies*, 2 (1975), pp. 5-23

Charlotte Brontë (1816-1855)

(i) *Works*

Jane Eyre. 1847 (Oxford University Press, Oxford and London, 1976)

Shirley. 1849 (Penguin, Harmondsworth, 1979)

Villette. 1853 (Penguin, Harmondsworth, 1983)

The Professor. 1857 (Everyman, Dent, London, 1983)

(ii) *Critical and Biographical Studies*

Allott, Miriam (ed.). *The Brontës: The Critical Heritage* (Routledge and Kegan Paul, London, 1974)

Gaskell, E.C. *The Life of Charlotte Brontë*. 2 vols (second edn, Smith, Elder, & Co., London, 1857)

Gérin, Winifred. *Charlotte Brontë: the Evolution of Genius* (Oxford University Press, London, 1971)

Jacobus, Mary. 'The Buried Letter: Feminism and Romanticism in *Villette*' in *Women Writing and Writing About Women*, ed. Mary Jacobus (Croom Helm, London, 1979), pp. 42-60

Moglen, Helene. *Charlotte Brontë: the Self Conceived* (Norton, New York, 1976)

Oliphant, Margaret. 'The Sisters Brontë' in *Women Novelists of Queen Victoria's Reign: a Book of Appreciations* (Hurst and Blackett, London, 1897), pp. 1-59

Rich, Adrienne. 'Jane Eyre: The Temptations of a Motherless Woman', *On Lies, Secrets and Silence: Selected Prose 1966-1978*, (Virago, London, 1979), pp. 89-106

Taylor, Helen. 'Class and Gender in Charlotte Brontë's *Shirley*', *Feminist Review*, 1 (1979), pp. 83-93

Winnifrith, Tom. *The Brontës and Their Background: Romance and Reality* (Macmillan, London, 1973)

Wise, T.J. and Symington, J.A. (eds.). *The Brontës: Their Lives, Friendships and Correspondence.* 2 vols (reprint, Basil Blackwell, Oxford, 1980)

Elizabeth Missing Sewell (1815–1906)

(i) *Works*

Amy Herbert. 1844 (new edn, Longmans, London, 1886)

Gertrude. 1845 (new edn, Longmans, London, 1886)

Margaret Percival. 1847 (new edn, Longmans, London, 1886)

The Experience of Life. 1853 (new edn, Longmans, London, 1886)

Katherine Ashton. 1854 (new edn, Longmans, London, 1886)

Ivors. 1856 (new edn, Longmans, London, 1886)

Ursula. 1858 (new edn, Longmans, London, 1886)

A Glimpse of the World. 1863 (new edn, Longmans, London, 1886)

The Journal of a Home Life. (Longmans, London, 1867)

Principles of Education drawn from Nature and Revelation, and Applied to Female Education in the Upper Classes. 2 vols (Longmans, London, 1865)

Note-book of an Elderly Lady. (Walter Smith, London, 1881)

Letters on Daily Life. (Walter Smith, London, 1885)

'The Reign of Pedantry in Girls' Schools', *Nineteenth Century*, vol. XXIII (February 1888), pp. 216–38

Extracts from a Private Journal Kept from 1846 to 1891. (St Giles' Printing Company, Edinburgh, n.d.)

The Autobiography of Elizabeth M. Sewell, ed. Eleanor L. Sewell (Longmans, London, 1907)

(ii) *Critical and Biographical Studies*

[Anon.]. 'Ivors and Other Tales by the Author of "Amy Herbert" ', *Christian Remembrancer*, vol. XXXIII (April 1857), pp. 291–348

——. 'Miss Sewell and Miss Yonge', *Dublin Review*, vol. XLV (September and December 1858), pp. 313–28

Coleridge, Christabel. 'The Works of Miss Sewell and Their Influence', *Guardian*, no. 3168 (22 August 1906), p. 1388

Foster, Shirley. 'Art and Autobiography: the Fiction of Elizabeth M. Sewell', *Dutch Quarterly Review of Anglo-American Letters*, vol. 6 (1976), pp. 191–215

Frerichs, Sarah Cutts. 'Elizabeth Missing Sewell: a Minor Novelist's Search for the *via media* in the Education of Women in The Victorian Era' (unpublished PhD thesis, Brown University, 1974)

Owen, Montague Charles. *The Sewells of the Isle of Wight* (printed for private circulation, Manchester, 1906)

Whitehead, C.M. *Recollections of Miss Elizabeth Sewell and Her Sisters* (W.J. Knight, Ventnor, 1910)

Elizabeth Cleghorn Gaskell (1810–1865)

(i) *Works*

Mary Barton: a Tale of Manchester Life. 1848 (Penguin, Harmondsworth, 1982)

Cranford. 1853 (Penguin, Harmondsworth, 1978)

Ruth. 1853 (Everyman's Library, Dent, London, 1982)

North and South. 1855 (Oxford University Press, Oxford, 1977)
Sylvia's Lovers. 1863 (Oxford University Press, Oxford, 1982)
Cousin Phillis. 1864 (Penguin, Harmondsworth, 1978)
Wives and Daughters 1866 (Penguin, Harmondsworth, 1969)
My Lady Ludlow and Other Tales. (Smith, Elder & Co., London, n.d.)
Lizzie Leigh and Other Tales. (Oxford University Press, London, 1913)
The Life of Charlotte Brontë. 1857 (2nd edn, 2 vols, Smith, Elder & Co., London, 1857)
The Letters of Mrs Gaskell, ed. J.A.V. Chapple and Arthur Pollard (Manchester University Press, Manchester, 1966)
(ii) *Critical and Biographical Studies*
Craik, Wendy. *Elizabeth Gaskell and the English Provincial Novel* (Methuen, London, 1975)
Dodsworth, Martin. 'Women without Men at Cranford', *Essays in Criticism*, vol. 13 (April 1963), pp. 132–45
Duthie, Enid L. *The Themes of Elizabeth Gaskell* (Macmillan, London, 1980)
Gérin, Winifred. *Elizabeth Gaskell. A Biography* (Clarendon Press, Oxford, 1976)
Lyall, Edna. 'Mrs Gaskell' in Margaret Oliphant, *et al.*, *Women Novelists of Queen Victoria's Reign: a Book of Appreciations* (Hurst and Blackett, London, 1897), pp. 119–45
Rubenius, Aina. *The Woman Question in Mrs Gaskell's Life and Works* (Uppsala University English Institute, Uppsala, 1950)
Wright, Edgar. *Mrs Gaskell: The Basis for Reassessment* (Oxford University Press, London, 1965)

George Eliot (1819–1880)

(i) *Works*
Scenes of Clerical Life. 1858 (Penguin, Harmondsworth, 1982)
Adam Bede. 1859 (Penguin, Harmondsworth, 1982)
The Mill on the Floss. 1860 (Penguin, Harmondsworth, 1979)
Romola. 1863 (Penguin, Harmondsworth, 1984)
Felix Holt. 1866 (Penguin, Harmondsworth, 1977)
The Spanish Gypsy. 1868 (Cabinet edn, Blackwood, Edinburgh and London, n.d.)
'Armgart' 1871, in *The Legend of Jubal and Other Poems* (Cabinet edn, Blackwood, Edinburgh and London, 1879)
Middlemarch. 1871–2 (Penguin, Harmondsworth, 1981)
Daniel Deronda. 1876 (Penguin, Harmondsworth, 1976)
Essays of George Eliot, ed. Thomas Pinney (Routledge and Kegan Paul, London, 1963)
The George Eliot Letters, ed. Gordon S. Haight (9 vols, Yale University Press, New Haven and London: vols I–VII, 1955; vols VIII–IX, 1978)
(ii) *Critical and Biographical Studies*
Blake, Kathleen. '*Middlemarch* and the Woman Question', *Nineteenth Century Fiction*, vol. 31 (December 1976), pp. 285–312
Bradbrook, Muriel. 'Barbara Bodichon, George Eliot and the Limits of Feminism', *Women and Literature 1779–1982* (Harvester, Brighton, 1982) pp. 49–65
Carrol, David (ed.). *George Eliot: the Critical Heritage* (Routledge and Kegan Paul, London, 1971)

Craik, Dinah Mulock. 'To Novelists — and a Novelist', *Macmillan's Magazine*. vol. III (April 1861), pp. 441–8

Cross, J.W. (ed.). *George Eliot's Life as Related in her Letters and Journals*. 3 vols 1885 (new edn, Blackwood, Edinburgh and London, n.d.)

Fernando, Lloyd 'George Eliot, Feminism, and Dorothea Brooke', *Review of English Literature*, vol. IV (January 1963), pp. 76–90

Haight, Gordon S. (ed.). *A Century of George Eliot Criticism* (Houghton Mifflin, Boston, 1965)

——. *George Eliot: A Bibography* (Clarendon Press, Oxford, 1968)

Hardy, Barbara. *The Novels of George Eliot*. (Athlone Press, London, 1959)

Holstrom, J. and Lerner, L. *George Eliot and Her Readers* (Bodley Head, London, 1966)

Linton, Eliza Lynn. 'George Eliot' in Margaret Oliphant, *et al.*, *Women Novelists of Queen Victoria's Reign: a Book of Appreciations* (Hurst and Blackett, London, 1897), pp. 63–115

INDEX

51, 52, 53, 54-5, 58; *A Life for a
life* 51, 53, 58, 64-7; *A Noble Life*
70n86; *A Woman's Thoughts*
45-6, 66; *Bread Upon the Waters*
59; *Christian's Mistake* 54, 55-6,
60; *Concerning Men* 47; *Hannah*
52; *John Halifax* 40, 44, 70n86;
Olive 53, 58, 62-4, 199, 200; *Plain
Speaking* 46, 68n7; *Sermons out
of Church* 47; *The Head of the
Family* 53, 57,.58, 64; *The Little
Lychetts* 64; *The Ogilvies* 40, 41,
54, 55, 57, 61, 118; *The Woman's
Kingdom* 52, 57, 61
Craik, George Lillie 45, 56
Craik, Mary 50
Cross, J.W. 186, 190, 192

Daily Telegraph 37n41
Davies, Emily 190
Dickens, Charles 148, 155
Dixon, William Hepworth 28
Dobell, Sydney 43

Edinburgh Review 7
Eliot, George 13, 36n30, 121, 122, 149,
159, 160, 162, 185-225
  fictional topics: angelic womanhood
  196-7, 201-2, 207, 215-16, 216-18;
  female heroism 203-4; female
  types: egoists 207-14, idealists
  214-222, rebels 198-207; images of
  femaleness 205-6; marital suffering 54, 195-6, 213, 217, 219-20;
  matrimonial commitment 193,
  202-3, 210-12, 215, 219, 220-2;
  spinsters 193-5; women artists
  199-200
  life: conflict of roles 186-7; marriage
  with Cross 186, 192; relationship
  with family 186; romantic disposition 190-2; union with Lewes
  186-8, 189, 191-2, 222n2; unorthodoxy 185-6
  opinions on: Craik 41; feminist
  activity 188-9, 193; matrimonial
  idealism 156, 190, 192; womanliness 3, 189-90; womanly independence 192; women's education
  141, 188-9; women writers 34, 189
  works: *Adam Bede* 183n59, 191,
  194, 201-3, 206, 207-8, 209;
  'Armgart' 199-201; *Daniel
  Deronda* 123, 175, 193, 194,

195-6, 197, 198-9, 206, 210-14,
222; *Felix Holt* 196, 208-9,
214-15; 'Janet's Repentance' 194,
195, 215-16; *Middlemarch* 24, 56,
127, 151, 175, 178, 194, 195, 197,
209-10, 218-22; 'Mr Gilfil's Love
Story' 207; *Romola* 160, 216-18;
'Silly Novels by Lady Novelists'
189; *The Mill on the Floss* 127,
205-7, 213; 'The Sad Fortunes of
the Reverend Amos Barton' 197;
The Spanish Gipsy 203-5, 206;
'Woman in France' 190
Ellis, Sarah Stickney 6, 36n21, 190
Englishwoman's Journal 188
Evans, Marian *see* Eliot, George

feminism
  attacks on sexual ideologies 28, 32,
  72, 73
  mid-Victorian ambivalence 10-12,
  37n61
  mid-Victorian radicalism 8-9
  reforms demanded 12, 183n68
  'the woman question' 8, 10, 20, 188,
  189
  women's rights 9, 21, 29, 116, 142,
  185-6
feminist criticism 14, 78-9, 167
Fields, James, T. 44
Forçade, Eugène 4
Fox, Eliza (Tottie) 137, 139, 140, 142
Fry, Elizabeth 215
Fuller, Margaret 191

Gaskell, Elizabeth, 14, 45, 77, 107,
121, 136-84, 185, 187, 188
  fictional topics: angelic womanhood
  145, 153-4, 159, 164-5, 173; fallen
  women 153, 183n50; female self-
  assertion 145-7, 149-50, 151-2,
  155, 159-60; industrial unrest
  143-4, 147-8; male tyranny 57,
  152, 154-5, 160-1, 168-9, 179;
  marital suffering 54, 156-7, 160-1,
  178-9; matrimonial commitment
  144-5, 147, 148-9, 152-3, 155-62,
  172, 180-1, 183n57; sexual duality
  150, 166; spinsters 162-78 *passim*,
  self-dependent 165-6, 167-9, stereotyped 52, 163-5, 170-1, 177-8
  life: childhood 184n82; conflict of
  roles 137, 138-9, 140, 182n28;
  marriage 136, 181n2; relationship

LEARNING RESOURCES
CENTER

ILLINOIS CENTRAL COLLEGE
MCMLXVI

East Peoria, Illinois